Like a Moth to a Flame

The Jim Reeves Story

Michael Streissguth

RUTLEDGE HILL PRESS®

Nashville, Tennessee

Published by Rutledge Hill Press®, 211 Seventh Avenue North, Nashville, Tennessee 37219.

Distributed in Canada by H. B. Fenn & Company, Ltd., 34 Nixon Road, Bolton, Ontario L7E 1W2.

Distributed in Australia by The Five Mile Press Pty. Ltd., 22 Summit Road, Noble Park, Victoria 3174.

Distributed in New Zealand by Tandem Press, 2 Rugby Road, Birkenhead, Auckland 10.

Distributed in the United Kingdom by Verulam Publishing, Ltd., 152a Park Street Lane, Park Street, St. Albans, Hertfordshire AL2 2AU.

Cover design by Ernie Couch / Consultx; page design by Harriette Bateman
Typesetting by E.T. Lowe, Nashville, Tennessee

Library of Congress Cataloging-in-Publication Data

Streissguth, Michael.
    Like a moth to a flame : the Jim Reeves story / Michael Streissguth
        p.   cm.
    Discography: p.
    Includes biographical references (p. 221) and index.
    ISBN 1-55853-607-8 (hc.)
        1. Reeves, Jim.   2. Country musicians—United States—Biography.
    I. Title
    ML420.R3S77   1998
    782.421642'092—dc21
    [B]   98-15921
                                                                        CIP
                                                                          M

Printed in the United States of America

1   2   3   4   5   6   7   8   9—00   99   98

Contents

Preface

Somewhere in the middle of writing my biography of Eddy Arnold, the notion of considering Jim Reeves's life and career began to take form. Each owed so much to the other that a Jim Reeves biography would be a natural companion to the Eddy Arnold biography. Arnold, of course, dominated the late 1940s country music scene with his sweet, unaffected baritone voice, confirming that nasal twangs and elaborate western outfits were not the only ways to reach a country fan's heart. With songs like "Anytime" and "Just a Little Lovin' (Will Go a Long, Long Way)," Arnold also lured followers in northern and urban audiences who previously had either snubbed or knew nothing about rural music.

At an Eddy Arnold show in the mid-1990s, I sat next to a sixtysomething woman who had connected with the "Tennessee Plowboy" after hearing his "Bouquet of Roses" almost fifty years earlier. Ironically, "Bouquet of Roses" played on the radio in her New York barrio home—a long way from Tennessee. In the late 1950s, Arnold's appeal to country and pop audiences slipped considerably as he eschewed any hint of country sounds in favor of wobbly attempts at pop standards. There were a few bright spots in his pop pursuits, but torrents of rock and roll dimmed them. His large constituency in the record-buying markets dwindled from the late 1950s until the early 1960s.

Enter Jim Reeves. While Eddy Arnold vainly mined for gold in New York recording studios, Jim Reeves's singing was being processed in Nashville by Chet Atkins's golden production engine. Reeves had perfected a warm, purring baritone that Atkins used to represent the smooth, countrypolitan style that would become known as the

"Nashville Sound," one of the city's answers to rock and roll. Like Arnold, Reeves generally remained within his vocal range and sang without much embellishment. Almost single-handedly, Arnold had made such a vocal approach acceptable in country music. But Reeves seemed to be Arnold's heir apparent, representative of the possibilities of singing country music "nice." If Eddy Arnold was the "Pioneer of the Nashville Sound" (also the title of my biography of the artist), Jim Reeves was the "Voice of the Nashville Sound."

With beautifully executed, pleading ballads such as "Am I Losing You" and "Four Walls," and the playful, country-oriented hits "Overnight" and "Billy Bayou," Reeves stepped to the forefront of country music in the late 1950s and soon found a home in pop markets. And when RCA Records chose an emissary to promote its line of country music in Europe, the company dispatched Reeves on a series of concert dates there. He developed an international following and opened new markets for American country music abroad, just as Arnold had pried open urban areas ten years before. The 1960s were no less abundant for Reeves. He continued to place songs on the country and pop charts, and amassed a following across the Atlantic that rivaled—and, in certain cases, surpassed—that of Elvis Presley.

Even death could not slow Jim Reeves's momentum. Within fifty-four months of his death in 1964, five of his posthumous releases reached number one on the country charts. Reeves posted five chart toppers *before* he died, but those came sporadically over seven years, 1953–1960. RCA Records generated a string of successful posthumous Reeves hits by dubbing his demo vocals over new instrumentation, and, incredibly, placed a Jim Reeves song on the U.S. country charts as late as 1984—twenty years after the artist's death. In contrast—and draw whatever conclusion you might—RCA only managed to keep Elvis Presley's name on the American singles charts for six years after his death in 1977.

On the other side of the Atlantic and, in fact, around the world, Reeves's record sales have remained healthy, outpaced only by the growth of his legend. Over the years, active fan clubs in Great Britain and the Netherlands have kept the flame flickering, and in some foreign markets, Reeves's legacy has acquired a life of its own, requiring little in the way of organized promotion. For example, as writer Mark Schone recently noted in the *Village Voice,* Reeves's music appeals to black people from Africa to the Caribbean even though there are no present-day efforts to market the singer to those audiences. "The entire African diaspora loves *Gentleman Jim*," wrote Schone. Although "entire" maybe overstating his influence (the African diaspora in the United States on the whole is not enamored of Reeves), his music does carry a weight among certain black audiences that has confounded scholars from New York to Nairobi.

From our vantage point in 1998, we can also see that Jim Reeves repaid the debt he owed to Eddy Arnold. When Arnold finally emerged from his doldrums with the roundly popular hit "Make the World Go Away" (1965), he did so in the wake of Jim Reeves. Reeves had remolded the country troubadour image for the 1960s, allowing others—most notably Arnold—to fill the mold. Poor Eddy Arnold was accused of taking advantage of Reeves's death, when, in fact, a new manager had begun packaging him à la Jim Reeves a few months prior to Reeves's death. However, Arnold could hardly deny that flecks of Reeves's sparkle had drifted down into his midst, and when he began collaborating with arranger-conductor Bill Walker in the studio and on the road, the debt became more obvious. The Australian-born Walker had come to the United States at Jim Reeves's request to be his musical director, but a few days after Walker arrived, his new boss's plane crashed.

From Eddy there was Jim, and from Jim there was Eddy reborn.

Eddy Arnold lived to reinforce his interpretation of his life and career, and to affect how others would tell his story. Jim Reeves had no such opportunity. It became the burden of his widow, Mary, to interpret his life, and she did so by giving countless interviews, shepherding thousands of fans through the Jim Reeves Museum in suburban Nashville, and working with RCA to keep his voice on the radio and in record shops. She certainly deserves much of the credit for maintaining the economic viability of Jim Reeves's name and his "Gentleman Jim" image. She was a quiet advisor-administrator while her husband lived, and we can assume that her role then was valuable, particularly when viewed in tandem with her canny and determined efforts since his death. Kudos also to the late Harry Jenkins, a former RCA executive, who helped Mary construct a business around her deceased husband. Unfortunately, as this book goes to press, Mary Reeves sits in a Nashville nursing home, unable to muster the strength and acumen necessary to preside over the Jim Reeves Enterprises she created.

The Jim Reeves story that Mary and others once close to Jim have cultivated generally runs along Horatio Alger lines: boy overcomes impoverished youth, fails in his first vocation (baseball), and finally scrapes his way to the top by following his real destiny (music). This interpretation is generally correct. After all, what interesting life story does not follow Horatio's highway to some degree? The official story even illuminates some of the singer's foibles. Everyone admits, for example, that Reeves's temper could blow like steam from a nineteenth-century locomotive. But many of the "official sources" who once surrounded Jim have seemed reluctant to say much else. Through them, we see a contradiction: a generous, talented man who also exhibited an ugly temper and intransigence. But how could generosity and ungraciousness coexist? We haven't heard or seen a deeper explanation of the man's character. Many of the "official sources" to whom I turned for insight refused to speak with me. They said they are waiting to sell their story (quite understandable), but they probably also fear that the wrong word could tarnish Jim Reeves's legacy.

But Jim Reeves's legacy is secure. His voice marked an important turning point in the history of country music, and I can only hope to document that contribution in an entertaining fashion. However, I believe the official Jim Reeves story lacks sufficient detail and does not provide a proper explanation of his confounding character. So, from the memories of those who knew him and worked with him, and from material gleaned from various archives and personal collections, it is my intent to bring together in one source a fuller interpretation of a remarkable life and career.

Michael Streissguth
Columbia, Maryland
1998

Acknowledgments

I am indebted to the following individuals who generously offered their recollections of James Travis Reeves and his times as I was writing this book: Norman Bale, Shep Baron, Lawrence Birdsong Jr., August Blume, John Bolin, E. S. Bouge, Cloyd Boyer, Gordon Bossin, Harold Bradley, Luckey Brazeal, Bobby Brenner, Al Brieda, Dick Broderick, Paul Brown, Clyde Brewer, Cliff Bruner, Jack Burgess, Cy Coben, Alan Cross, Elmo Davis, Jimmy Dennis, Dollie Denny, Danny Dill, Ray Edenton, Bob Ferguson, Leo Ferguson, Tillman Franks, Jack Gale, Bobby Garrett, Dave Glover, William Graham, June Graves, Mary Graves, Charles Grean, Bobby Greene, Charles Greenberg, John Grimes, Charley Hall, Margaret Hamlin, Burton Harris, Jim Harris, Kenneth "Little Red" Hayes, Don Helms, Billie Jean Horton, Leo Jackson, Steve Kamas, Anita Kerr, James Kirkland, Al Kubski, Charlie Lamb, Sleepy LaBeef, Billy Livingstone, Horace Logan, Jack Logan, John D. Loudermilk, Caesar Massey, Bob McCluskey, Tom McCusker, Louie (Reeves) McNeese, Jeff Miller, Bill Morris, Jimmy C. Newman, Louis Nunley, Frank O'Donnell, Frank O'Hare, James O'Gwynn, Jenny Lee O'Reilly, Frank Page, Clive Parnell, Milton Payne, Felton Pruett, Bill Pursell, Ed Ramigoz, Douglas Reeh, Floyd Reeves, Joe Reeves, Margaret Reeves, Vic Reinagel, Bruce Rhiddlehoover, Carey Rhiddlehoover, Jerry Rice, Hi Roberts, Johnny Rosica, Del Roy, Jane Rugge, Chuck Seitz, Roy Shirey, Herb Shucher Jr., Katherine Shucher, Chris Sidaris, Russell Sims, Goldie Smith, Peter Smith, Velma Williams Smith, Hugh Sooter, Sam Sorsby, Henry Strzelecki, Chester Studdard, Ben Sullivan, Jerry Thompson, Elvin Tappe, Virgie (Reeves) Thomas, Charlie Thompson, Mitchell Torok, Art Trieschman, Gabe Tucker,

Barney Vardeman, Art Visconti, Bill Walker, Billy Walker, Marvin Walker, Mary Walker, Irving Waugh, John White, Jim Willis, Gene Wortham, Ginny Wright, Leroy Youngblood, Alex Zanetis.

My thanks to the following persons, who helped in equally valuable ways: Billy Deaton, Roberta Edging, Myrna Ellis, Arie den Dulk, Tom Kirby, Don Mackin, Charlotte McGrath, Patrick "Nuggy" McGrath, Larry McGuire, Alanna Nash, Neilus O'Connell, Hugh Rutherford, Pee Wee Walker. Propers to: Frank Anderson, who opened his Jim Reeves collection to me; D. J. Cagley and Corey Seeman at the National Baseball Hall of Fame and Museum; Kevin Coffey for his insight into the Texas music scene; Claudia J. Depkin and Chick Crumpacker at the Bertelsmann Music Group; Linda Dykstra for her vocal lessons; Kent Henderson and John Rumble at the Country Music Foundation; Mike Henry and Mike Mashon at the Library of American Broadcasting in College Park, Maryland; David Kurtz of the *Times of Acadia*, Lafayette, Louisiana; Judy Norwood of the South African Film and Television Institute; Paul Leslie of the Evangeline Baseball League History Project at Nicholls State College in Thibodaux, Louisiana; Marius Moolman of the Embassy of South Africa in Washington, D.C.; Teresa Payne of the Federal Aviation Administration; Wesley H. Saunders of the Rapides Parish (Louisiana) Library; Richard Weize of Bear Family Records; the staff of the Panola County (Texas) Historical and Genealogical Association.

I am especially appreciative of Jack Julian, who traversed the Southland with me; Steve Andreassi of the IUP Lodge and Convocation Center in Hoboken, New Jersey; Larry Stone and John Mitchell at Rutledge Hill Press for their support of this project; and, of course, my wife, Leslie Bailey Streissguth, who sees what I cannot see.

Like a Moth
to a Flame
The Jim Reeves Story

1

Perhaps no child is categorized, preened, or chastised more than the last-born child. Psychologists make assumptions about the character and personality of first-born and middle children, but no child is more often explained by his order of birth than the one who emerges last from the womb. Depending on a child's familial environment (and which doctor one consults), the last born can be tagged with any number of labels: competitive, lazy, adventurous, gentle, mistrustful, extroverted, rebellious, extreme. He can be overshadowed and trampled upon by older siblings, or, in other families, doted upon and cherished. Sometimes he experiences both kinds of treatment within the family. It is hard to make any general statement about such children. But many have grown to be the most prominent of people—esteemed and not so esteemed.

James Travis Reeves arrived last in his family. Born on August 20, 1923, in the vast state of Texas, he followed seven other Reeves children: Beuford, Hulan, Ivy, Louie, O. D., Alton, and Virgie. Another daughter born between Louie and O. D. died after living just two days. By most accounts, young Travis, as he was then known, found indulgence among his older brothers and sisters. He needed it. Just nine months after Travis's birth, his father, Thomas (Tom) Middleton Reeves, died of brain cancer. Travis's mother, Mary Beulah, had little time to devote to her new son while she cared for her ailing husband in the months preceding his death, and when Tom finally expired in May 1924, she collapsed from exhaustion. The worrying and caring she had expended on her husband left her weak and confined to bed. So, when the infant Travis screeched and squealed in the night, and when he cried out for food in the day, it was the older children who stepped in for Beulah.

Initially, the words Travis heard and the words he imitated were those of his siblings. Beuford and O. D. whooshed the tot back to his feet when he fell on the dirt ground, and the sisters soothed him when he fell too hard too many times. "I was a second mother," recalled sister Louie, Travis's third-eldest sister. "When he was born, I carried him on my hip a million miles because my mother was in bad health. He hung to me."

When Tom Reeves died, there was little prosperity to which Beulah and the children could cling. They sharecropped a modest patch of East Texas land that belonged to Tom's brother-in-law and lived in a wooden frame house that bulged and buckled from the size of Beulah's brood. Eight children and a widowed mother squeezed into two bedrooms, a meager existence and belying the dreams that Tom's and Beulah's fathers had imagined when they settled in the region decades earlier.

Tom Reeves's family can be traced back to England's Elizabethan Age, a period marked by that nation's imperial explorations of North America. Inhabiting the area around Oxford, members of the Reeves family resisted the lure of the New World for some sixty-five years after Sir Walter Raleigh first spearheaded English settlement of Roanoke Island in the late 1500s. The Reeves people of that time and place appear to have enjoyed a degree of wealth and status, and probably saw little need to leave their mother country.

It may have been England's ancient laws of primogeniture, which bestowed a deceased's inheritance solely on the eldest son, that led the first Reeves to the American colonies. In 1652, as Oliver Cromwell enforced his anti-Catholic, anti-Anglican military rule over England, Scotland, and Ireland, a sixteen-year-old William Reeves agreed to a period of indentured servitude in order to travel to Surry County, Virginia, with the Littleton Scarburg trading company. Born in 1636 at Woodstock, England, William was the last-born child of Timothy Reeves.

By 1684, records indicate that William had fulfilled his servitude and could pursue life in Virginia as a freeman. His descendants took the Reeves name into the colonies of North Carolina and South

Carolina, and in the mid-1800s a number of William's people meandered into Georgia and Alabama. A great-great-grandson of William's, also named William, moved with his father from South Carolina in the early 1800s and got as far as Lineville, Alabama. That William J. Reeves ventured even farther west, setting his eyes on Texas ten or so years after it was granted statehood in 1845. Texas promised cheap, available land, a seduction outweighed only by another western magnet, the California gold rush.

But William Reeves chose Texas and, as a part of America's great westward migration, he most likely entered the state on an old Spanish road that passed through Natchitoches, Louisiana, and continued into the Piney Woods region of East Texas. Beginning in the mid-1700s, people of Hispanic origin had raised cattle in the then-Spanish-dominated Piney Woods, and they were followed in the early 1800s by white pioneers and Indian tribes like the Creek, Choctaw, and Cherokee who also raised cattle.

Like William Reeves, many who originally came from the Carolinas stopped in the Piney Woods instead of continuing west because the land so reminded them of home. The tall pines and prairie grasses that resembled the vegetation of the Carolina coastal areas waved their greetings to the newcomers, inviting them to stay. How could Reeves refuse? The large, open tracts of forest that the pines shared with black hickory, ash, and dogwood trees seemed God-given for lumbering, and the equally expansive plains promised bountiful harvests to anyone who wished to cultivate them. Thus, William J. Reeves settled in the newly formed Panola County in the new state of Texas.

The area that Panola County wrapped its boundaries around had been a land in limbo during the years leading up to statehood. When France sold the Louisiana Territory to the United States in 1803, the Washington government found itself in conflict with Spain, its chief rival in North America. Inevitably, a border dispute flared, with President Thomas Jefferson claiming that the Louisiana Purchase granted the U.S. land as far west as the Rio Grande River, while Spain contended that those rights extended only as far as the Red River (just east of present-day Texas). The two nations began to buff their cannons and move soldiers toward the disputed region.

However, with the United States keeping a suspicious eye on Britain, and Spain stamping out the fires of revolt in its colonies, both nations knew that hostilities would leave them vulnerable on other fronts. As a result, the two parties agreed to a neutral boundary some fifty miles in width that extended from the Sabine River in the west to the Arroyo Hondo River in the east. But the agreement put off a final resolution and had the unintended effect of opening a vast no-man's land to every sort of ne'er-do-well and fugitive. Smugglers, army deserters, and other rogues scampered to the land between the rivers, drooling over the prospect of living unencumbered by legal authorities. Honest folk who inhabited the Piney Woods resorted to their own firepower and ingenuity to keep the unsavory types at bay.

The Piney Woods region remained in limbo until Texas snatched its independence from Mexico in 1836, fifteen years after the Mexican Revolution had ejected Spain from the region. The United States and the short-lived nation of Texas surveyed a definite boundary, but even then the matter of lawlessness in the former border area remained high on the peaceful inhabitants' list of concerns. The opening of the neutral area attracted hard-working settlers, but the region's relative isolation also meant the arrival of more bandits and reprobates. "Those who sought to make land claims and become permanent settlers soon found themselves harassed by thieves and swindlers," wrote one historian of Panola County.

It took a small civil war—the Regulator-Moderator War—in Harrison and Shelby Counties to help bring law and order to the former no-man's land. In 1840, six years before Panola County was forged from portions of Harrison and Shelby, an angry debate raged in the two counties over how to bring justice to the region. Two sides—each with practical and justifiable aims—hopped over the fences of their cattle ranches and farms to battle over the issues. The Regulators advocated immediate vigilante justice, horse-whipping an alleged cattle rustler with no questions asked, for example, while the Moderators demanded a system of due process for accused criminals. One participant later summed up the spat this way: "Regulating is taking the criminals out and hanging them or otherwise giving them deserved punishment. Moderating is trial before the Courts which were at the time little more than a farce!"

When the Moderators took up arms to oppose their adversaries, the Regulators had already put their form of justice to work by destroying property of those they determined to be guilty and imposing other controversial and often extreme penalties. Guerrilla warfare rumbled across the land, with bullets zipping through the normally quiet groves of pines and rag-tag bands of zealots dragging men from their homes and executing them in front of their wives and children. Terror swept through the counties and seeped to other areas of the Piney Woods. Few families dimmed their lamps before bed without praying for God's protection through the night. Then the Texas authorities stepped in.

About 1844, the republic's president, Sam Houston, ordered between five hundred and six hundred militia men to East Texas, and with force and the suggestion of force, they dissolved the two factions. According to historians, hard feelings persisted for decades, but by the time Panola County was formed in 1846, East Texas was more or less a safe place to live. Fighting had ceased, and a more structured legal system curbed rampant criminal activity.

Such was the state of affairs in East Texas when William J. Reeves arrived from Alabama in the late 1850s. During the early 1840s Reeves had married a Chickasaw woman in Alabama, and the two produced nine children within eleven years. Although it is unclear when, the most certainly exhausted Mrs. Reeves died, leaving William to eventually find another spouse (whose name is lost to history). Records show that Reeves and his second wife had a child in Panola County in 1860, and then William is listed as marrying for a third time, in 1867, to a Viney Haney. She, too, bore children, including Thomas (Tom) Middleton Reeves—James Travis's father— who was born on November 12, 1882. The William Reeves family settled on a large and fertile tract of land in eastern Panola County where they farmed and likely raised cattle.

After the U.S. Civil War, while William Reeves established himself in Panola County and had a third series of children with Viney Haney, one Lorenzo Harris Adams entered East Texas from Sevier County, Arkansas, with a number of his younger brothers and sisters in tow. Lorenzo had entered the futile and protracted broadside against the Northern states in 1865 at the age of sixteen, in place of his father, Wyatt Woodruff Adams, who had been excused from military service because of bad health. Lorenzo had been in the army only a few months when family events beckoned him back to Sevier County.

Lorenzo's mother was a Choctaw woman named Martha and, according to Adams family lore, either she or the second wife of

Wyatt Woodruff Adams had poisoned Wyatt to death during the final year of the Civil War. Informed of the news, Lorenzo had rushed home from battle and dealt out his younger siblings to various families in the area. When hostilities finally ceased between the states, Lorenzo collected his family and joined the large post-war migration to Texas. Lorenzo was not out of his teens, yet he had a strong paternal sense of responsibility.

The new head of the Adams family probably followed the well-traveled Trammel's Trace into Texas. Immigrants from Arkansas and Tennessee had trod the path since the 1820s, and Lorenzo likely saw many of his war buddies and Sevier County acquaintances light out on it, too. Trammel's Trace carried the Adamses along the western border of Panola County, and it was there that Lorenzo decided to stop. Finding land not far north of William J. Reeves's property, Lorenzo Harris Adams and his kin settled near the community of Logan. He married Arminta "Sug" Sinclair, a Louisiana girl, on Valentine's Day 1869 and over the next fifteen years amassed two hundred acres of land. Arminta and Lorenzo had eight children, including Mary Beulah Adams—who would later become Tom Reeves's wife and James Travis's mother.

Lorenzo would have seven more children by a second wife and, maintaining his deeply instilled notion of responsibility, served one term as a magistrate and sixteen years as a deputy sheriff. Like William J. Reeves, whose ownership of a large tract of land accorded him a healthy degree of status in eastern Panola County, Lorenzo Adams also was viewed as an important figure in the regional community.

Along the eastern edge of Panola County, most people knew the Adams and the Reeves families, and, naturally, the two families knew each other. Actually, they shared a connection through marriage. In or about 1889 one of the grandchildren of William Reeves's second marriage had wed a daughter of Lorenzo Adams's first marriage. This union between the families carpeted the aisle for another. William's son Tom and Lorenzo's daughter Mary Beulah were only two years apart in age and probably met via their family ties as there were plenty of opportunities to get to know one another at church suppers, candy breakings, and country dances. On April 5, 1903, Mary Beulah and Tom were married, pulling the Adams and Reeves families even closer together.

By the time Beulah (as Mary Beulah was then known) and Tom started their East Texas life together, the material legacy of Tom's father had become somewhat diluted. William Reeves had passed on before the marriage, and Tom—the last-born—could not claim a piece of the original tract that William had staked out and farmed after he arrived in Panola County. Three or four surviving brothers preceded Tom, and one or more of them presumably worked the bulk of William's land. It seems plausible that Tom had to make his own way. Beulah also appears not to have received any land from her father (who was still living), and the newlyweds eventually moved into a house on land owned by one of Beulah's brothers.

A modest structure, the house had two bedrooms, a side room, a kitchen in the back, and a porch running across the front. Situated between the hamlets of Deadwood and Galloway, the house sat well back from the main road up a narrow, curving lane. In the summer of 1923, under its splintered, low-slung roof, the Reeves children cared for newborn James Travis.* A few months later, Tom Reeves died there.

As Tom slipped closer to death and Beulah focused on him, the older children—as well as nurturing Travis—managed the cotton harvest. When Tom died and Beulah took ill, they sprinkled new seed for the 1924 crop. The oldest son, Beuford, was in his late teens when his father died, and he assumed the paternal role in the Reeves family. He tended the fields and negotiated at harvest time, when a portion of the crop was due the landowner. While Travis was still a toddler, Beulah, who had not fully recovered from her physical breakdown (she really never would), decided to move the family a couple of miles down the main road that ran through Galloway and Deadwood on the way south to Logansport, Louisiana. Like a mama dog moving her pups into the shade on a searing day, Beulah led her children down that narrow, curving lane from their home. They crossed the Socagee Creek to Gus and Sally Barnett's land, which was closer to Galloway. Perhaps they could farm more acreage there or maybe the Barnetts offered a more desirable sharecropping arrangement.

The arrangement within Beulah's family, however, remained the same: Beuford and the older children worked the land and held up the

---

*Birth records place James Travis's birth in Logan, Texas. Beulah probably delivered him at her family's home.

Reeveses' part of the sharecropping agreement. But sharecropping merely provided a place to stay and a little cash. In order to eat, the family grew and canned corn, yams, peas, beans, and potatoes, and kept a cow and a few chickens for milk and eggs. They also picked wild berries in the woods and meadows, and probably had a few fruit trees around their house, like many in Panola County. The Reeveses rarely could afford to buy foodstuffs from the small country store up the road, but if they had a good cotton crop and sold a few eggs or pears, Beulah could periodically send one of the children to the store for sugar, flour, salt, and pepper. However, most of the family's food came directly from the land. Beulah's and Tom's grandfathers had been wise to stop in East Texas, where fish from Socagee Creek and small game animals like rabbit and opossum were plentiful.

By standards that William Reeves or Lorenzo Adams may have employed, Beulah's family seemed to have little. But compared to the other folks who lived in quiet eastern Panola County, the Reeveses were typical; life just required a bit more inventiveness and the co-operation of neighbors. For instance, when Travis's birthday arrived, Mary would bake a cake every other year and share it with a neighbor boy whose birthday fell near Travis's. In the intervening years, the neighbor boy's mother would bake for the two youngsters.

"We had plenty to eat, a few clothes to wear," remembered sister Virgie, the sibling closest in age to Travis. "That's all we knew back then. Everybody else was in the same predicament. We didn't know nothing else, but we were happy. We had a big time, enjoyed life." Everybody found outlets and "big times" around the farm. The Reeveses and their neighbors rarely went into town (the county seat of Carthage) because that meant a winding, time-consuming journey of some fifteen to twenty miles. Nobody, of course, owned an automobile, so almost everybody stayed near home. The Methodist church the Reeves family attended hosted most of the community's formal social events. People went to church on Saturday nights and again on Sunday morning, and enjoyed periodic church suppers.

For many, though, a Saturday night church supper was the first course in an evening that usually ended with a country dance. The rustic sounds of fiddles and guitars regularly spilled from homes into the East Texas darkness. And that's not all that spilled. Plenty of bootleg whiskey frequently accompanied the music. Bootleggers often would set up their white lightning next to the coffee and iced tea the local women served. Although bootleggers hosted a few dances, it was the regular folks who usually pushed the furniture out of their sitting rooms and, for a quarter, welcomed people for a night of music and local hooch. The music sizzled and the patrons rollicked. One night, the fiddle reels and dancing literally slid a house off its moorings, recalled John White, who played guitar at such dances and later wrote about his 1920s East Texas upbringing: "The band must have had good rhythm along with the dancers because at a certain point in time, the house fell right off its foundation blocks. This broke up the party."

Despite the ever-present white lightning, the dances were peaceful and family oriented—save the occasional donnybrook that would send the dancers fleeing. When fists flew, the music halted, and one band member usually had the duty of collecting and protecting the instruments. He would push the guitars and fiddles into a corner and drape his body over them while blows and bottles glanced off his back. Such brawls exploded whenever booze and bravado mixed, and they illustrated part of what was not so nice about Panola County.

In retrospect, the bountiful land and the resourcefulness of its people cast an idealistic glow over the county, but East Texas could be a dark place, too. After all, it was the home of the Regulator-Moderator War, and people still argued over the conflict. Bullets still whined through the pines, although they came not from Regulators or Moderators but from bootleggers defending their stills. In shameless defiance of the federal prohibition, coppery mash makers gurgled and dripped in the woods throughout Panola County. The Carthage newspaper routinely ran stories about raids, indicating how robust the bootlegging trade was. In fact, one quart of the Piney Woods pulp could bring thirty to forty dollars. Just days after Travis's birth, the paper reported that authorities had raided one his mother's relations. "The six stills were found on the Claude Adams farm in Panola County," the paper noted. "Three of the stills had a capacity of fifty-five gallons, two had a capacity of fifty gallons and the last, thirty gallons. A large quantity of mash and equipment used in making liquor was taken and destroyed."

According to the article, the law arrested five "negroes" who were tending the stills and hauled them a few miles north to Jefferson, Texas. One must wonder what kind of justice they received because East Texas barely recognized the Emancipation Proclamation, even in the 1920s. Where Travis grew up, if a black man so much as appeared alone in the Deadwood-Galloway area, residents would chase him away. According to John White, black field hands who worked for white farmers in East Texas could expect to be treated like chattel.

"Several white farmers that I knew still whipped their black field hands to keep them in line," wrote White. "Most of the farmers who still worked black families kept them in debt and forbade them to move as long as they were in debt. I know of some blacks who left, and the farm owner went after them and brought them back—all within the good graces of the law enforcement officer. When a black field hand got put in jail for anything—being drunk, disturbing the peace, killing another black person, beating his wife, or anything else that did not pertain to annoying white people—it was customary for the man he worked for to go to the sheriff and pay a minimal fine and bring the prisoner back to work."

It was in this environment defined by naked intolerance, steely self-reliance, and close community ties, that Travis Reeves became a young boy. Not burdened by the heavy farm work put on his older brothers and sisters, Travis jumped wholeheartedly into the games and frolics the other area children enjoyed. Landing the nickname "Jay-bo," which was derived from his first name, the pug-nosed kid fished and skinny-dipped in Socagee Creek, rolled old car tires down the road, and helped build "flying jennys," a whirling amusement ride. To make a jenny, which was much like a primitive merry-go-round, the kids would cut down a long sapling, bore a hole through the middle, and attach it with a peg to the top of a tree stump. The kids would straddle each end of the sapling while it spun like a propeller.

As he grew older, only a few chores kept Travis from his play. With his brothers and sisters, he pumped well water, brought in logs for the wood stove, and filled the kerosene lamps that illuminated the house at night. Although some children in the area picked cotton before they reached school age, Travis could rely on his older siblings to do that.

When most children around Galloway turned seven, they attended a two-story school house located near the community's Methodist church. Four teachers worked at the Galloway School, and when Jim started in 1930, he was put in a class with teacher Esther Tompkins, a sweet but strict woman. "When she said something, she meant it," said Marvin Walker, the boy who shared birthday cakes with Travis. "She didn't joke with you. She meant it." Still, Ms. Tompkins treated the youngsters as if she were their second mother, and Travis did his part to play the good son.

There occasionally were exceptions, as distant cousin and schoolmate Margaret Barnett recalled. "He was a good student, and he got along with everybody, except he was the baby of the family, and he liked things done his way." In school, Travis and the other boys controlled the daily baseball match-up like bouncers outside a floating crap game. They forbade the school girls to join in, urging them to go off and jump rope or something. Margaret, though, liked to shag a fly ball or two from time to time and one morning told Travis to expect her on the dirt diamond at recess.

"We only had one bat and one ball," she remembered. "The boys would take it where the girls couldn't play. . . . We got in a squabble over it that day. Whoever got the bat could play at recess. Of course, I beat him to the door and got the bat because I was closer to the door to start with. He decided to take it away from me. It wouldn't work." Rather than baseball, a wrestling match between Travis and Margaret became the main feature at recess that day—until Ms. Tompkins grabbed the scruffs of their necks. "Then the teacher wouldn't let none of us play," said Margaret.

Sharecroppers and others who had no option but to live with little during the 1930s often say they never knew about the Great Depression, that their lives would have been just as gaunt—even without the national economic calamity. Many in Panola County and across the nation who experienced those lean years look back as if to say, "What was the country whining about? We always had it tough!" A look back, however, reveals another accounting of the times. In Panola County, the Great Depression tightened the vise another few turns.

"Panola" is a Native American word for cotton, and if the white, fibrous fluff could be said to be "king" anywhere, it was in the county named "cotton." Some forty cotton gins dotted the county, and almost every sharecropper raised cotton, only cotton. At the end of 1928, production in the county had reached a healthy 27,500 bales, but despite the strong crop, signs of harder times ahead stained the fields. Decades of farming cotton was fast depleting the soil of nutrients, and pesky boll weevils had regularly invaded the fields throughout the decade. By the end of 1930, the year Travis began attending school, the harvest had dropped to 18,940 bales, and the price of cotton had dropped with it. A pound of Panola County cotton that sold for eighteen cents in 1928 was spiraling toward the sickly price of a nickel.

Extension agents and newspaper editorials urged those farmers who planted only cotton to diversify and plant feed corn, onions, and other vegetables for market. Many did so reluctantly or not at all, refusing to believe that "king" cotton would let them down, but cotton *had* become unreliable, and not just in Panola County. Throughout the South, farmers coped with the astonishing, depression-induced drop in cotton prices. Even crop diversification was of little help because the price of other crops had plummeted, too. Farmers could only wonder what lay ahead. Reports of unemployment lines, food kitchens, and crashing markets only darkened their outlook.

The Panola County newspaper, while reporting the depression's havoc, also tried to raise its readers' spirits. "Panola County isn't lost yet; not if the people are willing to help themselves," an editor wrote in the September 3, 1930, issue. "Here is the only relief as we see it: We received a nice rain last week, and will in all probability receive several more in the near future. Panola County had good land and frosts are late in this section, as a rule. We believe that every man in the county that is physically able, and most of them are, can plant and harvest, if he will, a good garden this fall. . . . Fatten a hog for winter if you have one. Last but not least, plant every available acre to feed for your stock."

In the same commentary, the editor later admonished: "As long as farmers and laborers spend their last nickel for a set of tires and gasoline for a dilapidated old car, forgetting their family's welfare, and sit around town and gripe and grumble, just that long will poverty be with us. You cannot blame the situation on God or politics. The people are to blame for the hard times, if there be hard times, and the relief rests with them."

If the Reeves family read this Hoover-esque, pull-yourself-up article, they may have laughed. Sure, they raised a garden. But feed for livestock? What livestock? All they had was an old milk cow. They grew cotton, and thrived or tumbled depending on their crop's fortunes. All the Reeveses knew was cotton, but it was becoming increasingly difficult to grow it. The state of Texas placed restrictions on cotton farming starting in 1931, but the sale of cotton brought in precious little cash, anyway. Others crops, the family observed, were just as worthless. Circumstances mired the Reeveses. Sharecropping had become a means to a dead end.

2

olumbus "Dad" Joiner had operated a store in Tennessee, dabbled in politics, and drilled unsuccessfully for oil in Oklahoma before he arrived in East Texas in 1925. An Alabama native who dreamed of tall, spraying oil strikes, the wildcatter had come unwittingly close in Oklahoma, stopping his drills some two hundred feet above the layer where black gold would later be tapped. With the image of riches still surging within him, Dad Joiner turned his eyes toward East Texas, where he owned leases on 320 acres of fields in Rusk County.

Rusk abutted Panola County's western border, and, like its neighbor, relied almost solely on agriculture to support its economy. Few in Rusk County imagined that oil might flow beneath their feet. It was well known there that explorers and whatever magical divining rods they used had created oil cultures in Beaumont to the south and in Wink and Desdemona to the west, but those places were so far from Rusk County they might as well have been in another country. Joiner suspected that the oil culture could seep into Rusk and tracked down an old compadre to confirm it. That compadre was Doc Lloyd.

An amateur geologist and professional hawker of tonic, Lloyd had directed Joiner to the Oklahoma boondoggle years earlier, but Joiner's faith in the man had never wavered. He trusted his friend's nose for oil. The two teamed again in 1926 when Joiner needed to sell a few of his leases in order to keep his so-far-fruitless explorations going. To convince prospective buyers of the land's potential, Joiner asked Lloyd to draw up a few surveys and reports to make the pitch appear more official. However, to the big oilmen,

Lloyd's work looked to be anything but official. He had pinpointed the location of every major oil field in the United States and had—arbitrarily, it seemed—drawn lines from each so that the lines intersected in East Texas.

One oil company executive found the report to be nothing short of preposterous. The incredulous man recalled that Lloyd's two-page report included such gems as: "Gentleman, all these major oil trends, intersecting as they do here in East Texas, bring about a state known in the oil business as the apex of the apex, a situation not found anywhere else in the world." Lloyd's off-the-cuff reports notwithstanding, Joiner managed to sell a few leases, and for four years he punctured the Rusk County landscape like a man stabbing at quicksilver.

The lines Lloyd had drawn intersected outside Henderson, Texas, where a widow named Daisy Bradford owned a farm of almost one thousand acres. Joiner was convinced (or rather Lloyd had convinced Joiner) that oil could be released from Bradford's land, but the only stream that anyone saw was that of cash going to Madam Daisy for the leases. Day after day, she watched while Joiner's men fruitlessly rammed their equipment into the ground. Two deep holes had failed to percolate oil, and money was running so short that, for a time, Joiner drilled only on Sundays—the day his investors and creditors were likely to take a leisurely drive by his rigs.

Joiner began drilling a third hole in the summer of 1929, and that too seemed barren of oil. The drill bored farther and farther down, but it only brought up fodder for those who ridiculed Joiner. Then, in the late summer of 1930, the lead driller on Joiner's team noticed that the hole had coughed up gritty, oily sand, a certain sign that the pure stuff was down there. The news buoyed Joiner, who watched excitedly as workers turned the hole into a full-fledged well site. By early October, the derrick had been completed, and crowds from East Texas and beyond invaded Daisy Bradford's farm to see the spectacle of surging oil that could erupt at any moment.

Finally, on October 5, 1930, a deep gurgle bellowed through the well. An oil scout—one of the many who had traveled to Daisy's farm—heard and saw everything and later recounted the events for researchers Roger Olien and J. Conrad Dunagan. "They got in the hole just about sundown, just dusk. They dropped [a testing tool] in there, and man, here comes gas and oil, gurgling and going on. And about that time here comes the oil, over the derrick, and all the pine trees downwind from us for several hundred yards were just soaked with oil."

Texas crude gushed from that third hole at a rate of sixty-eight hundred barrels a day, sparking droves of wildcatters and oil companies to follow Joiner's path into Rusk and the surrounding counties. Newly erected, towering derricks soon seemed more plentiful than pine trees. One observer colorfully likened the scene of innumerable new oil rigs to bristles in a hairbrush. En masse, the oil industry swept into the Piney Woods, and suddenly Desdemona and Beaumont didn't seem so far away from the Piney Woods. Dad Joiner's strike on Daisy Bradford's farm had tapped into the vast East Texas Field, at that time the largest reserve of oil ever discovered in the United States.

When the oil industry swept into East Texas in the first chilly days of the Great Depression, it did so with a swagger. Much of East Texas, including Panola County, was on the brink of becoming another Appalachia, a society with little means to support itself. Land dependence had become no dependence at all as crop prices plummeted. But the burgeoning oil industry changed everything as jobs on rigs and pipelines offered alternate ways of earning income to many people who previously seemed to have no options. Yes, concerns about the environment and overproduction accompanied the discovery of oil in East Texas, but oil also saved the lives of many East Texans. Oil saved Travis Reeves and his family.

In the early 1930s, Travis's older brother Beuford had gone to work for the United Gas Company, which in the wake of Dad Joiner's strike had built several oil production sites around Panola County. Beuford had married and moved north of Galloway to Latex, Texas, near the larger town of De Berry, leaving the farming to his younger—yet capable—brothers and sisters. Shortly after, in 1932, he moved Beulah and the children closer to him. Beuford had done so well at United Gas that he could afford to own a house in De Berry while living with his wife in Latex. Beuford moved his younger siblings and mother into the De Berry house, snatching them from a worsening outlook in Galloway. "He told my mother that she could live there as long as she wanted to," said sister Virgie. "And he didn't charge us anything." That was oil money at work. Beuford had not become an oil baron, but his job at United Gas transformed his and his family's lives in short order.

Travis was perhaps nine years old when the Reeveses moved up to De Berry, and there he found that his age could no longer shelter him from work. With marriage whittling down Beulah's brood, and Beulah herself becoming less able to expend much energy, more was expected of Travis. The family farmed a patch of land in back of their house that provided their food and some income, and there Travis could be found picking weeds or toting a cotton sack. He worked classes into his schedule, too, enrolling at the De Berry School, where he held on to his twister-like reputation. "He'd fight a circle saw for me," said Virgie. "When we were going to school, nobody better not bother me, or he'd hit him."

Travis's new school, like the Galloway School, consisted of four rooms and was bursting with boys hungry to play baseball at recess. "We had a couple of softballs," said Chester Studdard, a schoolmate and neighbor. "We knocked those things around until the guts started coming out of them."

When he could escape work and school, Travis often hitched rides to Galloway to play with his old friends, and as he approached his teens, he played more and more baseball with the De Berry boys. He also began dabbling with a new hobby: music. Travis had been drawn to a variety of musical talent throughout his life. Early on in Galloway, he had heard local fiddlers and guitarists at various events, and at home, O. D. often picked up a fiddle or guitar to play a few tunes. In De Berry, the family acquired a wind-up record player, and Travis marveled at the sounds of rural troubadours that emanated from the device with its spinning, felt-covered turntable. He hummed and sang along with the recorded musicians, wondering how all those people could fit in such a small box.

Travis's tastes were especially honed by Jimmie Rodgers's various blue yodels and records by the Carter Family and Panola County native Tex Ritter. He also surely heard a host of singers like Gene Autry and Vernon Dalhart, who employed a more urbane, full-throated approach to singing than did Jimmie Rodgers or the Carters. Their 78-rpm records, and those of pop singers Bing Crosby and Kate Smith, spread to rural communities throughout the South by means of mail-order catalogs and furniture stores, which sold record players and thus sold records.

Radio also stimulated Travis's interest in music. When electricity arrived in De Berry a few years after the Reeves family moved there,

At the De Berry School. James Travis stands in the top row, second from the left. (Courtesy: Frank Anderson)

a radio became a centerpiece in his life. In the evenings, Travis pulled in such distant programs as the *National Barn Dance* on WLS in Chicago and the *Grand Ole Opry* on WSM in Nashville. Stations closer to home featured a smattering of hillbilly music and western swing, which Travis digested along with the broadcasts of popular, urban dance bands of the day. Several styles floated on the airwaves around him: the local country dance sounds, the polished voices of Dalhart and Autry, and the harsher stylings of Jimmie Rodgers and the Carter Family.

Sister Virgie recalled that Travis often had a song on his breath. "When we were working in the field hoeing cotton or picking cotton, he would just stop and he would start singing and whistling. And my brother'd tell him, 'Come on, we got to finish this patch today.' But he wouldn't do it, he'd just start to humming and singing. He just picked it up. He was just born to sing, I guess."

Sister Louie said the singing and humming soon required accompaniment. Travis wanted a guitar. "He got his first guitar from a boy that had an old guitar that he didn't care anything about," she remembered. "It was laying out in his yard. My mother gathered a bushel of pears, and he gave the [boy's family] the pears for the guitar. It didn't have no strings on it, but he managed around and bummed him some strings and fixed it up, and that was his first guitar." Louie recalled that Travis learned to strum a few licks from Bill Price, a man who was married to her and Travis's first cousin. Price worked on a nearby gas pipeline and lived in Logan, according to Louie. And there were other teachers as well. O. D. certainly shared some tricks with his younger brother, and Virgie frequently saw Travis and a black farmer who lived down the road playing their guitars.

By Panola County standards, Travis became relatively proficient on guitar as he entered his early teens, and people in and around De Berry often danced to his performances. On weekends, he sometimes headed for his grandmother Adams's home in Logan, where, in the evenings, he would sit next to a fiddler named Robey Pyles and entertain family and neighbors from all around. A wide hallway ran down the center of the house, and Travis and Robey would play at one end while dancers jammed the rest of the corridor. Young Jenny Lee Wimberly lived across the pasture from the Adams place and almost always showed up to see Travis play. The two were sweethearts, and Travis often walked her home after the dance.

The town's youngfolk usually lollygagged home in a large pack, some on foot and others on horseback. They often would stop to tell a story or throw rocks into the dark woods. "Some of the girls and some of the boys, they'd all be singing," said Jenny Lee. "That was just a way of life." Jenny Lee and her beau often strayed from the dawdling group, seeking a quiet spot where Travis could set her on a tree stump and serenade her. From his repertoire, Travis often wooed Jenny Lee with "Nobody's Darling But Mine," a popular song for Jimmie Davis in 1937. And after the song, there would be a tender moment. "He was a good kisser," sighed Jenny Lee.

With his guitar, Travis joined a fraternity of local, mostly amateur pickers who gathered to chase away the occasional boredom of rural life. Through 1938 and '39, he became acquainted with musicians such as Rusty Courtney, Homer Barnett, Dewey Yount, and Ernest Singleton, who often lugged a trombone as well as a guitar to the impromptu jam sessions. Among that group was a Carthage boy named Carey Rhiddlehoover, who was a few years older than Travis and played mandolin. He and Travis shared some musical tastes and became especially close musical partners.

"We weren't playing regular or anything like that," recalled Carey, "but we just loved it so much we just liked to get together and play. A lot of times on weekends, we just got together. We'd get out on a porch on a Sunday afternoon and just play everything. One person would play one and somebody else would play one, and a lot of the neighbors came around and listened." The two boys also delighted in crashing country dances, more to watch the bedlam on and off the floor than for the music.

Carey idolized two young Texas pickers named Joe and Bob Shelton,* who appeared regularly on KWKH as the Sunshine Boys, and he worked the guitar-mandolin duo's songs and styles into his jam sessions with Travis and other local musicians. The Sunshine Boys had matured musically in the late 1920s by playing virtually non-stop for oil workers around Longview, and by the early 1930s, they had recorded as the Lone Star Cowboys for RCA Victor and backed Decca Records' Jimmie Davis. In 1935 they had started recording for Decca while maintaining regularly scheduled shows on radio stations in Dallas-Forth Worth and Shreveport. Like countless other radio performers throughout the South, the Sheltons found they could use their on-air spots to solicit and promote live appearances within the station's listening area. East Texas, they discovered, was a rich land for mining twenty-five-cent admissions.

Carey recalled that he first stumbled upon the Sheltons one evening in 1935 or '36. "I had been to a ten-cent movie in Marshall, and I was walking down the sidewalk and I heard this music, and I finally got around to see where it was coming from. I got fascinated with the mandolin. This Joe Shelton was quite an accomplished mandolin player." Subsequently, Carey tried to catch the Sunshine Boys whenever they made live appearances at Panola County school houses, and he was so inspired by Joe Shelton's playing that he rounded up a couple of beat-up mandolins and learned to play himself. He would trip through what he knew of the Sheltons' catalog and asked Travis to join him.

Rhiddlehoover had met Travis during a visit to what he called the "backwoods between Deadwood and Logansport, Louisiana." That was Travis's old home place, and Travis must have been back visiting old friends when Carey first encountered him. "He had a

---

*Shelton was the maiden name of Bob and Joe's mother. Their actual surname was Attlesey.

cheap guitar hanging around his neck," said Carey, who then put the young picker out of his head until his Shelton-inspired interest in music blossomed a year or two later. Carey became reacquainted with Travis after another chance meeting in Carthage, where Carey's father ran a painting and wallpapering business. "We was probably eating a five-cent hamburger and listening to a jukebox."

The meeting, wherever it took place, led to regular jam sessions between the two. "He was one of the most down-home people I ever met," said Carey of the backwoods boy. "He had a good sense of humor. He liked to laugh about something that someone would do that was funny. He didn't talk a whole heck of a lot." In fact, Carey recalled that Travis could be absolutely bashful—reluctant, for example, to sing in front of groups of people if the situation required.

Although Rhiddlehoover and Reeves (they had no group name) mainly played for fun, they did enter amateur contests in the county and picked up occasional jobs. Fiddlin' Bob Davis, a sixty-ish De Berry musician who lived near Travis and performed at local schools and churches, frequently asked the boys to back him. Davis had been a familiar source of music in Panola County since the turn of the century, and the large-framed fiddler's style and songs suggested as much. "He wasn't a breakdown fiddler," observed Carey. "He played mostly smooth, like two-step, four-four time stuff." In an age of modernizing music, Davis's rags, waltzes, and marches brought to mind old sheet-music covers with idyllic scenes and silhouettes.

"He played what they called two-string harmony," explained Carey of Fiddlin' Bob's style. "I learned that from him. I played that [harmony] on the mandolin, on slow tunes and tunes with a moderate tempo." Carey and Travis swayed along with Davis through old parlor favorites like "Let Me Call You Sweetheart" and "Missouri Waltz" as well as a number of sacred songs the fiddler also liked to perform. The boys added those old-fashioned standards to their own front-porch repertoire that included more recent, generally popular songs like "Harbor Lights," "Rosetta," and "Red Sails in the Sunset" as well as such Gene Autry/western favorites as "Mexicali Rose" and "Tumbling Tumbleweeds."

The pair experimented with a wide variety of songs and musical styles. "We played stuff back in those days that would be considered bluegrass," said Carey. "Of course, we didn't play it wide open and tune our instruments up so high that the strings would break. . . . There used to be an old newspaper called the *Semi-Weekly News*. I don't know where on earth that thing came from, but it would have songs and the words of songs. People all over the state of Texas would send in these songs. I remember one of these things had 'Bury Me Under the Weeping Willow' [a favorite recorded by the Carter Family in 1928]. We played that kind of music a lot."

According to Rhiddlehoover, the work with Bob Davis led to a circuit of performances with a one-legged traveling entertainer named "Peg" Chadwick. A magician and ventriloquist, Chadwick hired local musical talent to embellish his act. In Panola County, Davis and his boys warmed up the crowd, helping to build anticipation for Chadwick's stage entrance. Travis and Carey also caught the eye of a couple of local would-be agents who tried to lasso the Panola County musicians and book them at area events. Carey recalled that the entrepreneurs, Joe Forbes and Harvey Lawless, each sought to make his living by promoting local performers, but only Lawless—a De Berry man who worked for United Gas—appeared to have any luck.

One Saturday night in 1940, Lawless placed a number of Panola County players on KWKH Radio's new *Saturday Night Roundup*, during the Sunshine Boys' segment of the show. "There was a whole bunch of people: I believe Fiddlin' Bob Davis, [guitarist] Ernest Singleton, and a piano player named Pete Majors, and [Travis] and myself," said Carey. "We went over there and played a few numbers. I can't even remember what we did, but we had a lot of fun." The KWKH appearance probably was not the last contact Travis had with Harvey Lawless. Chester Studdard, a baseball mate and friend of Travis's from De Berry, recalled hearing Lawless present regular appearances by the De Berry guitarist on Shreveport's KRMD in 1941. Travis's appearances likely aired after February 1941, when Carey Rhiddlehoover was drafted.

Travis had become an integral part of the local music community. But he played mostly for fun, earning a dollar a night at most for his work with Rhiddlehoover behind Bob Davis. The farm required that he keep his boots in the fields, particularly after the death of his older brother Alton in 1939. A thunderstorm had swept over De Berry one afternoon and hurled a deadly bolt of lightning toward Alton. "He and O. D. was across the pasture and it came up . . . ," remembered sister Louie. "They was coming across the pasture back to the house, and they went under a big sweet gum tree, and it struck the tree and killed him."

Forced to be even more resourceful after Alton's death, Beulah began taking in borders, usually pipeline workers. She also asked her youngest son to stay home from school to work on the family farm. So, in 1939, when most of his peers were starting their first year at Carthage High School, Travis was helping to plug dikes on the Reeves farm. His sister Virgie also dropped out of school to care for their mother and work on the farm.

Just because Travis turned his attention to his family's livelihood and a growing interest in music doesn't mean he forsook his earliest love. When time allowed, he often chose baseball over music, tearing into marathon hours of play with De Berry youngsters Chester Studdard, Ralph Allen, Junior Barnett, Dee Lawless, and Marlin Lampworth. Most of the town's boys, though, had begun attending Carthage High several miles down the road in the county seat and had joined Coach E. B. Morrison's baseball team there. Travis's heart almost certainly sank as he watched his buddies go off to school and play ball on an organized team. He remained out of school—picking guitar and cotton—and probably never would have returned to the classroom had it not been for baseball.

As E. B. Morrison cranked up practice for the 1940 season, he observed a shallowness on the Bulldogs' pitching roster. He had capable arms in De Berry native Ralph Allen and a boy named June Graves from the Old Center community, but Graves was the only real starter. Allen basically pitched in relief. The coach needed another strong starting pitcher if his team was to succeed over the twelve-game season and make it into the playoffs. Morrison, who taught Spanish and history, had a good relationship with his players. He took an interest in their lives and seemed to look on the boys as sons. The youngsters could approach him and probably felt perfectly at ease in suggesting a solution to his pitching deficit.

A member of the De Berry gang nominated Travis Reeves to fill the hole in Morrison's pitching staff. A right-hander who could hurl a snapping curveball, Travis would surely return to school if he knew that baseball was part of the package. Because Morrison listened to his players, he met with Travis and invited him back to Carthage to try out for the high school team. The sixteen-year-old jumped at the chance and must have convinced Beulah Reeves—perhaps with Morrison's help—that returning to school was the best thing he could do. In any event, by early March 1940, Travis Reeves had landed back in the classroom and was preparing for the team's opener in late March.

Beulah may not have realized the extent to which baseball would consume Travis's time when she released him to E. B. Morrison and Carthage High School. Morrison scheduled spring practices in the afternoon, which meant that Travis would often arrive home after dark, if at all. De Berry was some twenty miles from Carthage, and although a bus carried the town's students to and from school, it did not wait around to take Reeves and his De Berry teammates home after practice and games. They would hitchhike home or stay overnight with students who lived in Carthage. Beulah got her son back for the summer after baseball season ended, and since the season started in the spring, Travis was able to be on hand for the fall cotton harvest.

Playing conditions at Carthage High were primitive. The field had been carved out of a cow pasture near the school, and a home-made backstop often failed to prevent foul balls from disappearing into the surrounding pine thickets. Baseballs were scarce, and periodically a game or practice would stop cold so the players could search the woods for errant balls. The team found that out-of-town fields could be just as rough—if they could get there at all. Coach Morrison often came close to forfeiting games because it was so difficult to transport his team to other communities.

"Back in those days," said Chester Studdard, "the school did not own any school buses; they were privately owned. We had to get to distant [games] the best way we could, and oftentimes some professor would volunteer to take us to the game." If the teachers failed to come through, parents and fans would form a convoy of automobiles for the trip out of town.

Before one out-of-town game, Morrison told interviewer Cody Pierce, he appeared to have no options. "There was no transportation, and I was about ready to go to the telephone and cancel the game. One of the boys said, 'Well, I can get my daddy's pickup truck.' So I said, 'Bring it around.' The driver and I got in the front seat and the rest of the boys just piled in the back the best way they could. It was kind of crowded. We were toddling down the road . . . and a highway cop stopped us. I wondered what was going to happen. I said, 'Officer, what have we done? We weren't breaking the speed limit.' He said, 'Well, I'll tell you. You're driving a vehicle here which has a farm license on it. And number two is, you're not supposed to haul anything except farm products, and those boys sure aren't that.' He let us go on. He wrote out a ticket, then tore it up."

To play baseball, the boys gladly endured such indignities. In fact, they loved the game so much they would almost be willing to dive through a barbed wire fence to play it. On Opening Day against Tatum High School, Coach Morrison placed Travis in right field, and the youngster batted 2–for–5, a respectable plate performance in his team's 17–1 victory. But Morrison had figured Travis to be one of the team's top pitchers, and when he sent him to the mound in relief of June Graves a few days later, Travis showed his stuff. He held the nearby Gary team scoreless until he, in turn, was replaced by another pitcher. The three hurlers combined for a one-hitter in a 37–0 drubbing of Gary. Travis appeared on the mound again to pitch a five-hitter against the San Augustine Wolves in mid-April, but then his season collapsed.

The *Panola Watchman* first reported that the team's promising pitcher had injured his right shoulder in a car accident, then a few days later noted that Travis had come down with the mumps and later said he had contracted whooping cough. Travis's value to the team had vanished in an incredible series of injury and illnesses, and while the Bulldogs scratched their way to their league's championship game, they lost to hated rival San Augustine. "Wait till next year," as the old baseball adage goes.

The 1941 season opened with Travis in robust health and the team more optimistic that they could outpace the Wolves of San Augustine. The Bulldogs also could look forward to playing on a brand new diamond at the Carthage fairgrounds—although it looked as if the ball field might not be ready in time for the home opener against Garrison High. "Even if the infield will be torn up and the outfield uncertain," the newspaper cheerfully reported, "there is one thing we can depend on: our pitchers Reeves and Graves. Both boys are due to be among the best high school pitchers in the state. Last year Reeves began the season under the worst conditions imaginable . . . this year he seems to be in good condition and is anxious to redeem himself."

And redeem himself he did. Word of Travis's potential reached the New York Giants, prompting the major league team to dispatch a scout to his 1941 pitching debut in the home opener. The appearance of a big-league scout toting a notebook would have rattled most high school players, but Travis was unfazed. The man's presence only supercharged his day. In a 3–2 victory over Garrison, he struck out thirteen batters and allowed just four hits. In early April he threw a two-hitter against San Augustine, and by the end of the month, Morrison's De Berry pitcher had led the team to a 8–0 start. As in 1940, San Augustine and Carthage were sprinting down the home stretch toward the league championship, and it would be the Wolves that delivered Reeves's and the Bulldogs' first loss. But it was too late to stop the Carthage nine's momentum.

In May, with Travis toeing the rubber, the Bulldogs blanked the dreaded Wolves in the league championship game. Travis again was mighty, giving up only one hit and fanning eleven. Sounds of bats whooshing through empty air replaced the sharp crack of hits whenever he appeared on the mound. The Bulldogs' next stop was Dallas and the state championship tournament. A Piney Woods team comprised mostly of boys from De Berry had won a chance to be the best in Texas. "We played together at De Berry in grade school all the time," said Chester Studdard. "It carried over into high school. We knew each other's moves. Our chemistry was there."

It was unlikely, however, that the Bulldog chemistry would bring home a championship flag. At the time, the state did not classify sports teams on the basis of school size. It may have been more equitable if Carthage had been able to compete at the state level against schools of its own size, those with the same kind of tenuous playing and practicing conditions and access to a similarly small pool of boys. But in Dallas, Carthage would face the big schools from wealthier school districts. To finance the team's trip there, Coach Morrison resorted to asking folks around Carthage for donations.

In the first round of the Dallas tournament, Carthage drew a bye. The team saw its first action on the morning of Friday, May 16, against a strong Hondo High School team from South Texas that boasted the so-called "Hondo Hurricane," pitcher Clint Hartung, who would go straight to the major leagues after high school. Hartung's team was the defending state champion and had defeated Austin in the first round of the tournament, but surprisingly, the much-heralded hurler and his team melted under a fierce Bulldog hitting

With the 1940 Carthage Bulldogs. Travis is bottom, right. (Courtesy: Mary Graves)

attack. "We jumped all over him," pitcher June Graves told an interviewer, "and beat him and the Hondo team."

It was Travis Reeves, not Hartung, who was king of the hill that
day, allowing just four hits in his team's 8–2 victory. The Bulldogs
remained potent as they entered the tournament's third round that
evening against McKinney High School. With just a few hours' rest,
"the rugged little Carthage sluggers" and fireballer June Graves
buried the McKinney squad and qualified for the state championship
game the next day against Sunset High of Dallas. The Bulldogs had
traveled two hundred miles to Dallas and then to the championship
game on the strength of Travis Reeves's and June Graves's pitching,
but they would go no farther. Although Travis struck out eleven
batters, Carthage fell to Sunset 6–1.

The Panola County newspaper grumbled that the Sunset players had enjoyed a day's rest before the game, while the Carthage
squad had played Hondo and McKinney the previous day. However,
the paper and the entire town of Carthage took pride in the rag-tag
collection of boys who had trouble getting home after practice and
the coach who relied on his wits to transport the team to away
games. The Bulldogs had shown why Americans of the 1940s so
loved baseball: It was a game of underdogs. If nine guys could pitch
and hit, a team could go anywhere—despite frayed uniforms and a
primitive home field.

The 1941 dream season transformed the Carthage players into
local celebrities, and if the kids in school had not known Travis
Reeves's name before the season, they knew it afterward. The *Panola
Watchman* splashed the team's Dallas adventure across its front
page, and word spread quickly when Travis and Chester Studdard
made the all-state team. In school, the younger students just stared
at Travis the baseball hero. Success on the diamond had helped him
shed the timidity that Carey Rhiddlehoover had observed when the
two first began playing music together. Travis had become a confident young man with an erect posture and a voice that rose loudly
and clearly above the noisy hallways and lunchroom.

"He was never bashful or embarrassed about anything," said
friend and fellow all-star Chester Studdard. "He was real dry-witted.
. . . He'd have been a great stand-up comic." Many of Travis's mates
recalled that the youngster was frequently called to the front of the

classroom by the English teacher to read poetry and recite passages from classic works. Travis bellowed out the prose and poems, his voice betraying the nasally cadence so common in the speech of many East Texans.

Travis's classmate and occasional date Margaret Rhiddlehoover (Carey's sister) attributed his confident, pleasing voice to Q. M. Martin, the superintendent of schools and a teacher at Carthage High. "He had a lot of influence on Travis," she said. "He taught classes in speech, and that's when [Travis] really learned to speak like that. [Travis] had a beautiful speaking voice." Travis exhibited a slight bravado when he stood before his classmates, and he never refused when the school's principal asked him to play guitar during assembly programs. Travis often toted his guitar to school, strumming and trying to sing above the clattering of the bus. He continued to work the land in back of his De Berry home and at the end of the day frequently scurried off to play music.

In the summer of 1941—amid his farm work, schoolhouse gigs, and hoopla over the fantastic baseball season—Travis turned eighteen, an age when many young men in Panola County had begun to put a finger on their future. Travis's older brothers had followed Beuford to the United Gas Company, but Travis harbored no such ambition. "He told my brother he wouldn't ever work for United Gas," said sister Virgie. "That wasn't what he wanted to do." But what would he do? Farming held no appeal for him. In fact, the Reeves family was scaling down its dependence on farming, and Beulah now relied mostly on United Gas money her children carried and sent home. If Travis was considering a professional music career, he kept his aspirations to himself—had he aired such a notion, derision would have followed immediately. "There's only room for one Tex Ritter in East Texas," many surely would have said. The pickers Travis knew would starve to death if they relied solely on the money they made playing dances. Music making was strictly for fun.

It seemed altogether plausible that Travis would play professional baseball when he finished high school. A year or two earlier, that route would have seemed as ridiculous as the musical one, but throughout the 1941 season, major league scouts had continued to drop by to catch his mound appearances. Agents of the St. Louis Cardinals, in particular, had hovered about during the season, watching closely as Travis and fellow hurler June Graves struck out batter after batter. The Cardinals were intensely interested and approached both boys prior to the 1942 season with offers to try out for their minor league club in New Albany, Georgia.

The overture must have sent the boys to heaven. After all, the Cards had just missed going to the World Series the previous fall. With men like Enos Slaughter and the spanking-new sensation Stan Musial, St. Louis was one of the top teams in all of baseball. But if Travis and June accepted, they would have to drop out of school and report to New Albany just as the Bulldogs' 1942 season was opening. That would deal a serious blow to Carthage's hopes of finally capturing the state baseball title (a fate worse than ignorance, perhaps!). On its front page, the *Panola Watchman* bemoaned the bittersweetness of the Cardinals' offer: "Friends of the Carthage pitching stars are proud for them, but view with alarm the serious effect their decisions to accept the tryout offers would have on the Carthage baseball mine. The [1942] team is calculated to annex the championship flag in Dallas this spring with Graves and Reeves alternating on the slab."

The boys were tempted, but in the end, E. B. Morrison interceded and asked the Cardinals to back off their offer. In a letter to Graves dated March 30, the Cards' vice president of minor league clubs urged the boy to stay home. "Mr. Morrison's letter of March 9 said that you and Travis were still in school and that you were very important cogs in his high school team this spring. If I were you, I would not walk out on my coach." Travis probably received a similar note.

Travis and June's sharp turn away from professional baseball surely invigorated Morrison and his boys, not to mention the towns-people. The team and the town geared up to hang the state championship banner in Carthage, and on Opening Day against San Augustine, Travis Reeves fueled their optimism. With his ever-strengthening and elusive curveball, he showed the Wolves that the Bulldogs would be 1942's team to beat. The curve—which was probably Carthage's best weapon against opponents—bamboozled almost every batter that day. Travis risked straining his young arm with the jerking pitch, but as long as the opponents struck out, he continued to serve it up. The players were accustomed to fastballs that steamed fat and straight down the center of the plate, but curves surprised them.

"He had wiry fingers," said Chester Studdard, who watched Travis from his shortstop position. "His fingers were longer than the palms of his hands. He could throw a curveball that most high school pitchers couldn't throw. He [threw] that curveball at right-handed batters just about at their head, their left ear. They thought it was going to hit them, and it would curve over the plate. He struck a lot of people out who were just standing there thinking it was going to hit them, and it would curve over the plate."

Discussions of postseason play reached an uproarious magnitude around Carthage when the Bulldogs returned home victorious from an April 10 exhibition game against the University of Texas's freshman baseball team. It may have been Travis's finest moment in a season of fine moments. The college coach had chosen Ralph Allen (who had graduated from Carthage High in 1941) to play first base for him, and in order to get look at the other Carthage players, he paid the Bulldogs' expenses to the game in Austin.

According to the *Panola Watchman*, the Texas coach got an eyeful, especially of Reeves. "Behind the brilliant pitching of Travis Reeves, Carthage defeated the University of Texas [freshmen] here Friday afternoon on the Clark Field diamond, 3–1. Using a curveball that cracked like a whip, Reeves struck out nine Yearlings." The Bulldogs' victory over the UT freshmen was akin to felling a giant, and afterwards, the college coach talked with Travis and teammate Chester Studdard about their plans for the fall of 1942. They'd be hearing from him.

Predictably, the Bulldog juggernaut continued to amass wins, easily pocketing the league title and returning to the state tournament. With donations from businessmen and other Carthage boosters, the team traveled to Dallas in a line of sedans to find that the baseball intelligentsia there expected the Bulldogs to win it all. "Carthage is rated favorite because it lists among its victims the strong University of Texas freshman nine as well as other outstanding schoolboy clubs," reported the *Dallas Morning News*.

At 7:00 on Thursday evening, May 21, the Bulldogs took to the diamond at Dallas's Reverchon Park to face Whitharral High School of West Texas. Travis was handed the starting duties and, true to predictions, he and the Bulldogs pounded Whitharral. The next day, June Graves maintained the momentum, blanking Mesquite High 6–0 in nine splendid innings of no-hit baseball. The victory moved the East Texas boys into the state championship game, and although it appeared that the Bulldogs might play Hondo High as they had in the 1941 tournament, the Hondo nine fell to the Adamson High Leopards of Dallas.

No Adamson High team had captured a state championship in any sport since 1924, and it seemed likely that Carthage would extend the school's dry spell for at least one more year. Travis Reeves's name in the lineup further dimmed Adamson's hopes of winning the state baseball title, but the Leopards had performed mightily up to that point in the tournament. In the first round, the Dallas club had scored twenty-two runs after just two innings, disgracing their opponents and causing them to forfeit before the start of the third. Then, in the second round, Adamson had sent a powerful Hondo team packing by a score of 4–2.

On Saturday, May 24, Travis started the game against Adamson and in the top of the first inning took a rare sting. The fans at Dallas's Rebel Stadium had barely settled into their seats with their popcorn and hot dogs when Adamson scored four runs on two hits and a pair of walks. Reeves returned to the mound in the top of the second after a scoreless Bulldogs side and was able to conjure up his old form. He held the Leopards scoreless in both the second and third innings, and then, in the bottom of the third, the Carthage offense began to stir. The Bulldogs put runners on second and third, and appeared to be on the verge of scoring, but they failed to capitalize on the opportunity. In the fourth inning, Travis again blanked the Leopards, and the Bulldogs again had runners at second and third—and again they failed to capitalize. Carthage was blowing its scoring opportunities and placing an increasing burden on Travis to prevent a larger deficit. He soon wavered.

"In the fifth," wrote the *Dallas Morning News*, "the Leopards broke out in another rash of runs, and June Graves . . . was rushed to the mound to put out the fire after three runs had been scored." Graves doused the red-hot Adamson bats, but Carthage's chances of bringing home the state championship wafted away on the spring breeze. After a sixth stanza in which the Bulldogs again stranded runners on base, the Leopards pushed the score to 12–0 in the seventh inning and were declared the winners (tournament rules stated that a game must be halted if one of the teams accumulated a lead of ten or more runs after the sixth inning).

Carthage's promising season had unceremoniously fizzled, but nonetheless—thanks to the victory over the University of Texas—it had been a season of highlights. The only problem was that, with Reeves, Graves, and Studdard all graduating, the Bulldogs would never again come so close to winning it all. The 1942 season, however, had enshrined Travis Reeves's name in the baseball lore of East Texas. He was the righty who came off the farm and helped forge a winning tradition in Carthage. Then, to the delight of all Carthage boosters, he had stunned the University of Texas and led his team to two state championships.

Whoever had thought to nominate Travis for a spot on Coach Morrison's spotty pitching staff had paved a path to the future for the young man from De Berry. Baseball had given Travis an avenue away from sharecropping and the oil fields he so adamantly wished to avoid, and E. B. Morrison had ensured that people knew about him. Morrison could have thrown up his hands at the lack of transportation and facilities for his team, but he refused to squander talent. He corralled his boys and shepherded them through the University of Texas game and into the state championship game, giving Travis a forum in which to impress coaches and scouts from across the state. After the 1942 season ended, the UT coach offered Travis and Chester Studdard baseball scholarships to attend the University of Texas. It was a distinct honor in the baseball-crazy state of Texas to play for the state university at Austin, and both youngsters accepted the offer.

On the class of 1942's graduation day, however, Travis's thoughts may have darted out past the University of Texas. While the superintendent passed out medals, scholarships, and honor pins, and the Carthage High band oom-pahed away, thoughts of Europe and the Pacific could not have been too far from Travis's mind. The United States' declaration of war against the Axis powers was almost six months old, and many of the boys expected to be called for military service at any time. Coach Morrison had gone to Sheppard Field, Texas, where—at the age of thirty-four—he had volunteered to serve as an Army athletic instructor and physical trainer. Carthage's young men would soon follow, biding their time on gas pipelines or family farms until the draft board drew their numbers. Travis could only wait, but while he did, he and Chester scavenged a few quarters for an Austin-bound bus.

3

Any sense of destiny that Travis imagined on his 350-mile bus ride to the University of Texas would have popped like a threadbare, wartime tire soon after he arrived in Austin. As Chester Studdard remembered, he and Travis lurched into town on the evening of August 15, 1942, and spread out over some chairs and floor in the bus terminal for a night's sleep. They had next to no cash, and expected to start in the university's summer program at the school's expense.

"Travis and I both enrolled," said Studdard. "We were only enrolled for about five hours. . . . Our scholarships weren't supposed to start until the fall semester of '42. We was down there and enrolled and the registrar's secretary told us, 'If you get a job and pay your way for six weeks, we'll pick you up in the fall.' We couldn't get a job. So we went back up to the registrar's office and said, 'Will you please take our names off the roll?' "

Perhaps the boys were impatient, but, from their perspective, staying in Austin would mean starvation. Anyway, they rationalized, Uncle Sam would certainly be calling before their UT baseball days began. The De Berry boys said good-bye to Austin and college baseball on August 16 or 17, then bought a bus ticket to Houston. It was as good as going home. Travis's sister Louie and her husband had settled there, and their Carthage teammate June Graves had landed a spot on a Houston baseball team and also worked at the Grand Prize brewery.

Once there, they decided to apply for jobs at the brewery. They moved in on June, munching his bologna and living rent free while they waited to hear about their applications. In the end, only Travis found a slot at the brewery; Chester gave up and headed home. Soon, however, the military collected June for service, and Travis followed Chester's path back to De Berry. During this time, Travis discovered he would not be following June's path to the military. Military doctors had identified a problem with Travis's heart.* He was classified 4-F.

Back in De Berry, Travis sought out that St. Louis rep who had approached him a year before and found that an open door still awaited him in the Cardinals' farm system. On October 24, 1942, Travis entered the professional ranks at the "D" level in Albany, Georgia. That season, the Albany Cardinals had lagged twenty-five games behind the league's first-place finisher, but that was of little consequence to Travis. The Cardinals organization had plucked him from uncertainty in Houston and plopped him down in America's most stellar farm system.

Baseball man Branch Rickey had just vacated the presidency of the St. Louis Cardinals to take over operation of the Brooklyn Dodgers when Jim signed with New Albany in 1942. (Rickey's name would later dry into historical permanence after he signed Jackie Robinson to a Dodger contract.) However, Rickey's impact on the Cardinals would be apparent for many years after he exited the organization. St. Louis owner Sam Breadon had given Rickey great leeway in running the operation, and with this freedom, Rickey had built an enviable farm system.

Before Rickey, most minor league teams operated independently of the majors and made a lot of money selling their players to the big leagues. Quite simply, the major league teams with the deepest pockets could outbid their rivals for the best players. Thus, cash-heavy clubs like the Chicago Cubs and New York Yankees could siphon off the sweetest players from the American Association and International League, for example, and leave the dregs to the less-endowed teams. The Cards had skimpy financial resources and watched talent pass them by, but Branch Rickey was an inventive man who knew that no matter how high the wall, it could always be circumnavigated.

---

*Studdard and Travis's friend Margaret Rhiddlehoover confirmed this. Margaret recalled Jim specifically telling her that he had rheumatic fever as a child and the illness had affected his heart.

In the 1920s and '30s, with Sam Breadon's blessings, Rickey established a host of Cardinals-owned or -controlled teams in the independent minor leagues of the nation, which allowed the Cards to groom their own prize studs and keep them in their own barn. As former *Sports Illustrated* Editor Robert W. Creamer wrote in *Baseball in '41*, Rickey collected teams as if they were golf hats. "By 1940 the Cardinals owned or controlled thirty-three minor league teams, and the flow of fine ballplayers from the minors to the Cardinals was astonishing." Through the years, the Cardinals would harvest from their system such greats as Stan Musial, Red Schoendienst, and Ken Boyer. Other major league teams copied Rickey's tact until it became common for big-league teams to have minor league arms.

Travis and his right arm had begun their initiation into pro ball at the worst—and best—of possible times. World War II had caused tremendous upheaval in the major and minor leagues, jumbling the careers of many players. First, major league baseball watched Detroit star Hank Greenberg go off to battle, and soon Ted Williams, Bob Feller, Joe DiMaggio, Stan Musial, and other heroes of the diamond fell into lockstep. Torn between patriotism and economics, owners everywhere cringed while hallmark names swapped their spikes for combat boots, and revenues dwindled.

But President Franklin D. Roosevelt had decreed that major league play should continue for the sake of the nation's morale. Owners dutifully coped by squeezing their resources. Youngsters—a couple as young as fifteen and sixteen—joined the pro ranks while the barn door was open, as did Pete Gray, a one-armed outfielder, and Bert Shepard, a one-legged pitcher. With such players, the big-league teams kept a splintered wedge in their open door, but not all minor league outfits could say the same. Teams and entire leagues collapsed. Of the thirty-two leagues that fielded teams in 1942, only ten had survived to see the opening pitch of 1943. Lack of manpower was the obvious culprit, but there were other woes, too. Gas shortages kept fans from driving or busing to the stadiums and restricted team travel to away games, while fear of German planes and exorbitant energy consumption limited the night games that had become so popular among day workers. Teams scrambled to remain competitive, shuffling men to fill unexpected voids and combing the country for suitable rookies. The Cardinals resorted to running advertisements, pleading for players with professional experience. The conditions were inglorious, but opportunities for a talented (but medically-unfit-for-service) guy like Travis seemed great.

Perhaps Travis would someday make it to St. Louis, but to do so he had a long road to travel. Albany's D classification lurked at the bottom of a rating system that designated its top teams as AA. D-level teams labored away in towns like Butler, Pennsylvania; Clovis, New Mexico; and Hickory, North Carolina, while AA clubs basked in Milwaukee, Baltimore, and Los Angeles—cities that would one day get major league franchises. Travis's view from the bottom of this towering ladder was intimidating, and when he looked up again at the start of his first pro season, the ladder shot up another few feet.

In April 1943, before Travis had pitched a single game for Albany, the Cardinals organization assigned him to Hamilton, Ontario, of the Pennsylvania-Ontario-New York (PONY) League. Unfortunately, the Hamilton Red Wings were in the process of folding their operation and relocating, victimized by the war that was fast snatching away American ballplayers. Travis had only to report to Uncle Sam Breadon, however, and Breadon's people wanted him in Jamestown, New York, where the Hamilton club was moving to be closer to competing teams. Travis had yet to throw a pitch in the minor leagues, and it appeared that he would have to wait much longer to get his chance. Records indicate that on July 22, 1943, Jamestown "suspended" him along with nine other players.

Whether injury or a dissatisfied coach stopped him on the ladder is unclear, but by midsummer 1943 Travis was back in Texas, and Chester Studdard had found him a job at Lockheed Aircraft in Dallas. Studdard, who would soon be drafted into the U.S. Navy, recalled that Travis pitched for the company baseball team and, while on the job, installed machine guns on B–17 bombers. By 1944 the pitcher who armed planes landed back in Panola County, where he likely found work with United Gas and surely sat in at the regular country dance sessions. Above all, though, he appeared to be marking time until he returned to baseball. On April 25, 1944, Travis penned a letter to his old pal Chester, who was stationed in Norman, Oklahoma. He seemed bored but in good humor as he joked about the scarcity of writing paper. "I had to get some out of the toilet. . . ," he quipped. "It ain't nasty and you'll tear it up anyway."

"I guess I'll try to play a little ball this summer with the Firemen in Shreve," continued Travis, referring to a softball team in

Shreveport. "Shine and Luther [Shine and Luther Lawless, Travis's friends] are going down and play with them too I think. Things are pretty slow around here now, nothing to do, but we get together sometimes and go fishing or play a little poker." Travis also mentioned that he was spending time with his old girlfriend Margaret Rhiddlehoover, who was attending college in Marshall, Texas. "We take in shows and the like on weekends when she's home."

Although Travis had dated many girls from Carthage High, he was closer to Margaret than many of the others. She spent many hours listening to Travis and her brother Carey play on the porch, and by virtue of her last name, she always had sat behind Travis in homeroom. When he could lay his hands on the family's old sedan, before he graduated from high school and after, he would whiz by the Rhiddlehoover home and pick up Margaret for a dance or movie. As they drove or danced, Travis confided to her his baseball plans and the frustration he felt about staying home while the other boys went to war. Afterwards, she—like little Jenny Lee Wimberly—often got the "treatment": a sweet song and a kiss. Whenever Travis returned to De Berry, he looked up Margaret. "She's as sweet as ever," he wrote to Chester in the summer of '44.

Travis again had to say good-bye to Margaret when St. Louis invited him back into its minor league fold for the 1945 season. He re-signed on December 15, 1944, and prepared to report in April to the 1944 Piedmont League champion Lynchburg (Virginia) Cardinals, a B-level team. It may have been desperation that forced the Cardinals to offer another tryout to Travis because by 1944 the war had seriously hampered the team, siphoning away almost three hundred players from the once-noble minor league system. The ranks had slimmed, and, as Travis discovered, even spring training had acquired a new complexion.

Instead of merely hosting its own prospects, the Lynchburg Cardinals had to make room for the other St. Louis farm clubs. In keeping with the war effort, baseball had restricted the distance that a club could take its players for spring training, effectively scotching the always-anticipated trips to Florida. So, Cardinals management chose the best, most southerly site: Lynchburg, Virginia. Still, nighttime temperatures in the mountain city routinely dipped below freezing in early April, just as the players were arriving. Major leaguers who were unaccustomed to cold temperatures during preseason training shared the misery of their underling brethren. Boston's Braves and Red Sox fielded snowballs in New England, while New York's Yankees and Giants settled into resort towns along the New Jersey coast. "The teams went from the sublime to the subfreezing," noted writer Bill Gilbert.

In Lynchburg, the five teams trained in shifts at Municipal Stadium, and during down times, the players explored town or just hung around watching the other guys practice. Travis and his peers had signed for about one hundred dollars a month, but the specter of an ax hovered over them. Despite the shortage of men, they were not guaranteed a position. Although the Cardinals' minor league supervisor, Joe Mathes, watched more and more of his players pack green duffel bags, he and his managers still wielded a paring knife to trim the rosters. According to the local newspaper, Mathes and his men seemed to be having the most trouble settling on a 1945 roster for the Lynchburg team. "While all five clubs are having a certain amount of difficulty in lining up a tentative squad, our Cardinals . . . are more or less stabbing their way through the dark in their efforts to mold a concrete playing force."

Throughout April, Cardinal hopefuls fell by the wayside, but Travis remained on the roster, withstanding the chilly temperatures and the pressure to outgun his peers. He was still on the team when Opening Day arrived, although the Cards' prospects for repeating as league champions seemed as cold as the Lynchburg mornings. Player-coach George Ferrell found that the preponderance of inexperienced players cast a green pall on the club. The team lost early and often.

Travis first saw action on the mound on May 11 versus the Newport News Dodgers. He pitched in relief of Cloyd Boyer (from the Boyer baseball dynasty that included Ken and Clete), who had allowed twelve runs in the first three innings. "Jimmy," as the newspapers dubbed Travis, pitched the remaining six innings against the Dodgers, striking out four and allowing four runs—a relatively decent performance by that game's standards. Over the succeeding weeks, he appeared on the mound in vain attempts to clean up the messes left by starting pitchers. On May 19 against the Richmond Colts, starter Ken Price allowed seven runs in four innings before Travis applied the defensive stopper. "Jimmy Reeves took over the pitching," wrote the *Lynchburg News*, "and held the Colts scoreless over the rest of the route but the damage had been done."

By the end of May, Lynchburg had tumbled to next to last in the Piedmont League, and Travis continued to finish hopeless games, his effective pitching overshadowed by the team's lopsided losses. Forced to do something about his team's lackluster play, manager Ferrell signaled his complete dissatisfaction one night after weathering yet another drubbing by the Richmond Colts. It was June 6, and Travis had come to the rubber to douse another fire. But his curveball refused to behave, and he gave up four runs in two and two-thirds innings.

The *News* recounted the bleak night: "Wild pitching and erratic fielding gave the Richmond Colts another easy victory over the Lynchburg Cardinals. . . . After the exhibition, Manager George Ferrell cut loose all three pitchers who appeared on the mound. Don Shuchman went to Winston-Salem on option but Risinger and Reeves drew outright releases." Released outright. Ferrell had banished Travis from Lynchburg, giving him no option but to limp back to De Berry.

Almost three years had passed since Travis had ditched his University of Texas scholarship and begun chasing a major league dream—three years of minor league disappointment punctuated by softball, oil, poker, hometown girls, and music. It was nice to pop back into town after his adventures and to spin tales of snowy Lynchburg. But he was always returning, never latching on to anything in his journeys. Lynchburg and Jamestown were his Sicily and Normandy beaches—or, rather, his Battaan and Corregidor.

Travis had no real war stories like his returning friends, nor did he have much to show in the way of career accomplishments. Poor Travis! Not even Margaret Rhiddlehoover was around anymore to fill his weekends. She had begun seeing the man she would marry. What had Travis done to follow his victory over the University of Texas freshmen? Not much; no military service, no steady job, no wife. He continued to come home to Beulah. To his family, who lived under the rule of practicality, Travis may have seemed downright irresponsible, but he was the youngest child and needed time to find his way. That summer, he took his mind off baseball by working at a Firestone tire plant in Shreveport.

Travis, though, carried within him the desire to succeed at the profession of his choice. Resolve surely traded for something around Panola County, and Travis's eyes blazed with determination. Throughout his failures in the Cardinals organization, persistence had upheld him. Travis would know failure again, but drawing perhaps from his family's perseverance through Tom's death and their ensuing burdens, he too forged ahead. In April 1946, the Panola County pitcher landed back in spring training, vying for a spot with the Natchez (Mississippi) Giants of the Evangeline League.

With the end of World War II, minor league baseball was delivered to its heyday. Veteran ballplayers as well as young men who had honed their skills on sandy diamonds in the Marshall Islands or soggy football pitches in England swarmed back to the United States, seeking to play the sport of their childhood. Minor league clubs reorganized as quickly as they had folded a few years earlier. A radiant postwar economy created a bulge in America's pocketbook, and minor league franchise owners stepped up to the plate to collect the proceeds. People had cash to spend again; restrictions on rubber and gasoline had disappeared, freeing team buses to return to the road; and television had yet to lure people away from outdoor activities. Baseball, particularly minor league baseball, thrived. Major league teams—inspired by Branch Rickey's groundbreaking splash into farm ball—poured their postwar dollars into the minor leagues, partially fueling the renaissance of the farm circuits. By 1947, there were more minor league teams in America than before the war.

During World War II, seven cities in Louisiana and one in Mississippi endured four years without Evangeline League baseball. The league had been organized in 1934 and survived the Great Depression, but it faded during the war as its men entered military service. In 1946, though, the Evangeline League returned in sweaty, Deep South exuberance. Natchez, Houma, Alexandria, Thibodaux, Abbeville, New Iberia, Baton Rouge, and Hammond would see bat on ball and ball on leather. The Cardinal farm teams for the most part had survived the war and represented the small but polished and well-financed tier of bush-level play. However, the Evangeline League teams embodied all that was gritty and pungent in the minors. Virtually every myth and verifiable legend that grew up around minor league baseball existed in some form in the Evangeline League. It was called the "Tabasco League," for things were spicy down there.

Fans rallied around their players every year, inviting them to their homes and shouting their names from the stands: Visconti,

Okrie, Ramogaz, and Spears. Wild bayou lads on their own for the first time mixed with concrete New Yorkers who only thought they knew about heat and humidity. Ohh . . . the heat. On a midsummer night, the players often felt as though they were wrapped in wet sheets that trapped the heat within their bodies. There was no release, no dousing or relieving the simmering inside. The wool uniforms—hand-me-downs from the major leagues—would become saturated by the third inning and would hang on the youngsters like a sopping army blanket. And that was at night! Day games were played on Sunday afternoons, usually under a brutally hot sun and boiling humidity. All day, players battled sticky perspiration that stung their eyes and caked the fine dirt that settled on their faces and arms. A few—not all—drank at night, either faked or reached sobriety by the next evening's game, and then started all over again after the ninth inning. Owners counted out eleven peanuts to each concession bag and charged fans ten cents for each glass of water. Long, numbing rides in flapper-era buses carried the players to far-away games and brought them back at dawn. Women waited in the parking lot.

This was a league of throbbing backs and long, sweet home runs, of grime and glory, and of stories too good not to tell. One of the best tales wafted out of Thibodaux, a town hiding way down in the toe of Louisiana's boot. Since the town was so isolated that visiting teams could never hope to drive back home by dawn, management installed barracks at the stadium for opposing teams. Some Thibodaux players also took up residence there. The quarters were pleasant, with show-ers, clean linen, and big fans that stirred the dripping air. Shep Baron played shortstop for the Alexandria Aces and slept in Thibodaux a couple of nights.

"A boy by the name of Ravon played for Thibodaux [as did] Bum Akenhead, who was a hell of a ball player," recalled Baron. "This fel-low Ravon, if you said 'snake,' he would climb the wall, literally climb the wall. He was horrible about snakes, just any kind. Just say 'snake' and he'd git. He had a bad habit. They had a whorehouse there—Betty's—and he'd go over there and get drunk, come in about three o'clock, [with] everybody in bed, and turn the lights all on and grab them old army beds and pick them up and say, 'Get up fellows! Old Ravon's here! Everybody awake? Good night, fellas!' And he'd pull them sheets up over him, and he'd go to sleep.

"Well, old Bum Akenhead, he was something else. Right back of the ballpark there was a bayou, and Bum had gone out there and caught about a three-foot black water moccasin. He pulled all the damn snake's teeth out, so it couldn't bite you. We were sittin' in there playing hearts, playing a little penny poker and stuff to kill the day—nothing in a little hick town like Thibodaux to do—and he said, 'Well, before we go to bed, fellas, don't forget nobody go to sleep.' He curled that old snake up at the foot of the bed, petted it, and it went to sleep, and [he] pulled the sheets up about halfway.

"Old Ravon come in about two o'clock. 'Wake up, fellas! Old Ravon's here! Everybody awake? Good night!' He got in that bed and pulled that sheet over, and he wiggled his feet and woke that old snake up. That snake started coming up 'tween his legs, and when he got up to about his chest, that snake put its head up. You ain't never in your life seen or heard nothing like it. I'll never forget that. The bed went one way, the mattress went one way, the snake went one way, and Ravon was hollering and screaming, 'Bum Akenhead! I'm going to kill you, you son of a bitch!' And he tore the screen door off going out. We could hear him hollering. He was on the centerfield fence under the scoreboard, cussing Akenhead. . . . Brother, we never had no more trouble with Ravon anymore. He'd tiptoe in at night and go to sleep and look in his bed to make sure."

In the company of war veterans and wide-eyed teenagers, Travis headed for the west Mississippi river town of Natchez and the eccentric, rejuvenated Evangeline League. The Natchez Giants had joined the league in 1940 and were owned by a character named Jake Atz, whose surname really began with Z—according to locker-room tales. His father, while serving in World War I, had tired of being at the bottom of every list and roll call, and had decided to change his name from one that began with a Z to one that began with an A, or better yet, A To Z: Atz. The younger Atz had married, possibly in Europe during World War II, and the woman knew little English and even less about baseball. Players often peeked from the dugout to see her cheering the other team.

Travis learned quickly that the bleachers were not bolted tightly in the Evangeline League. He would soon read about the Baton Rouge manager who pulled his entire team off the field after a disputed call, and Thibodaux's player-manager, Zeke Banura, a onetime major leaguer on his way down, zinging a ball into the stands after being razzed by the Hammond fans. The ball hit a woman, and Banura, still smarting from the heckling, forfeited the next day's doubleheader against Hammond. Such chaos routinely erupted in the Evangeline and drew few protests from the league's sleepy president.

Travis got to training camp a couple of weeks late, his arrival delayed by a chipped bone in the middle finger of his pitching hand. Sometime before the start of spring practice, he had attempted to field a line drive from the mound and injured the digit. Although such an impediment may have ended his season in the highly competitive Cardinals system, it seemed not to matter in Natchez. Travis remained on the Giants' roster through spring training and well into the season despite the injury. Manager Merle Coleman finally scheduled his first pitching start for June 1. Ironically, Travis pitched the first game of a doubleheader against the Cardinals' farm club in New Iberia, striking out five and pocketing the win for Natchez. It was a bullish start for "Jim," as the papers and his fellow players now referred to him, and he capped the afternoon with a one-for-three batting performance. He threw brilliantly for the "Atzman" throughout June and early July, ranking among the league's top ten pitchers and helping to pull the team up to second place behind Houma.

Jim Reeves perked ears and arched eyebrows around the league with his shutdown pitching. During a game in Thibodaux, an Evangeline player witnessed the frustration Jim's curveball caused and noted, "Them old boys were biting at the lip trying to hit it." Reeves's record had improved to five wins against one loss when Art Phelan, the owner of the Alexandria Aces, approached Jake Atz about the mule kicking in Atz's barn. Although Alexandria was a C-level team, it was considered to be only marginally better than the D-level Natchez Giants. In fact, by that point in the 1946 season, the Giants had outpaced the supposedly superior team.

Alexandria needed pitching in order to make a run for first place, so the Aces threw a line out for the steady-rolling Reeves. With a relatively large wad of cash (by Evangeline League standards), Alexandria could easily persuade Natchez to sell its contract with Reeves. Just as their major league counterparts helped enrich the coffers of minor league teams by purchasing players, the better-financed minor league clubs often threw money at smaller, poorer teams in order to snag their star players. It was like the big fish eating the smaller one. The moneyed, unaffiliated minor league teams could acquire raw talent from the poorer teams, season those players, and then sell them to the majors at a nice profit.

Money stole the thriving pitcher from the Natchez fans. Now Reeves would pitch against them, dimming their hopes for a league title. Jim's pitching had burgeoned in the first couple months of the Evangeline League's season. Perhaps the competition lagged behind that of the Cardinals system, or maybe Jim just needed a chance to prove himself. Regardless, he finally had reached firm ground in professional baseball, first with Natchez and now with Alexandria.

At "Alec," Jim found the quintessential minor league team in the quintessential minor league. Almost everyone from the players on up to management guaranteed that life on and off the field would never be dull. Owner Art Phelan unlocked his purse to buy players, but the bucks stopped there.

"He was so tight he squeaked," said outfielder Frank O'Hare. That might explain why Phelan hated to lose baseballs almost as much as he hated to lose games. When a foul ball flew out of the park, someone would yell "Outside!" and the kids peeking in through the knotholes would dash for the stray ball. Whoever retrieved it would be allowed into the park for free. And if the balls became soggy on a rainy night, rather than disposing of them, the staff tossed them into an electrically heated box. "It would bake those baseballs as hard as a brick," claimed O'Hare. "If one hit you on your hand, on your fists, you'd feel you committed suicide."

In addition to soaking the balls, rain gave Phelan a reason to bathe the infield in a flash of fire. He hated rainouts because they often were made up as part of a doubleheader, meaning that fans could watch two games for the price of one. So, to prevent umpires from calling games because of a muddy field, he would splash gasoline on the turf and then dry it by setting it afire. The fans loved it.

Phelan dispatched his boys to away games on an old Chevrolet bus that seemed to incur a flat tire or an overheated engine every other road trip. Constantly shifting and jerking to find comfort on the hard seats, the players sweated off pounds in the stuffy bus and would try almost anything to kill time on the hours-long trips to opposing cities. A monkey—a live one—accompanied first baseman Cecil Harper on the bus rides, and New Yorker Art Visconti, "Old Banana Nose," belted out Perry Como songs to rude reviews from the front seats. To drown out Visconti's interpretation of "Prisoner of Love," pitcher Chuck "Popeye" Thompson often picked country and western tunes on his guitar. The conflicting rhythms ceased when the bus passed something more interesting—like a pretty woman or a tempting restaurant. "We pulled in down in [a small town]," recalled Thompson, "and there was a watermelon truck right beside the bus. So, we reached out the window and got us [each] a watermelon."

The Aces fizzed with such antics, but Jim mostly kept his distance from the bedlam, preferring to laugh at the real, live comic strip in front of him. He watched the party, just as he had leaned against the wall and watched the wild country dance nights with Carey Rhiddlehoover. The players found Jim to be a serious, somewhat moody man, not full of mischief like the other players. "He was kind of hot-headed," observed fellow pitcher Thompson, "but I never did see him get into a brawl or nothing like that. But he'd let you know right fast whether he liked it or he didn't like it. . . . He wasn't no loudmouth. He was kind of quiet, kind of reserved."

At Bringhurst Field, the team's home diamond, Manager Carl Kot cast his serious East Texas boy as a reliever among a cast of able starting pitchers that included Art Trieschman, Leroy Youngblood, and Jim's old De Berry buddy Ralph Allen. The hurlers—including Jim—were among the league's best and most competitive. Youngblood, nicknamed "Purina" because he ran a Purina feed store, recalled that Evangeline coaches instilled a warrior-spirit in the pitchers of the day. "When you came to bat against me, you had a little stick in your hand, and you was trying to take my paycheck away from me, and I had that little ball in my hand, and I was trying to take yours. If you hit a home run on me, the next time you came up, you better get ready to hit the dirt because I was going to try to hit you right in your ear. That's where they taught us to throw because you can't hit anybody in the ear."

Unfortunately, the tenacity of the Aces' pitching staff and all the fastballs, change-ups, and curves failed to translate into Alexandria victories. The team had sunk to eighteen games out of first place by the end of July. Then, Kot finally gave Reeves the chance to start, but the move appeared to make little difference. On August 1, a shower of hometown boos drenched Jim during the team's 11–2 loss to the first-place Houma Indians. He had struck out eight batters, though, which prompted the *Alexandria Daily Town Talk* to lash out at the

An Alexandria Aces pitcher at Bringhurst Field; probably not Jim Reeves.
(Courtesy: Evangeline Baseball League History Project, Nicholls State University)

Bringhurst boo birds. "A check of his performance . . . will show that he didn't do half bad. The loss can hardly be blamed on him. Although he gave up eight hits in the seven innings he twirled, only two earned runs crossed the plate before he left the mound, and he whiffed eight of the highly touted Indians. The scored should have read 2–2 when [the reliever] went in to pitch."

The jeering returned to greet Reeves a week later, on August 6 against the Baton Rouge Red Sticks. He allowed four runs in seven innings and then uncorked the spectators' displeasure in the eighth by permitting six runs. Volleys of wisecracks and hoots were aimed at Jim, and the fans saved a sack of venom for player-manager Kot because he had chosen Jim to start.

Soon, though, Jim's statistics regained some of their Natchez luster. Over the next week, he notched two wins for the Aces, and he also reeled off a few more good pitching days before the end of the year. Jim finished the regular season with a record of nine wins against seven losses, and an earned run average of 3.40. Behind Art Trieschman and Leroy Youngblood, he proved to be the Aces' third-most reliable pitcher. The team, however, ended the season in far worse shape.

While Jim's old comrades at Natchez managed to close out the summer campaign in second place, Alexandria finished twenty-seven games out of the lead. But the Aces had finished in fourth place, which earned the team a berth in the Evangeline League's post-season tournament. Unfortunately, their September play mirrored the rest of the season, and they promptly dropped four games of the best-of-seven series to the Houma Indians while winning only one.

During the course of Alexandria's losing season, as Jim became more familiar with his teammates, he softened his serious veneer a wee bit and introduced them to his other talent. On the bumpy bus rides across Louisiana, he joined in with "Popeye" Thompson on a country number or two. Chuck played while Jim sang. Jim got so comfortable playing and singing on the bus that he began passing out song sheets so the rest of the team could warble along. But the folksy music drove "Banana Nose" Visconti up the wall and absolutely provoked shortstop Shep Baron, who much preferred Harry James and Glenn Miller to Ernest Tubb and Al Dexter. Baron, who roomed with Jim at a boarding house and then at the home of Katie Luckett on Albert and Chester Streets in Alexandria, would groan whenever Jim produced his guitar, in their room or on the bus.

"It was horrible, that whaa-whaa crap," complained Baron. On a night that he had become saturated in more ways than one, he reached the breaking point with Jim's strumming. "We'd been across the street and got drunk at a club after the ball game one night. He always had a little silly grin. . . . I told him while we were staggering over [to Katie's] to go to bed, 'Jim, you go plucking on that damn guitar and all that country shit, I'm going to break it for you.' He said, 'You wouldn't do that to your pal.' I said, 'Just pick away.' Damned if he didn't—and I did.

"I broke his guitar," boasted Jim's roommate. "He went to old man Phelan and said, 'That crazy coon-head broke my damn guitar. Take it out of his paycheck.'" Whether Jim obtained a new guitar from Shep's garnished wages or in some other way, he showed up again on the bus with another flattop box.

In contrast to Shep, most of his teammates—even some northerners—found Jim's voice and strumming to be quite pleasing. When he struck a chord and sang on the bus or in the clubhouse, they turned their heads and hushed. And it was almost exclusively on the bus, in the clubhouse, or in his room that Jim sang and picked. Although the Alexandria area buzzed with venues like the Blue Moon Club in Bunkie, the Colonial Club near Hessmer, and the New Club Almack on the Marksville Highway, Jim never approached their doors with his guitar. For fun, he picnicked with girlfriends, necked at Valentine Lake, took in movies, shot craps at the Blue Moon, and played golf or pool, but he rarely brought his guitar along.

After the Aces' loss to Houma in the playoffs, Jim threw his guitar on his shoulder and packed away his most promising season in the four years since his graduation from high school. With reason to smile, he headed back to where everyone knew him as Travis. At home in De Berry, he probably latched onto pipeline work because by the time the Aces' spring training opened in March of 1947, the papers reported that "outdoor work" had left him feeling somewhat weak. For the third time in his career, Jim entered spring training battling injury or illness. The chipped bone had blighted the previous year's training in Natchez, and at the outset of his first Carthage High year, whooping cough and a host of other maladies had stymied him. "Reeves, after limbering up and exercising, pitched a short while in batting practice," the *Daily Town Talk* reported, "but didn't exert himself, having recovered from an extended illness." Presumably, Jim's illness (whatever it was), grew out of his "outdoor work" in the off-season.

Roommate Shep Baron observed, more specifically, that Jim's arm seemed to be wearing down—the result, perhaps, of the curveballs that twisted and strained a pitcher's arm. "I think his arm was bothering him when he came here. We never talked that much about it. [We'd say to him,] 'Oh your arm's all right. Put you some alcohol on it. Get your chewing spit on it and rub it in. Get you some dirt. There ain't nothing wrong with you.' But he wasn't throwing normal, and some nights he'd moan a bit." Jim kept on, however. He wanted to improve on his previous year's performance and, snubbing the pain, was desperately clinging to his job.

"He was a throwback to the old days," observed infielder Alan Cross, who shared quarters with Jim on the road. "You couldn't take the damn ball away from him, as far as a manager making a pitching change. He didn't want to leave that mound. He was a competitor."

As Opening Day 1947 approached, the Aces' fans and players looked forward to a much-improved season. "We have a club this year which will give us the best of them a fit," bragged the thrifty Mr. Phelan to the *Daily Town Talk*. "Those boys will be hard to beat." In the early days of the season, Phelan's remarks appeared to have credence. At the end of April, the Aces sat atop the Evangeline League, and Reeves was three and one. If any physical pain plagued Jim, he displayed little of it on the field. He performed solidly on the mound through most of May. But against the Thibodaux nine on Thursday, May 23, he fell apart.

Alec held a two-and-a-half game lead in the Evangeline League over the Hammond Berries, and the Aces were looking past the Thursday night away game with the lowly Thibodaux Giants to a two-game weekend series against the Berries. If they squished the Berries on the weekend, they would increase their lead over the other league teams to four and a half games. However, the sixth-place Giants weren't so easily felled and by the ninth inning of that rain-drenched Thursday night contest were clinging to 1–1 tie.

Starter Fred Baczewski had done his part to stifle the Giants, allowing only one run over the first eight innings and helping his own cause with a hit. But a ball smashed back to the mound in the bottom of the ninth beaned the pitcher hard, ending his night. Reeves came on in relief of the injured Baczewski and finished the inning without allowing a run. In the top of the tenth, the Aces scored two runs and appeared to have the game wrapped up, but Jim gave up a pair of runs in the bottom half of the stanza to knot the score at 3–3. Neither team scored in the eleventh inning, but the Aces surged ahead once more as they recorded three runs in the twelfth. Jim returned to the mound to preserve the lead, but in a horrible display of pitching allowed one run and loaded the bases. He was promptly yanked from the mound, and "Purina" Youngbood stepped in to retire the Thibodaux side and save the game.

Technically, Jim was credited with the win because the Aces had gone ahead while he was still in the game. But he had come dangerously close to blowing a game against one of the worst teams in the league. What might he do against the stronger teams? Art Phelan apparently didn't want to find out. A few days after the game and despite Jim's admirable record up to the Thibodaux game, the owner issued walking papers to Jim. Phelan had three strong starters in Baczewski, Youngblood, and newcomer Hugh Sooter. He could do without Jim Reeves.

Jim had weathered such an ousting two years earlier in Lynchburg, but this time, instead of scurrying back to De Berry, the twenty-three-year-old followed his determination to Marshall, Texas. He believed his arm could still muscle a few wins for a team, so he approached the Marshall Comets' manager, Jerry Feille, about a try-out. Feille agreed to a five-day evaluation and scheduled Jim as the starter for a game on June 3. Just eleven days after his fiasco in Thibodaux, Jim took the mound against Marshall's Lone Star League rival Tyler. Going the full nine innings, he allowed eleven hits in a 3–2 loss but scattered the hits throughout the game so Tyler was unable to build an insurmountable lead. Feille saw enough potential in Jim to sign him.

Compared to the Evangeline League, playing in the Lone Star League was like vacationing on the Gulf of Mexico. Most Lone Star teams were clustered in East Texas within twenty miles or so of each other, and that lightened the burden of traveling to away games. Back at Alexandria, Jim and his teammates often had to endure bus rides of 125 miles and more to their away games. The escapades that occurred in the Lone Star League paled in comparison to those that transpired in the Evangeline, but the short road trips were nice. Players could make it home after every game, avoiding the long rides that surely affected a man's performance. "This is the greatest league I've ever been in," a Lone Star batsman once said. "I can have my quart of booze after the game's over, go fishing every morning, and I don't have to go on any road trips."

It was a short hop down to Henderson for the new pitcher's next start a few days later. Jim redeemed his loss to Tyler, pitching a five-hitter against the Henderson Oilers, and for the next few games he pitched admirably as a reliever. Jerry Feille returned Jim to starting duties in July and watched his local boy energize the team. On July 13, a *Marshall News Messenger* reporter watched Reeves dispose of the Jacksonville Jax. "Jim Reeves, husky right-hander who looks better each time out, set the Jax down with four hits and struck out five to win his fifth game for Marshall this season."

Five days later, Jim and the Comets spanked the Longview Texans to move into first place. In the month or so since Jim's arrival, the team had bubbled up from fourth place to the top. He caught fire again, and when the league issued player statistics on July 20, Reeves claimed the third-best winning percentage among all Lone Star hurlers.

Thoughts of the Lone Star League championship drifted to the front of owner Feille's mind, and he began to adjust his roster for the season's home stretch—which, strangely, landed Jim in Henderson. In the third week of July, the Henderson Oilers traded a pitcher and a catcher for Marshall's hottest pitcher, and Jim packed his bags again. The minor league life kept him moving. Whether Jim was pitching poorly or well, it didn't matter—teams never kept him around very long.

In dealing away one of their most powerful hitters and a promising pitcher for Jim, the C-level Oilers placed remarkable trust in his ability to perform, and Jim seemed up to the task. Four days after his last appearance as a Comet, he picked up in Henderson where he had left off in Marshall. Starting on July 25 against the Longview Texans, Jim faced his old Carthage teammate and Houston landlord June Graves. The Texans and Graves never had a chance. Reeves struck out ten, and although he allowed the first home run over Longview's centerfield wall since the great Hank Greenberg accomplished the feat in 1932, the Oilers sailed to an 18–7 victory. But the next day nobody talked about Reeves's strikeouts or his reunion with June Graves.

In yet another display of minor league mayhem, a riot had almost erupted after an umpire threw out three Texans for disputing a call in the sixth inning. Longview's manager—one of the three ejected—attacked an umpire, and irate fans poured from the stands to join the fracas. It took the police to restore order, but according to the *Longview Journal*, which predictably damned the umpires' actions, tempers continued to smolder. "After the game," the paper reported, "[the umpires] sneaked into the dugout and hid until police could clear the field of spectators who stormed out of the grandstand after the scalps of the umpires. The umpires left the park under police escort after fans had tossed cushions and other handy objects onto the playing field in protest against their domineering and high-handed tactics."

Jim saw nothing quite so exciting again. He lost a tough game to Lufkin on July 30, and in early August he sustained a season-ending injury, the exact nature of which was not revealed by memories or newspapers. The *Henderson Daily News* speculated that Reeves might be back in action by mid-August, but he remained out of the lineup for the balance of the 1947 season. While the Oilers rued their July trade with Marshall, Jim Reeves turned his attention to some personal business.

4

In early 1946, after the Lynchburg Cardinals had expelled Jim from Virginia and before he signed with the Natchez Giants, he checked out a Saturday night dance in Marshall, hoping to find a familiar face with whom to share a few beers and pass the evening. Among the hot, whining sounds of a country and western band, Jim zeroed in on a Carthage guy he knew and sauntered over to talk with the man and his date. He sat down with them—as welcome as an intruding parent, perhaps—and chatted away, all the while taking intense notice of the handsome, creamy-faced girl who accompanied his friend. He stole a few dances with her, and then a few more. The girl—who lived outside Marshall—welcomed Jim's overtures and rudely disregarded her date's escalating indignation. At the end of the night, Jim left behind a smitten girl and one angry friend.

On the dance floor with his friend's date, Jim had whispered his desire to see her again and promised to call during the next week. When he did, they made plans for a double date to another Saturday dance. On the agreed-upon night, Jim and the other couple pulled up to the girl's home in a lashing rainstorm. He bolted from the car, dashed through one gate near the road, leaped over a swelling creek, hurried through another gate just in front of the house, and finally stood on the porch, dripping. Jim and his date ran back to the car and, after patting their clothing as dry as possible, drove into Marshall, where they danced away the night.

The girl who had inspired Jim to do in his Carthage friend was Mary Elizabeth White, a seventeen-year-old senior at Marshall High School. Over the next two years, through Jim's stints in the Evangeline League, they saw one another during the off-season and exchanged the occasional letter. And when Jim's great baseball adventure carried him to Marshall and then Henderson, their relationship became more serious. Not long after his season-ending injury in August 1947, Jim burst into the Marshall dime store where Mary worked and proposed an immediate marriage. Taken aback but fully interested, Mary agreed. She quit her job and the very next evening—Wednesday, September 3—exchanged marital vows with Jim. In an interview with reporter Dixie Deen that first appeared in 1966, she picked up the story: "It was a quiet ceremony, performed by a minister Jim liked very much at the Methodist church in Carthage. There was just the minister [and] his wife, who was the witness, and Jim and me. I was eighteen and Jim was twenty-four."

The *Marshall News Messenger* announced the union a few days later, noting that the couple planned to honeymoon in Nashville, Tennessee, then settle in Henderson. "We had planned to come to the *Grand Ole Opry*, of all places, for our honeymoon," Mary explained to Deen. "We still didn't have a car, and Jim's buddy had promised to lend us his for the weekend. The day before we were due to leave, however, as fate would have it, the boy wrecked his car and our honeymoon, too!" Mary had wed a man with little means and a frayed dream to succeed in professional baseball. Jim possessed not an acre of land nor a steady job. What could he offer but disappointment? Mary had met the challenge of her life: finding consolation in Jim's love and serenades.

In all of East Texas, though, there was not a woman more equipped to share Jim's zigzagging path. The youngest child and only girl in a family with eight boys, Mary early on developed a resilient sheath to repel life's adversity. Born at the outset of the Great Depression in 1929, she grew up in the hamlet of Teneha in Shelby County, on Panola's southern border. Her paternal grandparents, W. D. and Corine White, had migrated to the Teneha area from Louisiana in the 1880s (not long after Jim's maternal grandparents arrived in the region) and purchased a large chunk of land, which they farmed. Their son John married local girl Belle Holt a few years after the turn of the century, and in 1908 they produced the first of a line of children that ended with Mary in 1929.

Like his father, John owned a plot of land, but an asthmatic condition made it difficult for him to farm. He relied on his boys to shoulder much of the field work and to help Belle and Mary with other household chores. Their homes—the Whites lived in a few— were little more than log cabins that became ovens in the summer and allowed wind and snow through their cracks in the winter. Mary watched one of the Whites' homes burn when she was a child, but blessed with some financial resources, John White simply moved to another house and another plot of land.

Mary's mother, Belle, was an inventive woman who taught her children how to weather hard times. When the house burned, she placed her children with neighbors, urging them to be good and brave until John found another place to live and farm. In more settled times, she created tasty meals and treats out of the family garden's simple yield. Baked sweet potatoes swimming in fresh butter and fried pies of apple, chocolate, and peach made her children's mouths water and sweetened their rigorous life. With her mother, Mary canned and stored vegetables and fruit, and tackled the backbreaking task of washing clothes. On wash day, using only their hands and a washboard, mother and daughter washed, rinsed, and wrung the family's heaping piles of clothing.

In 1938, life dropped a far larger burden into the Whites' collective lap. After suffering from chronic asthma and heart problems, John died, forcing Belle to find a new way to support her family. Faced with a situation similar to what Beulah Reeves had encountered fourteen years earlier, Belle—like Beulah—looked to her older boys for help. Sons Fred, Ned, and Paul had moved out of the Teneha area to Marshall before their father died, so Marshall seemed like a logical place to go. Eldest son Paul worked at a dairy in the city and arranged for his mother and younger siblings to make the move. He found jobs for two of the boys at the dairy, which helped the transplanted household, and when Mary reached her teens, she became a carhop at a Marshall drive-in restaurant where Belle had gone to work flipping hamburgers.

When the Henderson Oilers' training camp got underway in the spring of 1948, newlywed Jim came out with the rest of players. Henderson still had him under contract, and the team's owners had their fingers crossed that Jim would wipe away their regrets over trading for him. On March 29, he appeared briefly in an exhibition game and nine days later followed up with a win. However, when the Oilers gathered for their team photo, the *Henderson Daily News* reported that Jim was too ill to attend. The paper never mentioned his name again in reference to baseball. Jim had pitched his last game as a professional baseball player in April 1948.* On May 10, Henderson placed him on the inactive list, and on July 31, the team officially dropped him from its roster.

Just how Jim fell from physical grace has become fodder for conjecture. Alan Cross, who roomed on the road with Jim during their days with Alexandria, blamed Jim's demise on a cluster of festering boils in his right armpit. The boils, Cross noted, sprouted in Alec and continued to ulcerate in Marshall and Henderson until they became unbearable. "They'd lance them and take all of this goo out of them," recalled Cross. "It ended his career right quick. . . . One was right in the middle of [the armpit], and the other was right under it. . . . It was raunchy."

Despite the soreness under his arm, it is more likely that an abrupt injury halted Jim's career. In interviews over the years, both Jim and Mary pointed to a leg injury that tore Jim's sciatic nerve, a sensory and motor nerve that originates in the back of the pelvic area and runs through the pelvis and into the upper leg. Such a tear would easily ground a ballplayer for an indefinite period and cause chronic pain in the hip or thigh area. This was probably the injury that ended Jim's 1947 season in Henderson. Years later, in an interview with a Texas reporter, he recalled having to "hobble" through his September wedding. During spring training in 1948, Henderson teammate and friend Leo Ferguson saw Jim become more cautious on the mound so as not to aggravate his leg. According to Ferguson, Jim hurt his pitching arm trying to protect his leg, a combination—with the boils added, perhaps—that finally ended his playing days.

It was Ferguson—a zany ballplayer who once wore a woman's skirt for an entire game—who showed Jim his next meal ticket. Word had reached Ferguson that radio station KGRI in Henderson needed to fill a few on-air vacancies. "One of the associates there wanted me to come out and audition for radio announcing during the off-season of baseball," said Ferguson. "[But I had a] job at this refinery, and I

---

*Although records show that a Jim Reeves pitched for the Sherman-Denison (Texas) team of the Big State League in 1949, it was, in fact, a Jim Reeves of Fannin County, Texas, not our hero, who played for the team.

told Jim about it, and he said, 'Well, take me out there and introduce me. I've had a little radio experience.' I did, and he got the job."

KGRI, whose call letters reflected its ownership by Goggin Radio Incorporated, had taken to the East Texas airwaves in 1947 and operated out of a big, barn-like building on U.S. 79 southwest of Henderson. The station had tripped its "on air" light during a boom period in Texas radio. Throughout the state in the 1940s, residents of small towns like Jacksonville, Jasper, Lamesa, Lampasas, and Littlefield watched radio towers rise in their midst for the first time. The growth of the radio industry in Texas was fueled by oil barons and politicians looking for investments. (In fact, one ambitious U.S. Congressman named Lyndon B. Johnson jumped into the radio game in the early 1940s by purchasing tiny KTBC in Austin.) Most of these small Texas stations broadcast during daytime hours only and, with about 250 watts of power, covered a modest patch of piney woods or prairie. KGRI was one of those stations, and while it was dwarfed by such powerhouses as KWKH in Shreveport or WBAP in Dallas, it nevertheless served as an important local source of music and information.

Jim's resonant voice, although not tailored for radio, was certainly adequate—deep, with just enough of a ringing quality to travel well through the ether. Marred occasionally by nervous stutters, mispronunciations, and a stiff delivery, Jim's on-air persona could nonetheless grab an East Texan's attention. Jim's high school recitations and brief appearances years before on KWKH and KRMD probably helped him make the transition to his new job. He had witnessed radio from behind the scenes and was no stranger to a microphone. Pitching and performing music in public surely helped give him the confidence to talk to KGRI's audience. The station dropped its new man into a full-time schedule, and Jim donned the many hats required of a small station personality. He read the news, called broadcasts of baseball and football games, and spun records— some country and some pop. Jim Reeves became the radio voice of Henderson. Jim's name—already somewhat celebrated because of baseball—entered a wider vernacular through KGRI.

"Everybody in town knew him because it was the only radio station there," said Douglas Reeh, who worked up the road at KSIJ in Gladewater. "It was up on a hill, and it had stairs that faced the street. If he had a tape or a long record, he would sit out there on the steps and shine his shoes. People would drive by and wave."

When Jim hit the air each day, he ran a one-man show. Unlike larger stations that hired engineers to operate the controls and turntable while the disc jockeys talked, KGRI relied on its on-air talent to operate the control board *and* keep the platters and patter spinning. Stations in Shreveport and Dallas hired announcers to introduce programs and read commercials, but at KGRI, Jim (or whoever was on duty) handled all the chores. KGRI did employ an engineer, one John Bolin, but he only monitored the station's signal and serviced its antenna and broadcasting equipment. So, Jim—like any deejay—looked forward to those times during a pre-recorded program or long record when he could shine his shoes or just kick them up on the table. He often plucked away on his guitar, which no longer competed with his oily, leather baseball glove for attention.

Leaning on the guitar in the control room, staring at the piano in the boxy, carpeted studio, Jim quickly saw how radio could meld with his musical interests. Gospel quartets and hillbilly bands—some regulars on KGRI and others just passing through town—constantly caravanned through that studio, and the sight of them led Jim to organize his own small combo. He corralled the station's program director, Frank Ledbetter, and Al "Rusty" Courtney, a member of Jim's De Berry music fraternity, to perform on the air, and on his own time, Jim sang with a band or with his guitar while John Bolin recorded him on KGRI's tape machine.

The tapes Jim recorded in 1948 have survived and reveal the amalgam of musical styles that influenced his later performances. Country numbers such as Jenny Lou Carson's composition "A Penny for Your Thoughts" and Hank Thompson's "Humpty Dumpty Heart" mingled on Jim's song list with hymns, old-time standards, and more current pop hits like "Naughty Angeline" and "When Did You Leave Heaven?" which were popularized by Dick Haymes and Guy Lombardo, respectively. Sprinkled among the cover songs are Jim's own compositions and others that he co-wrote with Rusty Courtney. These rough performances are the earliest recorded evidence of Jim's vocal abilities. He had obviously studied and practiced the art of phrasing pop and country songs, and he could convey a sense of tenderness or joy as the songs required. His voice hinted at the sweetness of the wildly popular Eddy Arnold, yet there was an ease and smoothness of delivery in Jim's voice that dwelt in the realm of Red Foley, Gene Autry, and even Bing Crosby.

KGRI Radio's Jim Reeves as Sonny Day. With Al "Rusty" Courtney and Frank "Cole Knight" Ledbetter. (Courtesy: Richard Weize)

Reeves's guitar work was plodding and thick when he accompanied himself on the tapes, but on those occasions when he assembled a band, the music sizzled. His prominence as a radio personality and reputation in the local music community evidently gave Jim access to capable local musicians, and he began to join them for live appearances around the area. Many evenings at sunset, KGRI's John Bolin watched Jim dash out of "dry" Henderson to meet some musicians in the nearby beer-flowing towns of Kilgore and Longview. Several times, however, Jim—with only Mary in tow—would haunt various nightclubs and honky-tonks in hopes of sitting in on a few numbers with the bands.

The corridor of East Texas running west from Marshall to Tyler was a tornado alley of musical commotion in the 1940s, and the eye of the storm revolved around the nightclubs that dotted the area. Country and western music wafted through the doors of tiny roadside taverns and cavernous dance halls. The dance halls—well known hubs like the Overpass Club (later the Reo Palm Isle) in Longview, the Shady Grove in Gladewater, and the Paradise in Kilgore—drew the most patrons. Their vast dance floors groaned under the weight of two-steppers, and their bands were among the best East Texas had to offer. Bands longed for long-term engagements, called "sit-down gigs," at these clubs because the large venues could pay as high as a hundred dollars a week per man for six nights and one matinee of playing. The Paradise in Kilgore even put up the musicians in cabins and offered meals to them at twenty-five cents a plate.

Fiddle player Caesar Massey regularly worked these clubs and frequently invited Jim to sing a few numbers with his Swinging Dudes. The Dudes—or the Village Boys, as Massey sometimes called his western swing outfit—were in the midst of a year-long stint at one of the clubs in 1947 when Jim first sat in. When Massey moved to the Reo Palm Isle in Longview, Jim often hopped out of the audience to join in there, too.

"The first time, somebody came up to me and said, 'You ought to hear Jim Reeves sing.' I said, 'Who's Jim Reeves?'" recalled Massey. "They said, 'He's a ballplayer from Henderson, and he sure does sing good,' I said, 'Tell him to come up here.' That was the beginning of it, and we liked each other and he'd come back. We knew what he wanted to do when he came in there. I'd announce that we had Jim Reeves, and he'd get applause."

Al Dexter, the Texas native who hit it big with "Pistol Packin'
Mama" in 1944 and remained popular thereafter, appeared on bills
with the Swinging Dudes, Massey remembered, and he and Massey
prodded Jim to sing full time. "He had a wonderful voice and sang
real great," said Ceasar of his frequent guest from Henderson. "I
always thought that's what he was going to do, but he didn't think he
was at the time. . . . Al Dexter, he had already got rich on 'Pistol
Packin' Mama,' a lot of times told Jim, 'Why don't you take that up,
Jim? You sing real good.' He said, 'Maybe I will someday.'"

Along with spot appearances on Massey's stage, Reeves nudged
his way into the ensembles of other Texas bandleaders. Bob Cross, a
Kilgore-based bandleader, and Barney Vardeman, a Nacogdoches
native, also often made room for the Henderson disc jockey. Both
names would figure in Jim Reeves's first effort to cut a record.

Barney Vardeman and his band enjoyed a modestly enthusiastic
following around Houston and throughout East Texas. They had
appeared on KWKH's *Louisiana Hayride* and, after meeting with
indifference from record labels in San Antonio and Houston, cut
some sides for a small, independent operation called Macy's. In 1949
Houston-based Macy's had begun waxing artists such as deejay-
singer Biff Collie, Charlie Monroe alumnus Tommy Scott, and a host
of other—mostly Texas—acts. According to Vardeman, he and the
three other members of his band were among the first to record for
the label. Macy's, he recalled, was run by the husband and wife team
of C. D. and Macy Lelia Henry, who had moved to Houston after
going bankrupt in California. The father of one of the boys in
Vardeman's band sent a tape to Macy Henry, and she invited the
group to Houston for a session and even opened her home to the band
members during their stay.

When the pressings dried, Vardeman began promoting his first
record, "Let's Call It Quits" (backed with "I Love Someone"), in every
way he knew how. "One of the first places I took one of the old 78
rpms to was radio station KGRI and Jim Reeves . . ." explained Vardeman. "I took the record to him, and he said, 'It sounds pretty good.
You know, I'd like to make a phonograph record. How do you go
about making a phonograph record?' I said, 'Well, this is a fine lady
who owns the company.' I knew that he sang and . . . he had already
gotten a little old band together [and was] playing a little bit around
Kilgore and Gladewater. I told him I was going down the next week

to appear on Cook's Hoedown which was a big, big place in the South then. . . . 'I'm going down next week, and I'm going to tell Macy that you want to come in for an audition. I'm going to tell them how good you are.' And he laughed. Sure enough, I went down the next week and spent the weekend in Houston and played Cook's Hoedown and told Macy about Jim. In the meantime, I had given him her phone number, and he made an appointment to come in."

At this point, Bob Cross—or rather his Troubadours—entered the picture. Cross's drummer, Bill Morris, recalled that when word reached Jim that Macy's would record him, Reeves corralled him, steel guitarist Billy Bob Turner, and guitarist Bobby Davis—two other Bob Cross players—to make the trip to Houston. Morris, who would actually play bass on the session, recollected that Jim borrowed an old Chevrolet in need of a valve job from a friend who owned a Henderson dealership, and he picked up the musicians after their Friday night set in Longview.

After chugging to Houston during the wee hours of the morning, the old Chevy crawled into downtown as the sidewalks were beginning to fill with shoppers. Among the pedestrians that morning, Jim spotted something that jarred his groggy mind: Margaret Rhiddlehoover, his attractive girlfriend from years before—who was now married—strolling down the sidewalk with her one-year-old son. Jim stopped the car, ordered one of the musicians to take the wheel, and jumped out to see how Margaret was doing. While the two visited, the three pickers circled the block again and again. Jim finally said good-bye to Margaret and her son, and then—much to Morris's displeasure—the group skipped breakfast and went straight into the recording studio the Henrys had booked, where they spent the entire day recording four tracks. "It was almost dark again before we started back," complained Morris. "Had to come back to [Longview] and play a dance. I think we were about five or ten minutes late. Had to play that dance before we could get any sleep."

On that Saturday in Houston, Jim recorded four numbers he had co-written with Rusty Courtney: "My Heart's Like a Welcome Mat," "I've Never Been So Blue," "Teardrops of Regret," and "Chicken Hearted." The selections ranged from mid-tempo to slow, and they steeped Jim's smooth yet cautious vocal effort in a lukewarm kettle of guitars—Turner's steel, Reeves's acoustic, and Davis's electric. As on his KGRI tapes, Jim performed much like a sweet pop singer, remaining within his tempered vocal range and allowing each enunciated lyric to linger. However, the similes and metaphors of Jim's lyrics ("hearts like welcome mats" and "chicken-hearted women"), as well as the instrumentation, would appeal primarily to country audiences. Only "I've Never Been So Blue"—which opened with a vocal introduction and proceeded with an acoustic guitar-driven, Ink Spots sound—leaned toward pop. Vocal introductions, the often slow preludes to many Tin Pan Alley tunes, were rare in country music, but they were frequently employed by pop singers and contemporary vocal groups in the 1940s.

Macy's released the four songs on two singles, placing the more country-styled "My Heart's Like a Welcome Mat" and "Chicken Hearted" on the "A" sides. However, encumbered with what amounted to bland vocal and instrumental efforts, the discs sold dismally. The record company's hapless promotional efforts also probably precluded sales. Paul Brown, who recorded for Macy's as the lead singer for the Bar X Cowboys, recalled that C. D. and Macy Lelia seemed more interested in finding a particularly gifted performer and selling him or her to a major record label. "They mailed [records] out to the radio stations, but they didn't push you like they would if they was really going for the gold."

Still, a record could translate to currency for performers like Barney Vardeman, the Bar X Cowboys, and Jim Reeves. They were now "recording artists," and although they hardly turned Texas music on its ear, they certainly became distinguishable from the typical dance club act. A few spins on the radio and some sightings of their records on jukeboxes and in the stores, and Reeves and the rest acquired greater entrée than they had previously enjoyed. For Jim, the Macy's platters helped serve up more club dates as well as a regular gig on a hoedown sponsored by KSIJ in Gladewater.

Every Friday after his KGRI shift, Jim would grab his guitar and rush to a junior high school auditorium in Gladewater where he would join a cast of local musicians and Station Manager Douglas Reeh, who appeared in blackface and jitter-bugged atop a giant Hadacol box. Reeh, who answered to the name "Draggy" when in character, figured that only about thirty people attended the KSIJ show, which was not broadcast because the station, like KGRI, signed off at sunset. Jim, said Reeh, led the cast. "We put that show on every Friday night, and he was our lead singer, more or less our star attraction because he had a couple of recordings. . . . Nobody else had a recording. We played his records on the air quite often."

In the two years since 1948, Jim's aspirations had clearly grown toward music. KGRI and Mary's job as a bookkeeper at Crim Truck and Tractor Company bankrolled their life on 609 North Marshall Street in Henderson, but Jim often spoke of shedding their jobs and home, and sinking everything in music. In an interview years later, Jim said he finally put his dilemmas in God's hands. "I was sitting at the radio station's turntable, and I said, 'Lord, you just don't make sense to me. You give me a desire that's making me miserable. Take this desire away so I can get some peace.' That night when I got home, I said, 'Mary let's go.' Within a week we had sold our house and I had quit my job. We drove out of downtown Henderson to the Dallas-Shreveport highway, and I stopped and asked Mary, 'Which way?' She said she didn't know, so I flipped a coin—heads to Shreveport and tails to Dallas. It hit tails so we went to Dallas."

The coin story smacks of legend-building, but it was one that both Jim and Mary told and re-told over the years—although the "heads or tails" part was difficult to keep straight. "He decided he didn't want to be a disc jockey anymore," Mary told author Alanna Nash in the early 1980s. "He wanted to be a singer. But where do you go to be a singer? . . . Dallas was a huge center for country music shows and they had recording studios there. Shreveport was in the other direction, and they had the same, but mainly the *Louisiana Hayride* was there. But we didn't know which way to go, to try first. So, we said, 'Well, let's flip a coin. If it's heads we go to Dallas. If it's tails we go to Shreveport. So, heads it was, and we went to Dallas for two weeks. And the money started running out, and we had to do something else. He hadn't had any luck there. So, we went back to East Texas."

The couple settled in Longview, just north of Henderson, where Jim took a job at KLTI, a stint that soon ended over a dispute with management about programming. Reeves was twenty-eight and pursuing a dream that seemed as elusive as major league baseball. His and Mary's families worried about him. His brothers repeatedly urged him to take a job with United Gas, and Mary's older brother John, who worked for Shell Oil on the Gulf coast, tried to persuade him to take employment with that company. John approached Jim on a visit home. "I went by to see Jim and Mary, and I tried to talk him into going back and going to work with me. Apparently, they weren't

*Gene Wortham and the Circle O Ranch Boys. From left: Doc Shelton, Curtis Kirk,
Kenneth "Little Red" Hayes, Wortham, unidentified, and Bobby Garrett. (Courtesy:
Burton Harris)*

making a living, hardly. Boilermakers' scale in Houston was two dollars an hour, and I told Jim, 'I can get you a job.' He said, 'No. I'm
going to stay in the music business.' " According to the son of Jim and
Mary's doctor, the Reeveses were so strapped for cash that they
exchanged their Macy's 78s for medical services.

Circumstances, though, would ultimately force Jim to take a
"real" job. He persuaded an insurance company to give him a position selling policies, but his heart and mind continually strayed
toward his dream of a career in music. "My boss could tell I wasn't
happy and he asked me why," Jim once told Nashville reporter Pat
Anderson of *The Tennessean*. "I told him I wanted to make my living
as a singer. He asked me what kind of a singer, and I told him folk
songs and country music. He told me that if I'd stay with his company, he'd arrange a business trip to Nashville so I could see the
Grand Ole Opry. It may sound egotistical, but I told him that the first
time I saw the *Opry* I was going to be up on stage."

Egotistical, perhaps. Determined, definitely. Jim soon abandoned the insurance business and returned to a track more closely

related to music. A small announcement in a February 1952 issue of *Billboard* magazine placed Jim back at KGRI, organizing a benefit for an ill singer named Cecil Green. He had, in fact, returned as program director for the small Henderson station. Over in Shreveport, Horace Logan, program director of KWKH, recalled that Jim visited him to audition for an on-air job at about the same time the *Billboard* item ran. Although there were no jobs available at the time, Logan found Jim to have a capable speaking voice and congenial personality, and promised to contact him should an opening arise.

Jim's employment situation spun like a revolving door, but he continued to pursue his musical aspirations. Around the clubs, he had become far more than the deejay who sat in with the band on Saturday nights. The "voice of Henderson and KGRI" frequently obtained long-term engagements as the lead singer with area bands, but some in the audiences decided his urbane style was a little too uptown for their tastes. "The people at the clubs found Jim too smooth," recalled Burton Harris, who played lead guitar for Gene Wortham, a bandleader who regularly hired Jim. "He was not as popular as some of the other singers we had."

Of all the bands in the East Texas caldron, Jim probably performed with Gene Wortham and the Circle O Ranchboys most often. Wortham, who managed the band and whose only musical contribution was the odd vocal or two, dressed his boys in cowboy duds manufactured in Midlothian, Texas, and stuck to a steady diet of pure country. The lineup included Burton Harris on lead guitar, teenager Bobby Garrett playing steel guitar, Leon Hayes on bass, and Curtis Kirk strumming rhythm guitar. Other performers who from time to time played under Wortham included fiddler Kenneth "Little Red" Hayes (brother of Leon) and bass man Doc Shelton (no relation to the Shelton brothers).

Jim Reeves also was an occasional member as Gene Wortham's cousin, Jimmy Dennis, owned the right of first refusal on the lead-singing duties. But Dennis was seventeen years old and at that rebellious age could not always be relied upon to make the show. Still, crowds seemed to prefer the teenager to the adult Reeves. "Jimmy Dennis could sing all the different styles, and he could mock," said Burton Harris. "He aped everybody. He was a Carl Smith and he was a Lefty Frizzell and he was anybody else. Jim was Jim."

However, Reeves found himself in the spotlight with Gene Wortham a good bit, and the association was invaluable for Jim. He became more visible on the club scene, and when he decided to try his hand at recording again, he had a band at his disposal. In Dallas, Jim scheduled and paid for a session at the Jim Beck studio in order to have some material to send to record companies. From Wortham's fold, he chose "Little Red" Hayes and Bobby Garrett, and he also tapped Leon and "Little Red"'s brother, Joe "Big Red" Hayes, who had played often with Hank Thompson's and Leon Payne's bands. (The piano player on the session may have been Connie Frable, who played in the Longview area.) Reeves mailed the resulting cuts—all of them self-penned—to various major recording labels, but while the backup musicians produced a livelier sound than that heard on the Macy's recordings, Jim came across as just another nice-singing boy. As a result, RCA Victor, Imperial, 4 Star, Capitol, and Columbia all sent him rejection letters.

Through his contact with KSIJ Radio in Gladewater and his scattered club work, Jim had gotten to know Tom Perryman, a KSIJ employee and promoter of country music shows. A South Texas native who had come from KEBE in Jacksonville, Perryman had helped open KSIJ in 1949. At KSIJ, which was owned by a partnership that included politician John Ben Sheppard, Perryman had spun records, read the news, sold advertising, and had quickly been promoted to station manager, a title he held when Sheppard and his friends sold the station to an oil man named T. W. Lee in 1950. Lee also owned a group of newspapers, and he brought in one of his publishers to run KSIJ. The new general manager kicked Perryman back down the ladder to be sales promotion manager, replacing him with a man named Joe Yowell. Not long after, though, the Korean conflict broke out, and Yowell, who had enlisted in the reserves, was called to military service. Douglas Reeh, who Perryman had hired ten months earlier to be chief announcer, rose to the station manager spot, leap-frogging over his former boss. "There were no hard feelings," Reeh recalled of the shake-up. "He hated [Yowell] so much that he was just tickled to death when I got the job."

Station manager or not, Tom had amassed a small power base in Gladewater. Because he booked performers from the *Louisiana Hayride* into the Gladewater area and arranged for local musicians to record demos at KSIJ, he had become an arbiter of talent. Perryman also hosted a country music show on KSIJ and tirelessly wrote to *Billboard* with his observations of artists and songs. "Tom Perryman, KSIJ, Gladewater, Tex.," a typical item in *Billboard* read, "reports that Slim Whitman, who has 'Indian Love Call' coming up on Imperial, is running neck and neck with Hank Williams for top station popularity." Almost every week, Tom announced his impressions and activities, and because record executives saw his name, they gathered him to be an important man on the East Texas music scene. He was. Perryman provided an outlet for droves of country performers from outside the region to reach music-mad, oil-rich East Texas. Anybody plugging country music shows or records or both in the Gladewater area considered Tom Perryman's show to be a necessary stop.

A freewheeling record label boss and talent manager named Fabor Robison always checked in with Perryman on his swings through Texas. An Arkansan who operated from a base in California, Robison managed a crop of artists who danced on the outskirts of widespread recognition: Les "Carrot Top" Anderson, Johnny Horton, Danny Dixon, and Billy Barton. He carried a scythe and a net, always ready to sign a singer or buy a song should he encounter either on his travels. In 1951, Robison had begun to wax several of his acts on a label he partly owned, Abbott Records. In 1952, Tom Perryman introduced Fabor Robison to Jim Reeves.

Perryman had known about Jim Reeves since 1949, when he gave "My Heart's Like a Welcome Mat" a few spins and saw Jim become a regular face on the East Texas dance hall and club scene. Reeves and Perryman had often spent Friday nights together at KSIJ's weekly hoedown, and around the fall of 1952, the two became coworkers. Jim had left KGRI again and returned to Shreveport to see Horace Logan about a job at KWKH. Finding nothing there, he drove back to Gladewater and knocked on Douglas Reeh's door.

"He came over to KSIJ and asked me if I'd put him to work there," explained Reeh. "I said, 'I just can't afford you.' And he asked me, 'How much could you pay?' [With] figures running through my head and all the expenses, finally I said, 'Jim. I can pay you sixty dollars at the most.' He was kind of grinning. He was leaning against the door. He said, 'Make it sixty-five.' I kind of laughed, and I said, 'Okay, sixty-five.' He went to work running a regular deejay show."

Jim and Tom now saw each other daily, and one evening after work when Jim was fronting the house band at the Reo Palm Isle in Longview, Tom went to work for his colleague. Fabor Robison was passing through Longview with his artist Billy Barton, who had just written "Dear John Letter." Barton—who thought nobody looked as good or sang as well as he—had finished a series of *Louisiana Hayride* appearances and was set to open at the Palm Isle in a day or two. Perryman implored both to catch Jim's performance there, and since that's precisely why Robison often drove through Texas, they accompanied Tom to the club. On the perimeter of the sprawling dance floor and among the resting, sweaty dancers, Robison and Barton sat with Perryman and listened to the distinct, straight-forward voice that belied the country instrumentals behind it. Something in the combination struck Fabor, but Barton was far less enamored.

"I seen this guy singing and he had a mediocre-sounding voice, and had this strap on," said Barton. "It was the sloppiest way to put a guitar on I'd ever seen in my life. I thought, 'What in the name of God is he doing with that strap?' He had it around his shoulder, but not around his neck. He was standing there playing, and he was bald-headed. His baldness went about halfway back. I said, 'He sounds all right, but he sure is sloppy looking. . . . Fabor wanted to record him. I said, 'Fabor, I don't know why you want to fool with him.'" But Fabor thought he saw the future. He liked the performance and, according to Tom Perryman, signed Jim to a record deal in the KSIJ offices.*

If Reeves failed, so be it. Robison approached the music business with a talent-loaded shotgun. He had already packed his shells with East Texas singers—never-will names like Wink Lewis, Freddy Frankes, and Curtis Kirk (from Gene Wortham's band)—and hoped one or two would hit the target. If Jim Reeves didn't, someone else would.

---

*Burton Harris, who was with Gene Wortham's band, has placed the location of this signing in the kitchen of the Mint Club near Gladewater.

5

The beer on the Palm Isle's floor had barely dried when Fabor Robison began releasing Jim Reeves sides. Fabor took the songs Jim had recorded earlier at Jim Beck's in Dallas—there were eight in all—and within weeks of meeting Jim put two on the street: "Wagon Load of Love" backed with "What Were You Doing Last Night?". Reeves had written both songs, and although his voice was in a pop vein on both, on "Wagon Load" he had sped up the tempo à la Hank Williams and Lefty Frizzell. Jim seemed to mesh confidently with the instrumental accompaniment that included Bobby Garrett and "Little Red" Hayes. He sounded at ease, far less cautious than on his earlier tapes and records. Reliable Tom Perryman reported in the December 27, 1952, *Billboard* that "Wagon Load of Love" was "showing promise."

However, Jim knew that the releases might show nothing more than promise and that Abbott could be nothing more than Macy's all over again. He held onto his disc jockey and announcing slots at KSIJ and turned to Shreveport for a third time to bother Horace Logan about a job at KWKH. "He called me and said he was coming back again," Logan recalled. "He said, 'I know you're not going to like this, but I'm going to audition again.' I told him, 'If I'm not going to like it, don't bother coming over.' He came over and brought his wife, and he didn't know it, but I had an opening at the time. I listened to him again and hired him on the spot as an announcer on a regular day shift and put him on as one of the four guys on the *Hayride*." When Reeves boarded the *Hayride*, it was as one of the four announcers who worked the Saturday night show, not as a performer. "I was aware that he had this record, but to be brutally frank, it was not up to the standards necessary," continued Logan. "He wasn't good enough to get on the *Hayride*. . . . He did not approach with the idea of being on the *Hayride*. He approached with the idea of being an announcer at KWKH."

Although Jim never asked to do so, the notion of appearing on the *Louisiana Hayride* must have been churning in his mind. Certainly, no other radio show on Jim's side of the Mississippi could boast a cast of the *Hayride*'s caliber. The great Hank Williams had wowed the Saturday night audiences until he left in 1949 for the *Grand Ole Opry*, the legendary country music radio showcase on WSM in Nashville, Tennessee. After Williams's departure, hit makers and rising stars such as Red Sovine, Slim Whitman, Webb Pierce, and others were glittering on the *Hayride* stage in Shreveport's Municipal Auditorium when Jim arrived in town. His brief appearance on KWKH in 1940 lingered in Jim's mind, and throughout the 1940s he had listened as the *Hayride* evolved from a showcase for local talent to become the "cradle of the stars."

Jim knew that a regular spot on KWKH's show could launch his name into a new dimension. At night, the station's powerful 50,000-watt signal stretched across the Southwest into California, spread like a fan across the Northwest, bounced across the Pacific Ocean to Australia, and also extended as far southeast as the Cayman Islands in the Caribbean. *Hayride* credentials opened doors and could be traded for major label recording contracts and—to the dismay of KWKH—*Grand Ole Opry* membership. In the world of radio stations, Jim entered the big leagues in December 1952.

The station that KWKH would become first crackled through the ether in early 1922, less than two years after KDKA radio in Pittsburgh transmitted the first scheduled radio programming. Engineer William E. Antony built the physical plant in Shreveport under the auspices of the Elliott Electric Company, and in 1923, a team of investors led by a retailer of radio sets purchased the station, dubbing it WGAQ. However, many who bought radios to listen to WGAQ found its signal was frequently unintelligible and wondered why they ever parted with their hard-earned cash. One of the investors finally solved the problem when he bought out his partners and moved the station to a spot just outside Shreveport, where its signal could be transmitted more clearly. It was entrepreneur W. K. Henderson who stepped forward, and in 1925 he modestly renamed the station KWKH.

William Kennon Henderson owned and operated the Henderson Iron Works and Supply Company in Shreveport and fancied himself an important man—and the radio station gave him a forum to let the whole world know it. At arbitrary moments during the broadcast day, he often would burst into the studio and grab the microphone from his startled announcer. "Hello, world, doggone you! This is KWKH at Shreveport, Lou-ee-siana, and it's W. K. Henderson talkin' to you." He would bellow forth his opinions on monopolies and national debt, and if critical telegrams came to his attention, he would shrug. "If you don't like my views," he often told listeners, "turn your dials."

Henderson sold his personal conduit in 1932, and in 1935 the station changed hands again, becoming the property of the *Shreveport Times*. Oilman John D. Ewing owned the *Times*, and in 1936 he moved the station to modern facilities in downtown Shreveport's Commercial Building. In 1939, the Federal Communication Commission (FCC) granted KWKH permission to broadcast on a clear channel at fifty thousand watts, the maximum broadcast power then permitted by law in the United States.

Such strength gave KWKH a vast audience. During the day, its signal penetrated east Texas and Oklahoma, western Mississippi, and most of Arkansas. At sundown, when most stations around the country left the air, KWKH surged into the void, attracting listeners throughout the country. More than anyone else, it was the musicians who performed live on the air who benefited from the extraordinary exposure. As far back as the 1920s, W. K. Henderson had invited local musicians to perform on KWKH, and that practice continued throughout the 1930s. Acts that Jim Reeves heard in the '30s, such as the Arizona Ranch Girls, the Rice Brothers and the Sunshine Boys, plugged and solicited engagements throughout the expansive territory the station reached during daylight hours. When the 1939 power surge dramatically increased the station's nighttime coverage area, musicians on KWKH could brag to record labels about their national and even international audiences.

Along with regular morning shows that featured a variety of so-called hillbilly performers, the station also aired live hillbilly music on Saturday nights. Starting in 1940, KWKH organized the *Saturday Night Round-Up*, which was broadcast from Shreveport's Municipal Auditorium and, on periodic occasions, from such towns as Monroe, Louisiana; Magnolia, Arkansas; and Henderson, Texas. After World War II, station management ordered Program Director Horace Logan to restructure the show so the Columbia Broadcasting System (CBS) could pick up a half-hour of the program for live, regional broadcast on Saturday nights. With the help of KWKH's commercial manager, Dean Upson, who came to Shreveport from Nashville after running WSM's booking agency and managing Eddy Arnold, Logan structured a tightly formatted, three-hour program from which CBS could pluck its thirty minutes. Over KWKH, the show emanating from the cavernous Municipal Auditorium on the north side of town initially ran three hours, from 8:00 P.M. to 11:00 P.M. but later was extended to 11:30 P.M.

The station's revamped Saturday night lineup debuted on April 3, 1948, and featured such cast members as the Bailes Brothers, who had followed Dean Upson to KWKH, and Johnnie and Jack and the Tennessee Mountain Boys, featuring Kitty Wells. (Johnnie Wright, Jack Anglin, Kitty Wells, and the band were also refugees from Nashville's WSM who came to KWKH on the heels of Upson.) Word spread as wide as the station's coverage area that KWKH had begun broadcasting a country music bandwagon that was being picked up by the national CBS network, just as the *Opry* was being picked up by NBC for a half hour on Saturday nights.

Hank Williams became a regular four months after KWKH christened its show, debuting to his shuffling hit "Move It On Over" and dueting on "I Want to Live and Love" with Miss Audrey, his wife. In the next few years, a host of upward-bound acts followed Hank and grabbed slots on the show. Behind Nashville's *Grand Ole Opry*, KWKH had the hottest griddle in country music radio. Astonishment overcame chief announcer Hi Roberts (to whom Reeves reported at KWKH) as the *Hayride* began to sizzle before his eyes. "There was no great effort behind it to make it become what it did become," he observed. "It just grew. The people were hungry for it, and they just loved it. So, it became very, very popular. Horace poured his heart and soul into that thing."

Jim arrived at KWKH during the *Louisiana Hayride*'s heyday. Although Hank had abandoned the show for the *Grand Ole Opry* in

1949, men who would help define the country sound of the 1950s crowded the Municipal Auditorium stage almost every Saturday night. Johnny Horton, Webb Pierce, the Wilburn Brothers, Red Sovine, and Faron Young enlivened the *Hayride* with fresh, vital music. Shucks! Even a worn Hank Williams had returned to his radio home in September 1952, but he died just as Jim had begun announcing for the station.

Most of the programming day, though, followed the format of a typical mid-size American city radio station. In the mornings, a few of the *Hayride* regulars joined the roosters to wake up the Ark-La-Tex (the tri-state region comprising the contiguous corners of Arkansas, Louisiana, and Texas), but the rest of the day was filled with CBS network programming: Arthur Godfrey, soap operas, variety shows. With ebullient Oklahoman Hi Roberts and the serious Frank Page, Jim Reeves took his turn introducing each show and reading commercials, becoming one of the anonymous, omniscient voices of KWKH. Soon, though, he acquired an identity. Horace Logan recalled that it wasn't long after Reeves arrived that he teamed Jim with Hi and Frank to announce on the *Hayride*. "They liked that because they got extra money," said Logan, "not much but some. Any money in those days was money."

Horace also assigned Jim to the *Red River Roundup*, a country disc-jockey show that aired weekday evenings and from 11:30 P.M. to 1:00 A.M. on Saturday nights after the *Hayride*. To keep their hillbilly high buzzing, hordes of *Hayride* faithful heading home on Saturday nights tuned their car radios to 1130 kilocycles and the *Roundup*. Many who listened at home remained glued their radio sets as well. According to Logan, Hank Williams was the first cast member to capitalize on this large post-*Hayride* audience by hosting the *Roundup* for a period in the late 1940s. In late 1952, when Jim arrived at KWKH, he asked for the weekday and Saturday night slots, Logan said. It was a wise request from a man who wished to be a recording star. Reeves's name would be associated with the station's largest blocks of country programming, the *Louisiana Hayride* and the *Red River Roundup*.

On the *Roundup*, Jim interviewed country artists passing through town and played the big records of the day, many of which were by the *Hayride* cast members he saw on Saturdays. Webb Pierce's "Back Street Affair" and "That Heart Belongs to Me" were among the hit tunes, as was Hank Thompson's "The Wild Side of Life" and Kitty Wells' answer to Thompson, "It Wasn't God Who Made Honky Tonk Angels." Surrounded by glass and sound board, as he had been since 1948, Jim sat at his broadcast perch and waited to join them. Perhaps lost in dreams of a *Billboard* hit, he seemed distant on his evening shifts. Engineer Bob Sullivan spent hours in silence with Jim as the records spun around and around and around.

"Jim was the type of guy that you really couldn't get to know too well. I would say that he really wouldn't go out of his way to be friends with you. . . . He and I used to do a night shift together. Back then the announcer did nothing but announce, and they had a guy in the control room play all the records, play all the commercials, and do all the other stuff. Even there, working with Jim at night, he'd come on at five or six o'clock and I'd come on at five or six o'clock, and we'd go till one in the morning. But I never did really get to know Jim. We would talk, but he was the type of guy who just wouldn't open up. . . . He didn't seem to talk about his family or anything. He just came in, did his job, and left."

Around KWKH, employees were used to easygoing announcer Hi Roberts, who always had time for a word, and Hank Williams or Webb Pierce, who would stop by, slap a co-worker on the back, and shoot the bull. But Jim stayed back, silenced by shyness, insecurity, or competitiveness. Back at KGRI, John Bolin had observed a similar on-the-job demeanor in Jim. "He was a good guy, but you know how certain people are: just hard to get to know." The small-town radio engineer saw in Jim a moodiness, a pleasant demeanor that could quickly ice over. Jim, in fact, had never been the personality that everybody loved. At school, on the back of the team bus, or in the studio, he was the serious one—good for a song and a drink or two, but always the guy who seemed to have something else on mind.

On the *Hayride* stage, Jim peeled away some of his reserve to keep the live audience engaged between acts. Wearing a white cowboy hat, the junior announcer delivered pat introductions and plugs for the various sponsors: Jax Beer, Bristol-Myers, Coca-Cola. He had to step outside himself to give a rousing introduction to a *Hayride* act, but he generally stood back from the antics of Hi Roberts and Frank Page, who goosed the audience with cheer leading or crazy dances. Early in the show, Page and Roberts primed the fans for a night of applause and laughter that, in turn, created a sense of

With the Hayride *anchors. From left: Frank Page, Horace Logan, Hi Roberts, and Jim. (Courtesy: Richard Weize)*

electricity for the listeners at home. The two often incorporated staff musician Buddy Attaway into the antics.

"Buddy was one of the nicest guys in the world," explained Roberts, "but he was certainly not one of God's more handsome creatures. . . . He had these real skinny legs, and in order to get people laughing, we were always doing things to get crowd reaction so they would laugh and yell and scream and whoop. So, when Buddy would be out there—he might be fiddling or playing his guitar and singing—we would come out and roll up his pant legs. You could roll them up all the way like they were short shorts because his upper thigh was just about the same [size] as his calf. He was not a pretty sight. But people would laugh. The people would just howl, and we would get great response. Then, when the acts came on, they were already in a receptive mood."

Hayride producer Horace Logan also pitched in to incite the crowd. Just before the on-air light flashed on and the mike cracked open, Horace would shout, "Anybody here from Louisiana?" and a section of the audience would roar. Then, "Anybody here from Texas?" and rest of the crowd—those who had crossed the border to get there—would explode into rebel yells and fevered applause. Seconds later, amid the cacophony, Logan would lean toward the mike again and herald, "the *Louisiana Hayride*," and the show would begin.

Carved and erect like a cigar-store Indian, Logan watched over his show with piercing eyes and never let anybody forget that the *Hayride* rocked in his cradle: "I produced it. I decided who would be on it, and who wouldn't be on it. The *Hayride*—good, bad, or indifferent, failure or success—was entirely due to my efforts and nobody else's." Actually, others helped Logan guide the show toward success, but Logan was the captain, and his dedication and coordination produced a tight, top-notch show that entertained countless thousands every Saturday night. Using a format similar to that of the tightly regimented *Grand Ole Opry*, Logan penciled in a couple of appearances for each artist throughout the course of the program and kept things moving, always careful not to let the performers exceed their allotted time slots.

"Artists gave me each Saturday night a list of the tunes they wanted to do the next week, and I picked what they would do and the order in which they would do them and when they would come on," said Horace. "The idea behind that was this: When you appear on the *Hayride* in that first two hours or the second two hours, you were scheduled to do two numbers. If you did an encore, you came back two hours later and did one number. You had to reestablish your eminence or fall on your ass every Saturday night. . . . I scheduled a radio show, not a stage show. It was a radio show with an audience is what it was. We did everything on air. We were always doing some tricks and stunts and never explaining on the air what was happening, and the audience was having hysterics. We actually had microphones hanging over the audience, so we could pick them up just as much we could the cast. We never explained what was happening. The people got curious and came to see what the heck was going on. That's the way we averaged 3,300 people every Saturday night, which ain't a bad crowd."

If the show strayed from the efficiency that the dour-faced Logan demanded, the East Texas-West Louisiana fans never seemed to notice. They returned week after week, invading the 3,800-seat Municipal Auditorium like football fans rushing into LSU's football stadium on a Saturday afternoon in the fall. There was a bazaar-like atmosphere within: devotees flashing their cameras at Webb Pierce's sparkling outfit, someone capturing the songs with a wire recorder, reunions among friends in the aisles and lobby.

"They were family," said Hi Roberts of the *Hayride* audiences. "Oh shoot, it was carnival time. People walking up and down. There's a baby there; there's old folks and the fiftysomethings—all different ages. They were very comfortable because it was okay. [It was almost like] that feeling in a church because people own it, and they're not stiff and uncomfortable. That's the feeling you had at the *Hayride*. It was their place."

And now it was Jim Reeves's place, too. Jim finally had a secure job with a superior broadcasting outfit and saw on a firsthand basis the lives and working arrangements of top-flight country performers. The only question now for him was whether he would ever perform on the *Hayride*. If he was counting on "Wagon Load of Love" to turn the *Hayride* spotlight on him, he had better forget it. Horace poo-pooed the song. Perhaps, though, he'd like Jim's next Abbott sides.

On one of Fabor Robison's talent-mining trips through Texas, he stopped in Nacogdoches, Texas, to poke around the night clubs. It was there, in January 1953, that he found Jim's next release. In his long Buick, Fabor pulled up to Johnson's Record Shop and asked the proprietors if any local musicians or writers were making noise. There was one, the Johnsons told him: Mitchell Torok, a college student at Stephen F. Austin State University who played football and sang Eddy Arnold and Hank Thompson songs every morning on KSFA, the college radio station. The Johnsons suggested that Torok's wife, who worked at the local newspaper, could track him down, so they telephoned and left word that someone from Hollywood wanted to see her husband. She called back and told Fabor to meet Mitchell at Stripling's drug store near the record shop.

When Torok dashed in and laid eyes of Fabor, he saw nothing but Hollywood. "He was sitting there with perforated shoes. . . ," remembered Torok. "He had on a brown sports jacket, some sand-colored slacks, and a big, open collar like you see from California, [and was] twirling his car keys, waiting." Inspired by Hank Snow's 1951 hit "The Rhumba Boogie," the rosy-cheeked youngster had just penned a fast-moving, Latin-flavored ditty about a freewheeling boy from south of the border. "I tried to get some of the radio stations to help me make a tape to send up there to Nashville," said Torok. "I guess I had Hank Snow in mind. I'm not sure. I didn't have any equipment, and I had very little money at the time. The radio stations, the couple of times I visited there in about a two-week period, didn't have time. They were busy doing something else. They said, 'Come back later.' These engineers I talked with, I was offering to give them half the song."

Then, Fabor showed up in Nacogdoches. "I've got a hit," Mitchell told the flashy visitor, and he offered to strum it for him. The two drove out to the Torok's one-room house on the Lufkin Highway, and Fabor lugged a bulky, wood-encased reel-to-reel tape recorder from his truck. "I put the lyrics on the floor and played it," continued Torok. "He said, 'Well, I kind of like it. I got this singer named Jim Reeves. You ever heard of him?' I said, 'Yes, we hear "Wagon Load of Love" ever so often on the radio.' He said, 'Well, I'm recording him tonight. I'd like to take this and do it.' So, he took 'Mexican Joe.' "

That night (actually, very early the next morning, January 18, 1953), Fabor had the KWKH studios booked to produce Jim's second session. As the station was the nerve center for country music in Shreveport, it was natural that producers would use its studios to record *Hayride* talent. KWKH charged $20 an hour and opened its studios for such services at 1:00 A.M., the hour it signed off the air. Singers and musicians had four hours to find perfection because the station began the next day's broadcasting schedule at 5:00 A.M. "I don't know how we did it," marveled Bob Sullivan, Fabor's engineer that night, "because there was no echo chamber. Just a flat, cheap broadcast board was all we had, but it sufficed."

Drawing deeper from the city's talent well, Fabor assembled a group of Shreveport-based musicians to back Jim: pianist Floyd Cramer, bass player Don Davis, steel man Jimmy Day, and guitarist Tommy Bishop. They joined the dual fiddles of Texas brothers Kenneth "Little Red" Hayes and Joe "Big Red" Hayes. Cramer, Day, and Bishop comprised the nucleus of Red Sovine's band, and they often backed Webb Pierce and had even accompanied Hank Williams from time to time. Davis was a stalwart in the *Hayride* house band, and the Hayeses, of course, were well-entrenched in the Texas music scene.

In those early morning hours, Jim probably struggled with the new material. During his first session in Dallas, he had recorded mostly his own compositions, songs he had lived with for a while, but in Shreveport that January night, Fabor handed him something completely foreign, and fast to boot. Opening with the Hayeses' twin fiddles, "Mexican Joe" moved too quickly for Jim's vibrato to linger. Jim as well as the backup band seemed to be rushing toward some undetermined finish line. In a delivery uncharacteristic of Jim Reeves, a lyric like "wondering" became "wandrin'." Jim clipped the words to keep up with the tempo, something he'd never really done before on recordings. Ultimately, though, the song fell into place. "It just kind of growed together," remembered "Little Red" Hayes. "Jim began to play an open-chord guitar, singing the song, and all of the sudden this rhythm pattern just kind of came in." The ensemble would tackle nothing else that night, and Fabor left the studio with two versions of "Mexican Joe."

Robison rushed back to California with the master tapes, coupled "Mexican Joe" with "I Could Cry" from Jim's Jim Beck session, and rolled the single into record stores by March.* Setting out from his office on North Argyle Avenue in Hollywood, Fabor left behind

---

*Athough the label read "Jim Reeves and the Circle O Ranch Boys," Gene Wortham's band, with which Jim had earlier played, had nothing to do with the "Mexican Joe" recording.

his small staff and wife Mary to buttonhole every disc jockey and distributor he knew throughout the nation. By month's end, "Mexican Joe" had made the record popularity charts in Dallas/ Forth Worth and Houston, and was beginning to steam up the national charts.

Charles Greenberg, an accountant who shared Abbott's North Argyle office and kept Fabor's books, watched "Mexican Joe" explode. "We all worked to ship the damn stuff out of the office," said Greenberg. "I remember at the end of the first month, I guess we had sold something like fifteen or twenty thousand records, and Mary looked at me: 'You know, Chuck, if we sold fifteen or twenty thousand records every month, we could make a pretty good living.' The next month it went haywire. 'Mexican Joe' sales really started coming in."

Gliding by such hot hits as Marty Robbins's "I Couldn't Keep from Crying" and Webb Pierce's "The Last Waltz," Jim Reeves and "Mexican Joe" approached the number-one spot on the charts in late April. Only the late Hank Williams's "Kaw-Liga," which had occupied the top notch for thirteen weeks, blocked "Mexican Joe" from its day in the sun. "Kaw-Liga" would surely falter soon, but sentiment over Hank's untimely death just a few months earlier, in January, was pushing his classic "Your Cheatin' Heart" up the charts. "Mexican Joe" just might run out of gas by the time the Drifting Cowboy was through with number one.

But when the May 9 record chart hit the newsstands, "Kaw-Liga" fell dramatically from the top spot to sixth, and since "Your Cheatin' Heart" had not yet mustered the drive to replace it, "Mexican Joe" became the top country single on *Billboard*'s country countdown. Fueled by a crisp—if rushed—vocal, Fabor Robison's promotion, and a country audience receptive to novelty songs, Jim Reeves had reached number one on his chart debut. Not even Hank Williams or Eddy Arnold had accomplished that feat.

As Jim watched this hot-sauce song speed up the *Billboard* charts, he waited for Horace Logan to give him the nod for a *Hayride* appearance. And he waited. No matter how many steps up the charts "Mexican Joe" took, Logan seemed in no hurry to put his junior announcer on the radio show as a performer. In fact, *Hayride* cast member Billy Walker, a Columbia artist who had yet to see a national hit in four years of recording, had begun performing "Mexican Joe"

on the show. Although Logan has said that he wasn't "averse to let-
ting him evolve as a singer," virtually everybody associated with the
Hayride in 1953 recalled staring with disbelief as Jim simmered backstage while Billy Walker rambled through "Mexican Joe." Certainly,
Horace could spot talent, but perhaps he needed more evidence of
Jim's. Or, having just hired Jim, maybe Logan didn't want to lose his
announcer and disc jockey. "Horace kind of liked to keep you in
place," ventured Hi Roberts. "He just really didn't make things easy
for you. I don't know whether he was jealous of Jim's ability. He was
just funny."

Although Jim respected that Horace had given him a big break in
radio, he began to fume a bit. Logan was not only blunting his song's
potential but his career as a performer as well. Billy Walker also
dropped down on Jim's hit parade. In Jim's eyes, Walker was no better than Logan, really. He was hitting a handicapped man. Heck!
Walker had even cut "Mexican Joe" at KWKH—with "Big Red"
Hayes, Floyd Cramer, and Jimmy Day backing him! But Walker and
his producer at Columbia saw it differently. It was common for artists
to "cover" songs, and—on the *Hayride*, at least—"Mexican Joe" was
withering on the vine.

"I thought 'Mexican Joe' was a hit song from the word go,"
explained Billy Walker. "The only reason I considered recording the
song was, there was another group of guys on the *Hayride*, a trio from
Monroe, that had cut 'Mexican Joe,' too. . . . And Columbia had
wanted to cover the song, so we did it." Jim avoided his competition
like the bad part of town, and according to Walker, never completely
forgave him. "I felt sorry for the guy," said Billy Walker. "The guy's
got a hit record out, and he can't sing it on the place where they got
him on. I thought it was an act of sheer stupidity for Horace Logan."

Despite Walker's version, Jim's recording of "Mexican Joe" ran
away as if it had no competition, and finally Horace Logan melted.
According to KWKH's Frank Page, Logan released Reeves to the
Hayride crowd on a night when an Arkansas rockabilly performer
named Sleepy LaBeef failed to show. (LaBeef recalled that his car
broke down four times in Texas on the way to Shreveport, and four
times he called Horace Logan to report his whereabouts.) When
LaBeef's replacement appeared, the people uncorked a thunder that
had been bottled since they first heard Jim sing "Mexican Joe" on the

radio. "Everybody just flipped," observed Hi Roberts. ". . . There was
a great response. Jim, right away, was well received because he was
already known."

Grudgingly, often in the waning moments of the show when
things were dragging, Horace began allowing Jim to sing his hit song.
In mid-April, the *Hayride* temporarily relocated to Little Rock,
Arkansas, where the *Shreveport Times* also owned KTHS, a radio station that simulcast KWKH's Saturday night jamboree. Events such as
a Billy Graham crusade or Shreveport's springtime Holiday in Dixie
festival periodically chased the *Hayride* out of Municipal Auditorium, so the station often moved the program to nearby cities such as
San Antonio or Oklahoma City. For a month—through late April and
early May, during Holiday in Dixie—the *Hayride* parked in Little
Rock. When the show departed Shreveport, KWKH was featuring in
its advertisements Slim Whitman and Goldie Hill, who recently had
a number-one hit with her "I Let the Stars Get in My Eyes." When the
show returned to its home base on May 16, Horace Logan finally gave
Jim Reeves his due—and top billing. "Mexican Joe" was just too hot,
and the audience's love of Jim was too strong to ignore.

Predictably, offers of show dates deluged Jim. He hired "Little
Red" Hayes to accompany him for his "live" gigs, and when Jim
could break away from KWKH, they met at club dates around Shreveport and across Texas. Hayes had played behind Jim at the Reo Palm
Isle until just before Jim left to take the announcing job in Shreveport.
Throughout the Texas club scene, Reeves and Hayes (who were often
joined by Bobby Garrett) fronted various pick-up bands, among them
groups led by Lone Star stalwarts Jimmy Heap and Charlie Adams.

For Hi Roberts, Jim's supervisor at KWKH, his announcer's new
popularity manifested itself in the frequent requests for schedule
changes. "He started really getting action. He came and he said, 'Can
I switch my things off?' He wanted to know if he could switch his days
off because he was getting feelers out there. People would call him
and want him to be on their country shows. So, he says, 'I can go
down to Honey Island, Texas, and sing three songs and make $250.' "

In Dallas on April 18, Jim headlined KLRD Radio's *Big D Jamboree*,
and the venerable *Grand Ole Opry* in Nashville invited him to appear
on May 23 during the highlighted NBC portion of the show. According
to a report in *Billboard*, "Mexican Joe" brought down the house during
Jim's *Opry* performance at the Ryman Auditorium. Before the month

ended, Jim took a leave of absence from KWKH and hoped he would never have to return as an announcer. He would continue to be a cast member on the *Hayride*, and he and Mary remained in the home they occupied in a subdivision on the west side of Shreveport. On June 1, 1953, though, Norman Bale, a disc jockey from Atlanta, Texas, joined KWKH as Jim Reeves's replacement.

Little more than a month later, as "Mexican Joe" finally headed south on the national charts, Jim and "Little Red" Hayes played the West Texas city of Lubbock on August 7, a date that would launch them toward a tour of California. After the gig, while the duo zoomed west from Lubbock in a new Buick that "Mexican Joe" had financed, "Little Red" watched in the quiet of the car as his boss absorbed the scenery—the hill country of West Texas and the dreamy, sun-splashed Sonoran Desert in New Mexico. Jim explained to his fiddler that he never had traveled much farther west than Dallas, and although baseball had revealed eastern sections of the country to him, he was glad to be discovering another part of America. "He was a happy, happy, happy man," surmised "Little Red" Hayes. "He was a very happy man, making a lot of money. Wasn't having to disc jockey for a living, having a good time."

6

Ntrepreneurs and business executives who seek to exploit
country music talent rarely have been credited with having
pristine reputations by the artists they represented. Their
moments of self-interest often pock the roads to success they
paved for their clients. Recording pioneers Ralph Peer and Art
Satherly, who have been enshrined for carrying country and other
musical styles to the masses, cannot escape the fact that they pock-
eted for themselves or their employers the lucrative publishing rights
to songs written by the unsuspecting artists they recorded. On
another front, WSM's brass charged *Grand Ole Opry* artists 15 percent of their concert grosses to bill themselves as *Opry* performers, a
practice the show's cast members deemed sheer robbery. The notorious and legendary Colonel Tom Parker lurks on the polluted river
bottom of music entrepreneurs, having at times dealt deceptively
with some of the biggest names in music: Eddy Arnold, Hank Snow,
and Elvis Presley.

But deep in the sludge—deeper perhaps than even the Colonel—
skulks the memory of Fabor Robison. Like Parker, who introduced
Arnold and Presley to universal fame, Robison exposed Jim Reeves
and other artists to a broad audience, but he warmed few hearts in the
process. Performers who worked under his umbrella complained of
lost royalties, missing concert payments, and sexual harassment, as
well as Robison's brow-beating, violent style. He was known to bran-
dish a revolver and would flout any wishes but his own. Cunning just
dripped from his greased-back hair onto his beige summer suits. He
could charm the habit off a nun—and trip her with it. However,

Fabor, for all the venom spit upon him, knew how to sell records and, with a meatless ditty like "Mexican Joe," could propel out of oblivion an anonymous performer like Jim Reeves.

Jim and his record, in turn, gave Robison reason to chortle after more than two years of hit-seeking. An Arkansas native, Fabor had traveled to California in the late 1940s to grab a little of Hollywood's glitter. He later would tell associates that he worked in the set department of a major Hollywood studio and was a stand-in for actor Robert Young, to whom he bore some resemblance. He would say that he labored as a cook in a Los Angeles hotel, but, Fabor generally revealed few clues about his past. Like Colonel Parker, who guarded the secret of his Dutch birth, Fabor seemed to be hiding something. His promotion man for a couple of years at Abbott—Del Roy, who drove miles and miles with his boss on promotional junkets—never even knew from what state Fabor hailed. "Fabor was a rather closed-mouth person," said Roy. "A very private sort of person. He did not put his business in the street." Robison's life and career came into sharp focus for only a few years in the early 1950s, the period of his greatest success.

Fabor and his wife, Mary, a New Yorker who played the drums, haunted the vibrant Southern California country and western music scene. Seeking to claim a larger chunk of the West Coast c&w action, Robison had caught wind of Johnny Horton and lured him into a management contract, and was also courting 4 Star Records' Terry Preston, who became better known later as Ferlin Husky. Robison had already signed Les "Carrot Top" Anderson and placed him with Decca Records, and he hoped to work similar magic with Horton. However, Fabor could only persuade the man with whom he shared his Argyle Avenue office to record his latest charge. Les McWain ran Cormac Records and waxed artists in the back room of 1653 Argyle, but a few months after recording Horton, the label collapsed.

Stuck with a talented, yet unsigned artist, Fabor decided to blast his own shaft to the record-buying market. He looked up Sid Abbott, the owner of a Los Angeles drug store chain whom Fabor had met while plugging "Carrot Top" Anderson. "Carrot Top" regularly performed at Abbott's store openings and other promotional events, and when Fabor needed cash to finance a recording session for Anderson, he had hit up Sid. Now, Fabor had a much heavier proposition in mind. With a countenance that alternately flashed wide grins and earnest expressions, he persuaded Sid Abbott to bankroll a record label. They called it Abbott Records, and the new enterprise provided Johnny Horton with a recording home. Out came mild-selling Horton cuts like "Done Rovin'," "Talk Gobbler Talk," and "Devilish Lovelight," and Abbott proceeded to ink South Dakota singer Danny Dixon and Kentucky native Billy Barton, who dueted with Johnny Horton on "Somebody's Rocking My Boat Again."

Simultaneously, Robison struck an arrangement with Sylvester Cross of American Music, one of the few music publishers truly interested in promoting western music. Cross owned the rights to such western classics as "Tumbling Tumbleweeds" and "Cool Water," and paid Fabor a fee for every new Abbott song Robison sent his way. In addition, Cross helped finance Robison's cross-country promotional tours, journeys that had the effect of selling Abbott records and thus filling American Music's coffers. Cross's funding, perhaps more than any other factor, helped Fabor construct the framework of Abbott's success with "Mexican Joe."

By the time Robison released "Mexican Joe," his tours across America had established a network of disc jockeys and record distributors who felt flattered when the president of a record company—the man who splashed advertisements and news items in their copies of *Billboard*—stopped by to visit and take them to lunch. The back end of Fabor's car sagged with boxes of Abbott discs. Del Roy, who joined Fabor as head of promotion in the aftermath of "Mexican Joe," frequently accompanied Robison. "Fabor bought two Cadillacs as company cars, and he gave one of them to me and he drove the big one," said Roy. "We pretty well traveled around the country, persuading the radio stations, the disc jockeys." Roy said he never gave a cent to a disc jockey on Robison's behalf, but Russell Sims, who was Billy Barton's cousin and had helped Fabor with recording and promotion, recalled that around disc jockeys, bills flaked freely from Fabor's wad. "We'd pay anybody to play a record, if we had any money," claimed Sims. "If we didn't, we'd get some."

Not long before the rise of "Mexican Joe," Robison had sold Johnny Horton's recording contract to Mercury Records and probably used the cash to buy out Sid Abbott's stake in Abbott Records. After that, Fabor's wad just grew. With the proceeds from "Mexican Joe," he moved his offices to Hollywood Boulevard, phased in a second record line (Fabor Records), disassociated himself from Sylvester Cross by forming his own publishing company (Dandelion Music), and chased frequently cockamamie investment schemes. He manufactured and tried to sell a coffin-like tanning bed that was designed to hold water and keep the sun worshiper cool, and, according to KWKH engineer Bob Sullivan, he tried to open a recording base in Brazil.

"He was just an oddball," said Sullivan. "He approached me one time during all this recording I was doing . . . and asked me if I'd be interested in moving to Brazil. I said, 'Good Lord, what for?' He said, 'Well, I've figured out I can go down to Brazil. They're building a city down there called Brasilia. They got all the recording equipment you need, and those guys there are so talented they can copy anything they hear. What we'll do is go down there and cut tracks so we don't have to pay the musicians [union scale], and we'll bring the tracks up here and dub in the singers.' " If Fabor thought expansively before "Mexican Joe," his aspirations stretched without limits afterward.

On Jim and "Little Red" Hayes's late-summer swing through the West, Robison introduced Jim around to the important disc jockeys and promoters, officially unveiling him to the West Coast establishment at a dinner on August 23. That night, Fabor also introduced sixteen-year-old Carolyn Bradshaw, a *Hayride* artist who was on Jim's tour and had recently recorded the inevitable answer song, "The Marriage of Mexican Joe." From California, Jim scampered back to Shreveport to fill an autumn complement of *Hayride* appearances and Texas gigs before rocketing north for a stint at the Roosevelt Lounge in Detroit. While seemingly out of the orbit of country music's influence, Detroit—like many northern industrial cities—had absorbed an influx of southern whites who had come to work in the city's auto industry. They loved their country music and welcomed Jim for an extended run.

Meanwhile, the road-mad Robison was motoring throughout the Great Lakes region, sniffing out talent and passing out discs. He planned to rendezvous with Jim in Detroit and then whisk down to Shreveport for Jim's fourth recording session. But first, Fabor had business in Cleveland. A few months earlier, Robison had traveled through Cleveland and met WSRS Radio's Jack Gale, a disc jockey who occasionally recorded artists on his tiny Triple A label. The two chatted briefly, and then Gale spun for Fabor a record he had recently waxed for teenager Ginny Wright.

The new Abbott artist. (Courtesy: Frank Anderson)

Jim surrounded by, from left, Carolyn Bradshaw, Fabor Robison, and Mary Robison in August 1953. (Courtesy: Richard Weize)

Originally from near the Georgia towns of Summit and Graymont, Ginny Wright had come north to Cleveland to live with her sister, and the two were working as waitresses at Manner's restaurant in town. Ginny sang weekend nights on a local barn dance and frequently dropped by WSRS to pester Jack Gale about recording her. She sounded like a female Hank Williams, she told him. Gale finally relented, and to his amazement, little Ginny's record dropped onto more than a few turntables in Cleveland and caught the interest of cowboy hipster Pee Wee King, who brought her on the local show he was hosting on WEWS-TV.

Like Pee Wee, Fabor perked up his ears at the sound of Ginny's piercing voice. He asked Jack Gale for a meeting with Ginny, saying that he could do more for her in the Golden State than Gale could do in Cleveland. Gale dialed Wright and put Fabor on the phone with her. The West Coast record man told her to tape ten songs and send them to him. Then Fabor vanished, and, although Ginny sent the tape, she nearly gave up hope while waiting for his response.

But Robison had not forgotten. It was early October, and he was cruising across northern Ohio, kicking up fallen leaves on the highway. Darkness had spread over Cleveland when he turned into Manner's. "I was working, and I had to make a whole lot of milk shakes for these jockeys who rode horses," said Ginny Wright of the night she first saw Fabor. "I was mad as heck, and I looked up and I saw this Cadillac pull up in front of the restaurant. I saw this guy pull up, and the car had a California license plate on it, and he had on dark glasses. Well, I reached back and pulled off my apron and laid it on the counter. My sister said, 'Where do you think you're going?' I said, 'I'm going to record.' She said, 'You're crazy!' I said, 'I bet that's Fabor Robison.' I met him at the door and said, 'You're Fabor.' And he said, 'You're Ginny. I've come by to get you.' I said, 'I'm ready to go.' He said, 'We'll leave out in the morning.' I was living with my sister at the time, and I went home and packed me a suitcase."

The two headed for Detroit in order to catch up with Jim at the Roosevelt Lounge. Once in town, Fabor found a hotel and walked into the office to check in. "He came back to the car and said, 'They ain't got but one room.' I said, 'That's all right. I'll sleep in the car.' He laughed at me and said, 'Get on out, chicken. I got you a room.'"

That night, after whatever excuse Fabor used to get the youngster inside the club, Jim invited Ginny on stage to sing "A Dear John Letter" with him. The song was written by Billy Barton and was incinerating the country and pop charts at the time for the duo of Jean Shepard and Ferlin Husky. It needed no introduction to Ginny. She knew it up and down, and the just-introduced Jim and Ginny received an enthusiastic reaction from the Roosevelt throng. Ginny then took the spotlight to sing Goldie Hill's "I Let the Stars Get in My Eyes," but she became tangled in the verse and struggled to bring the song to an end. She just backed away from the edge of the stage and quit. As she started to run toward the side of the stage, though, she felt Jim's hard, sinewy arms enfold her. "Don't let that get you down," he implored like a coach. "Go out and do another one." She did, and to Ginny, the incredibly famous Jim Reeves seemed to be developing a fatherly concern for her. She mistrusted Fabor and his cool, sly style, so she welcomed Jim's protectiveness.

"At intermission, he came by and sat down," remembered Ginny, "and this woman walked up to me—kind of a young woman. She had short bobbed-off hair, and she had pants on like a man. She was patting me on the shoulder and just putting her face in mine: 'You don't need a microphone. You got the strongest voice. Your voice is really strong.' . . . She was patting me, and Jim looked up at her and said, 'You get the hell away from her.' I kind of looked [at Jim] funny. I kind of opened my mouth. I didn't know that artists did fans like that. I said, 'Jim, she's a fan. What are you doing that for?' He looked at me and laughed. He said, 'Ginny, you don't know what she is?' I said, 'She's a woman. She's a fan. She came up here telling me that she liked my voice and everything, and I'd be a great singer.' He pulled up his chair by me: 'Honey, I know you're a little country girl, but I'm going to tell you about the birds and the bees. You stay away from women like that. "Of course, he explained to me all about it. I didn't know nothing about it. I just couldn't believe that a woman went with a woman or a man went with a man. I was just green."

The next day, Jim, Ginny, and Fabor drove straight through to Shreveport. Ginny remained under Jim's sheltering wing, fearing that Fabor might try something unsavory. "Fabor would drive a while, and Jim would sleep in the backseat," Ginny recalled. "I'd sit up in the front seat, and then when Jim would drive he would sing songs to me that he wrote." Almost immediately upon arriving in Shreveport, Fabor ushered the duo into the KWKH studio. After seeing Ginny and Jim glide through Billy Barton's "A Dear John Letter" in Detroit, he matched the two with Barton's: "I Love You." While the Hayes brothers and the *Hayride* boys picked, Jim—in a dead-serious tone—recited verses of unrequited love and Ginny—with her sharp, nasal style—sang the chorus over and over (*I love you you you. No one else will ever do . . .*).

On his own, Jim recorded two other numbers on this, his fourth session for Fabor: "Echo Bonita" and "Bimbo." The latter song, written and recorded by Capitol artist Rod Morris, had come to Fabor by way of Fred Stryker at Fairway Music and, although Jim was hesitant to touch it, Fabor saw a hit. Fabor had rushed Jim into the studio twice since the "Mexican Joe" session, but the two resulting singles failed to capitalize on the buzz over Jim's first hit. On this session, Fabor tied his hopes to "Bimbo," another novelty song that told the tale of a gummy-faced little boy. Per usual, Jim's home territory of

Texas embraced the song first and then herded it onto the national
charts in early December. In one month's time—and less than ten
months after hitting the charts for the first time—Jim corralled his
second number one hit.

When the "Bimbo" session broke up, Fabor left Jim at home with
Mary and packed Ginny Wright into his Cadillac for a trip to California. There, he would move the teenager into his home, escort her on
a round of publicity appearances, and put her to work with wife Mary
writing disc jockeys and packing records. "When I started to leave,"
recalled Ginny, "Jim come and bent over the car and said, 'Well,
Ginny, don't stay out there too long. We got a hit on our hands.' " Jim
hit it right. The duet—the first release on Fabor's self-titled label—
followed promptly on the Jim Reeves path, charting on January 9,
1954, (the week "Bimbo" hit the top) and percolating to number three.

In February 1954, Jim was in California for another Abbott session on which he would try to break away from the themes and delivery of his recent hits. He took six of his own compositions into the
Western Recorders studio in Hollywood and ran through them with a
crack lineup of much-used West Coast musicians: Roy Lanham and
Gene Mombeck on guitars, Speedy West on steel, Harold Hensley on
fiddle, Dusty Rhodes on bass, and Marion Adams on drums. The
songs, among them "A Woman's Love," "Hillbilly Waltz," and "Let Me
Remember (Things I Can't Forget)," eschewed the childish topics of
"Mexican Joe" and "Bimbo" and embraced the more mature rumina-
tions of love and regret. Jim's performance of the songs harked back to
the Jim Beck session in Dallas, when his simple baritone crooned
through "What Were You Doing Last Night?" and "I Could Cry."

Clearly, though, the upbeat, high-register style that Fabor
encouraged had improved Jim's delivery. Yes, Jim downshifted to a
comfortable tempo and sang within his range that evening in Hollywood, but his vocals had acquired an energy and versatility that
was non-existent on his pre-Robison recordings. Before linking
with Fabor, Jim's straight, unflavored singing threatened to induce
sleep. Now, his vocal embellishments and enthusiasm commanded
attention—although not the attention Fabor wanted. From this session, in which Jim had found a more perfect mix of sweetness and
vigor, Fabor released nothing. The snub surely inflamed Jim, for not
only was Fabor withholding from the public Jim's style of choice, he
was also denying Jim the added satisfaction of composer royalties.

To Robison's credit, he had molded Jim into a hit maker by injecting his capable voice into a high-velocity novelty format. But the combination was beginning to breed an ugly potion in the studio. While Fabor wrenched from Jim higher octaves and faster deliveries, Jim steamed. "Sing high!" Fabor shouted through the talk-back. "Scream it! Hit them notes as high as you can! Move it up! Raise it up an octave!" Jim hated to take his voice to unnatural levels, and according to Fabor's studio helper, Russell Sims, his protests often sparked screaming and cursing matches. "I had to go between them lots of times to cool them down," he said. "Seems like they didn't go [to the studio] to work. Seemed like they went there to hassle. They was notorious for hassling." In the end, Jim could do nothing but capitulate. Fabor had launched him, and Fabor promoted the black off a record. What could he do?

In Jim's next session after the un-Fabor-like Western Recorders respite, the boss dropped his singer back into the same old style: fast and funny. In Shreveport on March 16, 1954, back with the *Louisiana Hayride* house band, Jim faced the sour prospect of recording the utterly inane "Beatin' on a Ding Dong" and the slightly more palatable "Penny Candy." The tunes were Fabor's idea of hit material, and although he also slated a few songs more suited to Jim's preferences, "Ding Dong" and "Penny Candy" probably poisoned the session for Jim.

"Fabor kept wanting uptempo," recalled engineer Bob Sullivan, who manned the control board that night, "Jim's singing at the top of his voice. . . . Jim fancied himself as a crooner, but Fabor, all the material he picked was 'Mexican Joe,' 'Bimbo,' and stuff like that, that bordered on being comedy records. He and Jim used to get into it all the time about that." During the session, observed Sullivan, Reeves did not want to perform "Penny Candy," and throughout the ode to a bonbon-obsessed girl, repeatedly mispronounced Penelope, Penny's full name, singing it as "Pen-eh-lope." "Somebody said, 'Hey that's wrong,'" continued Sullivan. "Jim said, 'To hell with it. I'm not singing that song one more time.'" Despite Jim's indifference, however, "Penny Candy" found the country market's sweet tooth, peaking at number five on the *Billboard* country chart in late 1954.

KWKH's demand that *Hayride* cast members appear on at least two shows a month tied Jim and Mary Reeves to Shreveport, and except for the occasional jaunt north to Detroit or west to California,

Jim—through Tom Perryman or KWKH's small booking agency—
worked several Ark-La-Tex one-nighters with "Little Red" Hayes and
a pickup band or the *Hayride* house band. Often with Johnny Horton,
the Rowley Trio, Ginny Wright, Jack Hunt and His Rhythm Ranch
Hands, and others, Jim joined *Hayride* package shows that traveled to
nearby cities like Oklahoma City and Little Rock. When he wasn't
performing, Jim spent his days working in the yard, visiting with sister Virgie in Shreveport, writing songs, golfing, or—with Mary—
catching up on his correspondence.

A female booking agent named Luckey Brazeal, who worked out
of Carlsbad, New Mexico, opened a new performance circuit to Jim
in 1953 and 1954. A mutual friend introduced her to Jim after the
Hayride one night, and soon Luckey was booking him all over West
Texas and eastern New Mexico. El Paso, Lubbock, and Amarillo in
Texas and Clovis, Alamogordo, and Ruidoso in New Mexico became
as familiar to Jim as Gladewater and Longview. Brazeal, a motherly
figure to Carlsbad artists and to performers she booked who were
from outside the region, welcomed Jim and Mary into her home
whenever he worked for her. Hundreds of miles from Shreveport, Jim
could relax in Luckey's home, strumming with the musicians she
used as a pickup band and amusing the neighborhood children.

"Jim really wanted children, as much as he played with them,"
said Luckey. "He'd go around with khaki pants, barefoot with just
socks, and go out and play in the yard with my kids and the neighbors' kids." He led the local brood across the street for baseball
games, and would shower his affection on all of them. "I had a little
friend in a wheelchair," continued Luckey, "and he'd go out and
push her and play with her." Jim showed a fatherly interest in these
children, just as he had with Ginny Wright.

Ginny Wright also became part of Brazeal's extended family
when Luckey began booking *Hayride* packages in New Mexico. And
if Luckey was like a mother to her on trips out there, then Jim continued to play father. On the final night of a string of Brazeal-booked
shows in Hobbs, New Mexico, Jim and Ginny had elicited raucous
cheering from the audience with their renditions of "I Love You" and
"A Dear John Letter," and Ginny was on a high.

"This guy came up," recalled Ginny, "and he ran a night club, and
he invited everybody after the show to come to the night club and sing,
and he would furnish free drinks. Well, I went and got my guitar, got my

Chowing down with "Little" Joe Hunt. (Courtesy: Luckey Brazeal and Tom Kirby)

Clowning with Hayride member "Little" Joe Hunt at Luckey Brazeal's home in Carlsbad, New Mexico. (Courtesy: Luckey Brazeal and Tom Kirby)

Jim tinkers with the fiddle. Next to Jim is George Abraham, Mary Brazeal, and Jack Hunt. "Little" Joe Hunt sits strumming the guitar. The other men seated are unidentified. Abraham and the Hunts regularly appeared together on the Louisiana Hayride. (Courtesy: Luckey Brazeal and Tom Kirby)

little old cosmetic case, and I started heading out to the car, and Jim says, 'Ginny, where do you think you're going?' I said, 'I'm going with you all. I'm invited. I'm on the show.' . . . He said, 'You just go get in my car. I'm taking you back to the motel. You're staying with Mary. You all start packing up because we're leaving and going back to the *Hayride* right afterwards.' I said, 'Lookie here, who do you think you are? I got invited, too.' He said, 'You ain't going to that place.' He just looked after me. . . . It was so funny. I got mad at him, and I come back to the hotel and I'm crying, and Mary said, 'What's the matter with you?' I said, 'Jim won't let me go. They invited me.' She said, 'He knows what he's doing. You ain't got no business going to that place.'"

Mary Reeves shared Jim's parent-like compassion for Ginny, watching over her on the road and keeping her company when Fabor dropped the young woman in Shreveport for her allotment of *Hayride* appearances and local tours with the show's cast. "When Jim would be booking out by himself and I'd have some days to myself, Mary would come and pick me up and we'd go out to a movie and go out to eat," Ginny said. "We went to rodeos together and went on picnics together." She appreciated the attention, but Ginny was curious why Mary rarely attended her husband's shows. "A lot of times she would go with us," Ginny explained, "but she would never go to the show. She would go and stay in the motel. I asked her one time because I was kind of curious. We had a big barn dance in Hobbs, New Mexico, and Tibby Edwards was on there and Johnny Horton and me and Jim and several other people was on there. I said, 'Mary. Why don't you come along with us. She said, 'No. I don't want to go. I don't like to see the women messing over Jim. If I don't go, I don't see it, and I don't know anything about it. I'd just rather not.'"

Ginny understood Mary's concerns. As fatherly as Jim acted, he wasn't exactly the best role model. She had seen the caterwauling girls gather around Jim—and had watched him choose one and disappear. That first night in Detroit, she had seen a married woman disappear with Fabor and then with Jim. "At that time, I wasn't married. I was single. I was a virgin. I couldn't understand how people could live like that. But that's the way the world is. There she was with a husband, and she slept with Fabor and she slept with Jim. . . . I remember Jim telling me, 'Jenny, don't slip up and say anything about that woman.' I said, 'You'll never hear it from me.'" Ginny never divulged that secret to Mary, but Mary surely knew about Jim's infidelity.

In front of his new Buick with one of Luckey Brazeal's neighbors. (Courtesy: Luckey Brazeal and Tom Kirby)

Jim and Mary Reeves outside Luckey Brazeal's home. (Courtesy: Luckey Brazeal and Tom Kirby)

Chasing women had become a part of life on the road, as far as Jim was concerned. Women made themselves available from every dance floor of every honky-tonk and outside every stage door of every auditorium, and Jim plucked freely from what he saw as a fringe benefit of his newly found celebrity. At the *Hayride* particularly, a group of female admirers flocked behind the Municipal Auditorium like hens at feeding time, waiting for Horton or Pierce to come out for a smoke or a bite to eat at the diner across the street. They stood in line for Jim's attention, and he apparently obliged one or two. It all seemed so perfunctory—meet a girl, arrange a meeting—until a worried mother ushered her daughter into Horace Logan's office. Jim Reeves, the mother claimed, had impregnated her girl.

"That girl had been out with a lot of the guys," remembered Logan. "She was kind of freewheeling. Jim at the time had an application to join the Masons, and when the word got out, the Masons blackballed him and wouldn't let him in. But it was my understanding that, although Jim Reeves was not impotent, he was sterile. I knew damn well it wasn't Jim, and even if it was, it didn't make any difference to me." Still, Horace nosed around because Jim was a bit freewheeling himself, and he found that Jim had probably been with the girl, although many others had also.

From announcer Hi Roberts's vantage point, the girl had no claim against Jim. "The thing about it, she was supposedly unable to conceive because she had her tubes tied or something. So, everybody knew. She was a gal people always wanted to frolic with, if there was nothing better. She made herself so available." According to Roberts, Logan gathered virtually all of the *Hayride* staff to overwhelm the mother and daughter and proclaim Jim's innocence in the matter. He called the meeting in the Municipal Auditorium's dressing room. "He had all the 'Hayride' people in there," said Roberts, "I mean men and wives and girlfriends—the whole thing—in a great big dressing room. She came in, and we confronted her because Jim and Mary wanted children desperately. They had gone to doctors. Jim was unable to father a child." *

The issue faded right there in the Municipal Auditorium. "The little ole girl had the baby," continued Horace Logan, "and the baby

---

*Although numerous oral accounts corroborate Hi Roberts's and Horace Logan's belief that Jim was sterile, I was unable to locate medical records confirming that assertion.

looked so obviously like a fiddle player in one of the bands, there wasn't any question about who the father was. The joke was: put a bunch of instruments on the stage and put the baby there and let her crawl, and she'll crawl right over to the fiddle." Perhaps Jim forgave Horace Logan for the "Mexican Joe" ordeal right there. Jim had evaded a paternity charge, but nothing could excuse his unfaithfulness. How Mary Reeves reacted to that specific incident is unknown. In general, as had her widowed mother and mother-in-law, Mary maintained a stoic face and disposition. "She was a strong person," acknowledged Ginny Wright. "I don't think I could have handled it if it would have been me. She handled it really well. If she was ever jealous, she never did let on like she was."

In early 1954, "Little Red" Hayes parted company with Jim on the road and joined Blackie Crawford's Western Cherokees, a band with which he would remain until it evolved into Ray Price's Cherokee Cowboys. In Hayes's absence, Jim announced his plans to form a band. With an ever-growing number of personal appearances on his slate, and tiring of the blind-date-like experience of working with pickup bands, Jim figured he needed more consistency behind him. His search reeled in the man who, for the rest of his career, would be Reeves's closest musical companion: guitarist George Edward "Leo" Jackson.

A first-generation American of Greek descent, Jackson was born on October 22, 1934, in Meridian, Mississippi. Meridian, of course, is forever linked with the great country-blues singing guitarist Jimmie Rodgers, but the legend's aura seemed not to faze Leo Jackson one bit, at least early on. Unlike Jim Reeves, Jackson picked up the guitar relatively late in his childhood. His father, a restaurant cook, was in no way musically inclined, so it wasn't until his sister married into a musical family that Leo became acquainted with the instrument.

"Her husband's brother played steel guitar," explained Jackson, "and his brother-in-law played the electric guitar. I was over there one day and he plugged this guitar in the amplifier. That was almost unheard of in my part of the country, an electric guitar. He didn't play well. He just played chords. But he played an E chord, and I thought, 'Man, that's the prettiest sound I ever heard.' It was really just beautiful, so I had him show me that chord. And from there, I learned a few more chords. And then I got serious with it, after that."

The sixteen-year-old dashed into Peavey's Melody Music in downtown Meridian and bought an inexpensive Stella guitar. The boy practiced so hard picking out lead parts and playing melodies that the strings cut his fingers. Leo soon upgraded, trading his .22 rifle for a Harmony guitar and then, since he wanted an even better instrument, toting the Harmony into Peavey's and swapping it for a Gibson. "I played around on it, learning chords. So, I decided I better start playing some lead guitar. That's when I went and traded [the Harmony] to Peavey for the Gibson ES5, a big, blonde [electric] Gibson guitar . . . It was a beautiful guitar."

Leo amassed stacks of records by Chet Atkins, Les Paul, Jimmy Bryant, and Hank Garland, his favorite artists (in the order listed). Actually, though, it was the recorded sounds of Ernest Tubb's steel guitarist, Billy Byrd, that first excited him. "Wasn't for Billy, I probably wouldn't be playing. And then I heard Hank Garland and I almost quit playing." The men were the undisputed wizards of the guitar, and their picking jumped crisply and distinctly off the 78-rpm platters Leo bought. He would ratchet down the turntable speed when he played singles like Les Paul's "How High the Moon" and "Meet Mister Callaghan," and then copy the guitar licks. "My sister would be there ironing and listening until I got it, and she would say, 'That's it. That's it.'" When he could scrape together the change, Leo would watch the guitar players with country and western acts that filed through Meridian's Royal Theater, and then run home to emulate what he had seen.

"Word gets around," said Jackson, "and this guy called me one day. His name was Slim Free. He was playing a club called Sam's Place out on Highway 80. He said he needed a guitar player. I said, 'Yeah.' I had just bought that [Gibson] guitar. He picked me up one Saturday and we played. I did that for several months after that. I must have done something right. He sang a lot of Hank Williams and Webb Pierce. He was a big Hank Williams fan. He did them well. He played the bass run-type rhythm thing, and I played the lead. He played the bass pattern stuff that sold Hank's records . . . and I would play the steel guitar parts."

Slim Free soon lost the job at Sam's Place, but a fiddle player named James Parker had heard about Leo and invited him to join him at the Pine Stop, a rough, beer joint that sat in a clearing surrounded by pine trees. Although the rail-thin, seventeen-year-old had no business in such a dive, Leo furthered his education. He drank his first beer and graduated to a band. In addition to his own fiddle and, now, Leo's guitar, Parker's band featured a bass, steel guitar, drums, and a piano (played by a blind singer named Willie Brane). Leo remained with Parker for one year—long enough to learn the intricacies of band work—and moved on when his father left town to open a restaurant in Houston.

"I wasn't quite eighteen [when] I went to Houston, Texas, to work in his restaurant," Leo said. "That's where I met a guy that I had known in school back in Meridian. He had moved there, and he knew some people who had a daughter that was learning to sing, and said they would like to meet me because she needed somebody to play with her. She didn't play an instrument. Their names were John and Clara Lee Ross. I would spend the night there, and come to find out, they were best friends with Jim Reeves. They'd sit around writing, sending in requests to radio stations to play 'Mexican Joe.'"

The Rosses became like family to Leo, paying him to accompany their daughter and opening their home to him day and night. All the while, Leo stirred the soup at his father's restaurant and made a regular gig in a small Houston beer joint where he played lead guitar for a Native American who sang and strummed rhythm guitar.

Jackson had been in Houston about a year when the Rosses asked him to go with them to Shreveport to see Jim on the *Hayride.* They could have predicted his response, so on a Friday, after Leo's gig, the Rosses swung by the nitery; loaded his gear, guitar, and amplifier in the back of the car; and tooled out of Houston on a northeastern highway.

"We got to Shreveport early on Saturday morning," Leo recalled. "Jim was out doing yardwork when we got there. It was really early. For the first time, I saw him." The sight of the hottest new face in country music intimidated Leo. He mumbled a hello, and when the poised singer asked if he played guitar, Leo demurred. But John Ross piped up, bragging on Leo's guitar skills and urging Jim to give the young man a listen.

"Well, have you got your guitar?" Jim inquired.

"No," fibbed Leo.

Then John intruded again. "Yes he has. It's in the car."

Leo lacked confidence in his honky-tonk-honed playing and assumed that he in no way approached the level of perfection that a star like Jim Reeves would demand. "Jim had me sit there and play with him," said Leo. "Of course, I didn't think I was good enough. I noticed everybody left and left me and Jim in his living room. Jim got his guitar and sang. We were just noodling around, just not doing anything in particular. But on the way back Sunday, John said, 'I don't know whether you know it or not, but you just auditioned. Jim's thinking about starting a band.' Two weeks later, he called me and asked me to go to work with him."

Jim was scheduled to play in Meridian on May 25 and 26 for the 1954 National Country Music Jubilee, which honored the work of Jimmie Rodgers. "Jim had said something about calling me when he got back from the Jimmie Rodgers thing," Leo continued. "But I said, 'I'll be in Meridian, so why don't I just meet you there.' He told me, 'I'm going to be at Highland Park, so why don't we get together there?'" All keyed up, Jackson filled a suitcase and collected his guitar and amp for the bus trip to Meridian.

At the Jubilee, Leo sat on the bench while Jim played with a cast headlined by organizers Hank Snow and Ernest Tubb, and after the show, Jim told the wide-eyed guitarist that he could stay at his home in Shreveport and that he'd meet Leo back in Shreveport in a few days. "Jim had some other things to do. He was going somewhere else from Meridian. It wasn't to play a gig. He was going to do some medical stuff." Leo let Jim go on his way, and Mary and Tom Perryman's wife took him to Shreveport. "Boy, they were giving me hell because I was so bashful. My face would turn red at the least little thing. They teased me unmercifully, but I loved it."

When Jim returned home to Shreveport, he took Leo out on his route of regional shows and plugged him into his *Hayride* act. They headed for Memphis with Hank Thompson and Maxine Brown for two shows set up by promoter Bob Neal (who would soon manage a young buck named Elvis Presley), then bounced into Gladewater, Texas, for a week's worth of rodeo shows. In late July, while Jim's uncharacteristically tender "Then I'll Stop Loving You" floated up the charts for Abbott, Leo and Jim departed on their first extended tour together. Jim stopped the growth of his band at Leo. At least for now, he wouldn't need more musicians. The *Hayride*'s Rowley Trio also was booked on the tour and backed Jim. After playing so many *Hayrides* and package shows with Jim, the Rowleys knew his music as if it were their own.

Fabor Robison organized the tour, which would kick off in Baldwin Park, California, a western suburb of Los Angeles, and he packed most all of his Abbott and Fabor country acts on the bill. Joining Jim on what Fabor dubbed "The String Music Tour" were Ginny Wright, Jim Edward and Maxine Brown, Alvadean and Sandy Coker, Shirley Bates, the Rowley Trio, and Tom Tall. Reeves, of course, headlined but the lineup under him was solid. In mid-summer, Ginny was still milking the hoopla over her duet with Jim, and Jim Edward and Maxine Brown watched as their "Looking Back to See" edged up the country charts. Together they would snake north through California, Oregon, and Washington, remaining on the road for weeks—and all the while cursing Fabor Robison. Fabor had squeezed the shows so tightly together that there was little time off, and he didn't appear to be forthcoming with the pay he had promised the artists.

The shows, however, opened new audiences for Jim and the rest of the Abbott crew. Funny, though, it appeared that Fabor was trying to introduce audiences to himself. "Everybody stayed on stage the whole time," recalled Leo. "I don't know why. That's just the way Fabor wanted to do it. He stood out there and held a ukulele that he couldn't play. He just stood there and grinned at everybody. Sometimes we played a dance, and the whole four hours he was out there. He was a ham." It was amusing to watch the boss on stage, but his attempts to control the movements and schedules of his cast offstage caused an uproar. "All the girls on the show, at night Fabor would lock them up in the motel rooms where we were, and he would keep watch over them," recalled Leo. "He wouldn't let us intermingle with each other. He was afraid somebody was going to f--- somebody." Jim had set his eyes on Fabor's secretary, and one of the girls on the show wanted the gentlemanly Jim Edward Brown in the most desperate way. So, when Fabor tried to corral the girls and erect a fence around them, the tin cups began clanging on the prison bars.

"There was a lot of problems going on," admitted Ginny Wright, "but Fabor was mingling himself. He didn't mingle with me, but he was messing around. . . . He had pressured us so much, and he was making life miserable. We couldn't go nowhere. We couldn't even go to the swimming pool. He went back [to Hollywood] to record, and he caught a plane. It wasn't too long after we left on the tour. He told us not to go swimming. So, me and Shirley Bates and his secretary, we all wanted to go swimming, and we all went downtown and bought bathing suits. . . .

Then, he caught a plane after the session and came back. Well, [Alvadean Coker] told that we went swimming, and, man, he just raged and went on and carried on until Shirley Bates called her boyfriend. He came up and got her, and the police had to come out to the motel to keep Fabor from jumping on her boyfriend. I was going to leave, too. I wasn't going to put up with that. I was going back to the *Hayride*. I'm not used to taking stuff like that—somebody telling me what to do and clamping down on me like that. Jim came and talked to me and said, 'Jenny. You're the featured girl, and I'm the featured guy. Without me and you there's no show. Shirley we can do without because she's just a fill-in. We can't do without each other. You've got to stay.' I said, 'If I stay, he better keep his mouth off of me, and I mean it!' "

The tour concluded in September, and Jim and Leo returned to their spate of *Hayride* appearances and Ark-La-Tex shows. On September 20 and 21, they joined Ernest Tubb, Hank Snow, Jimmie Davis, and a retinue of other country notables for Hank Williams Day in Montgomery, Alabama, and soon after, left on a pared-down version of Fabor's String Music Show that featured—with Jim—only the Browns and the Rowley Trio. *Billboard* reported that Jim signed a one-year contract with the *Hayride* in late September, and at the end of the year, he would be leaving on an international USO tour headlined by actor Forrest Tucker. For three weeks during the Christmas holidays, the cast traveled through France, Germany, the Azores, and Newfoundland, landing back in New York in early January for an appearance on Ed Sullivan's *Toast of the Town* television show.

During Jim's overseas stint for the boys in uniform, Leo Jackson stayed in Shreveport, working on his adaptation of the Jim Reeves sound. "That gave me time to practice and learn. Mary was a big help there. She had all of Jim's records. It gave me a chance to practice and learn most of the stuff that we'd be doing. So, I was glad for the time." When Jim returned from the tour, he assembled a full band that, along with Leo Jackson and Bobby Garrett, included James Wordlow on drums, and Bill Morris on fiddle and bass. Jim, of course, knew Morris from Bob Cross's band and had met Wordlow at the Reo Palm Isle when Wordlow was playing with Texas bandleader Roy Shirey. Incorporating the title of his first Abbott release, Jim dubbed the band the Wagonmasters.

Underscoring the last months of 1954—before he toured Europe—was Jim's increasing disillusionment with Fabor Robison.

Claiming high expenses, Robison had sent both elements of the String Music Tour back to Louisiana with less than their promised pay, and his clashes with Jim became more heated with each row. And, as far as Jim saw, little seemed to be changing in the studio. Between the second String Music Tour and Jim's trek through Europe, Fabor recorded the artist on three thematically mature songs—"Where Does a Broken Heart Go?," "The Wilder Your Heart Beats the Sweeter You Love," and "Give Me One More Kiss"—but he still prodded Jim to shout and sing above his voice's natural comfort zone.

"He had Jim singing three octaves higher than he wanted to sing," asserted Leo Jackson. "Money was really the main reason [Jim] left Fabor, but that would come in a close second: the material he made him cut. Fabor had to have the publishing or some part of it [on] the songs he was doing. Jim really had to fight to do something he didn't have a part of. If Jim really liked a song, he really had to fight to get it."

Word wafted out of Los Angeles that Jim Reeves wanted a divorce from Fabor Robison, although his contract with Abbott Records ran through June 1956. Bob McCluskey, a former RCA Victor promotion man who in 1954 was with *Billboard*'s West Coast bureau in Los Angeles, knew Fabor's promotion chief, Del Roy, and heard that Reeves had begun casting about for a new label. Acting out of loyalty to his old employer, McCluskey picked up his telephone and called RCA Victor's Steve Sholes, the label's artist and repertoire (A&R) director in charge of country music. In his New York office, Sholes listened while McCluskey explained Reeves's unhappiness with Fabor's song selection, haphazard payments, and demanding, controlling style. Sholes listened and quickly dispatched his courting hooks toward one of the most explosive names in country music. Sholes contacted Jim, and during the String Music Tour, Cadillacs containing RCA regional representatives began showing up outside the troupe's hotels. Bob Sullivan, the engineer at KWKH, recalled Fabor returning to Shreveport moaning about RCA's romancing of Jim (and the Browns, toward whom Sholes had also cast his net).

Jim could always identify an opportunity. He had seen it in base-ball, in radio, in the dark dance halls of East Texas, and when RCA came into view, there was no question about the promise there. A major label could deliver a wider distribution and far greater resources in the way of promotion, and Steve Sholes seemed like a nice guy, not a Fabor Robison. On February 19, 1955, Robison announced that he had agreed to release Jim Reeves from his management and recording contracts. In return, Jim surrendered to Fabor performance royalties on any Jim Reeves recordings that Abbott released in the future.

Although the split seemed clean in the black and white pages of *Billboard*, a putrid acrimony marked Jim's transition from Abbott to RCA. Fabor boiled with indignation, damning Jim for leaving him after the buckets of sweat he'd expended to promote him. And Jim—emboldened by his pending departure—developed a short fuse in response to Fabor's verbal assaults. After almost two years together—two years in which they had benefited from each other—the relationship between Jim and Fabor culminated in a display of raw hatred. The scene was Fabor and Mary Robison's home in the canyons north of Los Angeles. On the afternoon of January 31, 1955, Jim climbed the series of twisting roads to a large log structure that almost seemed to be a compound in which the mad scientist Fabor hid. Within the walls, Fabor had transformed a room into a studio, and it was there that Jim would tape his final session as an Abbott artist.

One of the regular session musicians Fabor tapped for his West Coast dates observed that, on that night, the boss was in no mood for sentimental good-byes. In fact, Fabor's .38 pistol sat atop the control board, gleaming and threatening while the gathered musicians tackled two nondescript numbers, "Red Eyed and Rowdy" (credited to Reeves and Tom Perryman) and "Are You the One?" (a duet with Alvadean Coker). As the session limply and uneasily progressed, the first signs of inevitable friction arose, and when they did, the session crew watched Fabor's hands appear from behind the control board and grasp his gun. He charged in among the musicians, waving the weapon in the air. "You just like all the rest of them," Fabor shouted at his departing artist. "I go down there and get you out of them swamps, brought you to Hollywood. I get you out here, and you let me down. God damn it! If you gonna sing, sing now!"

Everybody knew that Robison carried a gun, but the combination of a gun and a white-hot temper sparked visions of Jim lying on the floor, bleeding. Jim remained calm and finished the session, according to the session musician, but when he saw the daunting pistol perched back on the control board, he crept up to Fabor, snatched the gun and grabbed his collar. "Look you little pipsqueak," spat Jim. "I took off of you all I'm gonna to take. You got six or eight songs of mine on the shelf. I'm gonna sign a contract tonight and give you those songs, royalty free. You're also going to sign a contract releasing me from your record company, or I'm gonna shove this damn pistol down your neck."

On March 23, 1955, Jim Reeves signed a pact with RCA Victor that allowed the label to renew the agreement after one year. From the West Coast, Fabor Robison told the press that he planned to concentrate on his pop talent roster. However, besides the DeCastro Sisters, who had approached number one on the pop charts in 1954 with "Teach Me Tonight," Robison's roster lacked real depth. Jim's career was beginning to take off like a rocket, while Fabor struggled in the vapor trail, desperate to find an act to replace Jim. Fabor Robison would never repeat the run of hits he had known with Jim Reeves.

7

teve Sholes's name cracked like thunder through country and western music when Jim Reeves signed with RCA Victor in 1955. The gentle, portly man with a probing eye for talent had raised four walls and a roof on the country and western foundation that field producers Ralph Peer and Eli "Obie" Oberstein had constructed for Victor Records in the 1920s and '30s. Peer had recorded the Carter Family and Jimmie Rodgers discs that Jim had heard as a youth, and Oberstein had recorded RCA Victor artists like the Delmore Brothers, Uncle Dave Macon, and Arthur Smith.

In the mid-1940s, Sholes picked up their glowing torch when he stepped in to supervise the record company's "folk and race" operations (replacing Frank B. Walker, who went to MGM Records), and with Eddy Arnold adorning RCA Victor's bow, Sholes navigated the company to preeminence in the country and western field. He had thrown the company's weight behind Arnold and watched the artist dominate the country charts in the late 1940s. And while the "Tennessee Plowboy" garnered cash and respectability for RCA Victor's "folk" division, Sholes ushered in a talented supporting cast. Hank "I'm Movin' On" Snow, Pee Wee King, Johnnie and Jack, Homer and Jethro, and others signed with the label in the late 1940s and early '50s, rounding out a team that pushed RCA Victor above all other wax purveyors of modern country music.

Of course, such a cluster of stars gains luster from the firmament that supports it. Within the gigantic Radio Corporation of America, Sholes had carved out an environment that allowed his hit makers to thrive, to perform in the style they loved with only discreet direction.

"He would leave all the musical decisions to the leader of the musicians in the studio," said Anita Kerr, a fixture in the Nashville studios who as early as 1950 played organ on Sholes's sessions. "He would just say whether he liked it or not, which was very good, too, because he always had very good taste, or as we used to say, 'a very good nose for what the public would like.'"

Sholes's placid demeanor inspired a collegial atmosphere in RCA Victor's country corner of the world. In the studio, he eschewed hysterics—he was, in fact, incapable of hysterics—and guided artists by suggestion and gentle prodding. If an artist mangled a lyric or a session musician flubbed a riff, Sholes would calmly proceed to the next take. He refused to admonish a musician over the studio's talk-back speakers. Rather, when he saw the need to correct a straying player, he would call a break and hold a casual, one-on-one conference. "He was gentle with everybody," observed Charles Grean, who assisted Sholes on most sessions. "He was just a real gentle soul. He never got terribly angry. In the control room, he was always calm and collected, and whatever dramatic situations came up, he would just calmly defuse them."

In addition to taking a fatherly approach to his artists and others with whom he worked, Sholes constructed and maintained an organization that almost guaranteed top-notch performances in the studio and access to good song repertoire. On the repertoire end, he snuggled with song-laden music publishers Julian and Jean Aberbach of Hill and Range and courted songwriters such as Cy Coben and Steve Nelson, who—despite their northern, urban origins—penned many country hits. To help match songs with artists and coordinate the music during the sessions, Sholes hired wisecracking Charles Grean, a onetime copyist for Glenn Miller. Sholes could blow a few notes on the saxophone, but he never considered himself a musician and thus hired Grean, who knew music and played bass, in the 1940s. On Steve's country and western sessions, Grean plucked the bass, wrote arrangements, and taught new material to artists. He was Sholes's right-hand man in the studio, and outside the studio, he helped him sift through the bales of songs that stacked up on the doorstep.

"Usually, we worked together," Grean said of the duo's song selection process. "I kept track of them. I had a filing system. I had a book, and as a song came in, I wrote it down and made comments on alphabetical pages. Like 'Anytime,' I would say, 'Great song. Good idea. Good for Eddy Arnold.' Then I had another sheet that had Eddy Arnold possibilities, and I had all those songs listed. So, when the time came for Eddy Arnold to record, Steve and I would get the book out, and we'd have maybe fifteen songs for Eddy Arnold. We would go over them carefully and figure out which ones we wanted and which ones we didn't want." The procedure illustrates the high degree of infrastructure that supported RCA Victor's country artists. To listeners, the Eddy Arnold, Hank Snow, and Lonzo and Oscar releases suggested down-home simplicity, but the foundation upon which they sat was built of corporate efficiency—softened, of course, by Steve Sholes.

Sholes responded to reliability and sought out people he could trust. Grean was his agent on the studio floor; a steady, veteran engineer named Jeff Miller could achieve the recorded sound Sholes wanted; and on his country sessions in New York and Nashville, Sholes assembled a journeyman group of backup musicians who pounded out steady rhythms and filled breaks with improvised flourishes. Standing out among the most-trusted was a gaunt guitarist from Luttrell, Tennessee, who reeled off licks as deftly as a preacher recites verses. Chet Atkins had introduced himself to Sholes in 1947, via an audition acetate of "Canned Heat," and he so impressed the A&R man that he copped an RCA Victor contract.

"Si Siman in Springfield, Missouri, he had a show called *Korn's A' Krackin'*," recalled Atkins, "and he would transcribe the show and sell it to stations. He told the guy in Chicago who did the pressing, 'Listen to this guitar player.' Well, he got Mr. Sholes to listen. This was in early 1947. Steve liked what he heard and wanted to sign me, but he called around trying to find me, and I had been fired from Springfield. I was out in Denver with a cowboy band, and he didn't find me for quite a while." Chet had hitched his wagon to KOA Radio, and when the RCA offer reached him, his bandleader, Shorty Thompson, demanded to be the featured singer on Chet's recordings. The young guitarist politely rebuffed his boss—and received a pink slip for his impudence.

Chet Atkins left for Nashville, and although his RCA Victor records only sold in spurts, Sholes found much to like about his new acquisition. In addition to being a phenomenal guitar player, Chet was retiring and modest—just Steve's style—and related to people with respect rather than bluster. By 1949, Chet had became a regular

The RCA gang in the early 1950s, before Jim's arrival. Standing, from left: Bob McCluskey, Steve Sholes, Chet Atkins, Betty Jack Davis, Skeeter Davis, Minnie Pearl, Charline Arthur, Grandpa Jones, Hank Snow, unidentified, Porter Wagoner, and Jethro Burns. Seated, from left: Homer Haynes, Pee Wee King, unidentified, Eddy Arnold, unidentified, and Ken Marvin. (Courtesy: Bob McCluskey)

instrumentalist on RCA's Nashville sessions, and if Sholes couldn't make it down for a recording date, Chet would coordinate everything. RCA brass had shuffled Charles Grean over to the company's pop department, so Steve began to rely on Chet's presence in the studio more frequently. Sholes had found a protégé, a status that by 1952 accorded the young Atkins the title of A&R assistant and, later, an office in the building where RCA housed its Nashville operations (the Methodist Television Radio and Film Commission building at 1525 McGavock Street).

It was into a highly productive and organized system that Steve Sholes plugged Jim Reeves: Songs came through established channels; Sholes's artists were mostly of high hit-making caliber; and arguably the best musician in Nashville—Chet Atkins—kept an eye on RCA's interests in Nashville when Sholes could not. Reeves would test his recording mettle for the first time as an RCA Victor artist on May 31, 1955, at the McGavock Street facilities.

On May 30, in the middle of a long road trip, Jim and his band trundled into town and checked in at a downtown hotel. Bobby Garrett, Bill Morris, and James Wordlow would join Jim in the studio the next day. (Leo Jackson had difficulty joining the Nashville chapter of the musicians' union and would have to stay away from the session.) Bobby Garrett recalled shivering with nervousness as he entered the studio, for right in front of him were the cream of Nashville session men: fiddlers Tommy Jackson and Tommy Vaden, and guitar virtuoso Hank Garland. "Here am I, a nineteen-year-old kid, just about scared to death, but at the same time thrilled to death," said Garrett.

But while his steel guitarist shook, Jim maintained his serious pitching face, the visage that had intimidated Evangeline League batters. "It was just the same old Jim," said Garrett. "He just went right on in there and took care of business." Like Garrett, Bill Morris's nerves jangled as he walked into the room. He had pleaded with Jim to find another bass player for the session, but Jim had prevailed, and Bill could only surrender as engineer Jeff Miller turned him toward the corner of the room, a position that—at McGavock Street—enhanced the bass sound. As Bill moved into position, his attention was drawn to a man who just seemed to be loitering. "By the door, there was some tall, lanky guy sitting in the chair, leaning back against the wall listening. Steve Sholes was in the control room along with the engineer. They're making this session, and I kept wondering, 'What the heck is that ole boy doing over there against the wall?' I asked Jim if he was looking for a job. He said, 'No, that's Chet Atkins.' "

Chet had only sauntered down the hall from his office to say hello and catch a few glimpses of the new artist at work. And what he glimpsed was a man whose distrust of Fabor Robison had bred a general suspicion of corporate authority. Jim was polite enough, it seemed, but his temper flared when songwriter Cy Coben attempted to guide him through one of the two Coben songs scheduled that day. Coben often traveled to Nashville with Sholes when his songs were to be recorded, and Steve permitted the writer to interpret his songs for the artists. "For some reason or another," recalled Coben, "Steve let me always be at the recording sessions, if it was convenient. If Eddy [Arnold] was doing something of mine, he let me be there. I'd say something to [Steve when] he was producing. He'd say, 'Go out and tell Eddy yourself.' I got into the habit of doing that. . . .

"Now, Jim's a new artist. He had just come off Abbott. I didn't know him, really. I said something to Steve, and he said, 'Go tell Jim yourself.' I went out there and said something to Jim. You got to give this guy credit. He turned to me and said, 'Look man, don't tell me how to sing.' Whatever he said, he said the equivalent of 'get out of here.' " Jim had tolerated the meddling of Fabor Robison, but he was damned if he was going to bend as easily at RCA—or anywhere else in all of Nashville. Sholes, Atkins, Coben, and the others in the studio that day saw that Jim planned to draw territorial lines that no one could cross. Coben slunk back to the control room and, needless to say, Reeves never again touched a Coben composition.

Jim recorded four numbers on that first day at McGavock Street: Cy Coben's "I'm Hurtin' Inside" and "If You Were Mine," Redd Stewart's "That's a Sad Affair," and Jim's own "Yonder Comes a Sucker." Playing it safe, Sholes decided to release "Yonder Comes a Sucker," a novelty song decidedly in the vein of Jim's Abbott smashes, and found that country audiences had made the transition with Jim to RCA Victor. They propelled the song to a twenty-week stay on the charts, where it peaked at number eight. The flip side, which featured Coben's ballad "I'm Hurtin' Inside," also popped up for a two-week flash appearance on the *Billboard* juke box chart.

Sholes called Reeves and his band back up to Nashville for an August 29 session at which they taped two fiddle-introduced novelties, "Ichabod Crane" and "Jimbo Jenkins," and two slow-tempo numbers, "I've Lived a Lot in My Time" and "My Lips Are Sealed." Sholes chose to follow "Yonder Comes a Sucker" with "Jimbo Jenkins," which Bobby Garrett had written alone, although Jim shared writing credit. ("I had to give Jim half of it to get him to cut it," remembered Garrett. "He told me that's the way it was done. I figured he must know what he was talking about.")

"Jimbo Jenkins" failed to make the *Billboard* charts, and in the months following the disappearance from the charts of "Yonder Comes a Sucker," RCA fell down in its efforts to paste Reeves back on the national countdown. Although a *Billboard* poll of disc jockeys ignored Jim's Abbott years and dubbed him the second most promising new country artist of 1955 behind Elvis Presley, RCA found itself in the midst of a dry spell with Jim—his longest fallow period between hits yet. Two singles released after "Yonder Comes a Sucker" failed to make the charts, which left RCA wanting more from the year's second most promising country artist.

While Jim searched for his footing as an RCA Victor artist, he made the next turn for any country artist on the way to more prosperous days: to the *Grand Ole Opry*. Jim's contract with the *Louisiana Hayride* was due to expire in September 1955, and the *Opry* was more than eager to pick up the two-year recording veteran who now had the confidence of RCA Victor. From the *Hayride*'s point of view, Jim's flight was hardly unexpected. Over the years, KWKH had watched the *Opry* lure away seveal big names, so when Jim's popularity grew sufficiently robust, Horace Logan knew it was only a matter of time.

"It was not a precedent," said Logan of Jim's departure. "He was merely following the steps that at that time perhaps a dozen or more artists had followed, starting with Hank Williams and Webb Pierce and Faron Young. It was just another step. It was a logical step, and I accepted it because I knew exactly what it was. . . . I did not think it was morally right to keep an artist under contract to the *Hayride* when he was capable of being booked nationally and internationally, and we were not capable of booking him nationally and internationally. Here's a guy that's got maybe the only chance in his life to make some real damn money, and we're going to keep him here? No. And I kept telling that to the people who owned KWKH."

With Jim's *Hayride* contract behind him and a string of national bookings on the horizon, Shreveport had become too small to hold him. Nashville was a multifaceted town with recording studios, music publishers, and, of course, the "Air Castle of the South," WSM, which produced and aired the *Grand Ole Opry* and booked *Opry* artists throughout the United States. Shreveport had only the *Louisiana Hayride*, and although labels like Abbott and Columbia swooped into town occasionally and recorded their acts at the KWKH studios, the station had limited means to book talent. In the late 1940s *Hayride* co-founder Dean Upson had established a KWKH artists' service bureau, and in the early '50s western swing bandleader A. M. "Pappy" Covington worked with KWKH to book *Hayride* performers. But, observed Logan of Covington's operation, "it was of no consequence. We had no connections, no way of booking them on a national basis. We could book them regionally, but that was it. Regionally was a couple hundred miles in every direction. But as soon as they got to the point where they could book in Oregon, we didn't know who in the hell to contact in Oregon. We had no booking agency, so their only recourse was to leave the *Hayride* and to go to Nashville."

WSM was well aware of the *Hayride*'s strengths and weaknesses. *Opry* manager Jim Denny observed the spring of talent that gushed in Shreveport and dispatched a clandestine talent scout to most every *Hayride* show. Sooner or later, Denny knew, a charismatic, talented *Hayride* performer would begin thinking of the *Opry*, and when they did, WSM would be waiting with a pen, a contract, and a stage that was the most prestigious in country music. Around the National Life Building on Seventh and Union Streets in downtown Nashville, the staff referred to their country cousins down south as the "*Grand Ole Opry*'s farm club." On October 22, 1955, Jim joined the majors, debuting as a regular on the *Opry*.

"Jim thought about that long and hard," said Leo Jackson. "He was scared about the move. But the *Grand Ole Opry*, you can't do any better than that." He had waved good-bye to a disappointed *Hayride* crowd on September 10 and took off for a tour through New Mexico, Colorado, Oregon, and Washington before stepping onto the Ryman Auditorium's stage in the billowing wake of announcer Grant Turner's introduction. No strangers to Jim Reeves, the *Opry* crowd—especially the women with the shrieking voices—reacted enthusiastically to the new cast member, a reception that would continue unabated through the years.

"Jim always got a very respectable amount of applause," said Don Helms, a Hank Williams band alum and staff steel player on the *Opry*. "He was a class act, I would say, and I think the audience felt that. He was somebody special, and they treated them nice. He, in turn, treated them nice."

When Jim's deal with the *Opry* became final, he and Mary pulled up stakes in west Shreveport and settled into an enclave of trailer homes off Dickerson Road in north Nashville. "I didn't think we would stay in Nashville long," Mary Reeves told reporter Dixie Deen, "because it was sort of a trial deal and, of course, Tennessee was six hundred miles from Texas, and our families were really upset because we moved so far away. However, we realized that this was where it was happening and that this was the major move if we wanted to be successful in the business. That's why we came here and that's why we stayed." Perhaps Mary viewed the move to Nashville as a temporary situation because Jim doubted the depth of his popularity. Nashville, RCA Victor, and the *Opry* could send him packing just as the baseball towns of Lynchburg, Jamestown, and Alexandria had done.

With a major record deal and a regular slot on the *Grand Ole Opry*, Jim had two strikes on the batter. A solid management arrangement would be the third strike, the one that would plant him firmly on his new mound in Nashville. Fabor Robison essentially had acted as Jim's manager during the Abbott years, so Jim had to be careful not to tumble into a similar unpalatable situation. In much the same way that he had confronted Cy Coben in the RCA studio, Jim came to Nashville with both eyes open and wary, never turning his back to the door, and suspecting virtually everybody of being another Fabor. Buddy Killen was working for Tree Publishing Company in 1955 and recalled in his autobiography that Jim displayed a palpable mistrust of publishers. Jim had decided to place the compositions "Yonder Comes a Sucker" and "Jimbo Jenkins" with Tree, and Killen met with him to sign the contracts.

"Mr. Reeves," said Killen, "I really appreciate you placing your songs with Tree."

"I might as well place them with you as anybody else," snapped Jim. "You're not going to pay me anyway."

The response stung Killen, and although Jim shortly thereafter became more conciliatory toward the Tree representative, it was obvious that he feared being taken advantage of by Nashville business interests. Killen would ultimately befriend Reeves and occasionally play bass for him on the road and in the studio.

With such deep suspicions guiding Jim, it would certainly be difficult for him to find a suitable manager. Between August and late November 1955, *Billboard* reported first that a Bill Henry had taken over Jim's management and then ran an item that placed Jim under the aegis of booker W. E. "Lucky" Mueller, who also handled Webb Pierce and Red Sovine. Apparently, neither relationship worked out, and it wasn't until Jim spoke with Charlie Lamb that a viable management arrangement presented itself. Lamb, a Nashville journalist and deal maker, wrote a column for *Cashbox* magazine and had first met Reeves as the singer toured on the gusts of "Mexican Joe." The two were already well acquainted by the time Jim and Mary moved to Nashville, so Lamb felt at liberty to suggest a manager for the singing Texan. For Reeves, who deemed nefarious anybody who wanted a part of his career, management was a necessary evil. He knew that he and Mary couldn't communicate with fans and fan clubs, book engagements, negotiate contracts, *and* produce a quality Jim Reeves performance. So, Jim perked up his ears when Lamb told him about a savvy, dedicated man in Boston who wanted to build some business in Nashville.

The man in Boston, Herbert L. Shucher, had introduced himself to Charlie Lamb as part of his master plan to find a place in the Nashville scene. Shucher managed Carl Stuart, a disc jockey and featured performer on WCOP Radio's *New England Hayloft Jamboree* in Boston, but thus far he had found little opportunity for his charge outside the northern city. Regardless of whether Stuart worked out, Shucher still wanted to move his operations to Nashville. He loved country music and, as a hobby, spun records of that genre for a Boston radio station. Shucher's love of southern-oriented music seemed unlikely in a northeasterner whose parents had immigrated from Russia and, in the home, spoke only Yiddish. Herb's father owned a blouse factory and expected his son to use his Boston College degree in political science to pursue a career in law. But immediately after his graduation, Herb found a position with the business information firm of Dun and Bradstreet and began to tinker with country music, spinning records and putting Carl Stuart to work around Beantown.

In 1954, Shucher placed a call to Charlie Lamb and asked for help in establishing a management presence in Nashville. Lamb said they could talk at the Jimmie Rodgers festival in Meridian, Mississippi, where Shucher would be introducing Carl Stuart around. A few weeks later, Shucher left Meridian with Lamb's promise to keep an eye open for him, and in 1956, Shucher left Boston for Nashville. Jim Reeves was the reason for the Bostonian's move. Charlie Lamb had hooked them up. "Herb Shucher was a very smart and shrewd individual," said Lamb. "He had all the necessary stuff to be a good manager."

Almost immediately, Shucher made his value to Jim apparent. He set up Jim's office in his Madison home, hired a secretary named

Joyce Gray to channel the paperwork, and formed a publishing company with Jim called Open Road Music. Then, he began courting Bobby Brenner, an agent at the Music Corporation of America (MCA), with the goal of working Jim into a succession of national radio and television shows. To a large extent, Jim enjoyed wide broadcast exposure over the *Grand Ole Opry* broadcast, but that was just one mass-media pipeline. Shucher envisioned a broader radio forum and a consistent presence on television, which had become the medium of choice for Americans who stayed home in the evening. An MCA relationship would be important, and it would come. Jim, though, still had to prove his viability. Could he make it in the big city, away from the relative small-town life of Shreveport, among a cast of giants at RCA Victor and the *Opry*?

Shucher had to raise Jim's profile before MCA and the national media would bite, so, in the absence of televised access to America, he packaged a Reeves-led caravan of country talent that hit the road for the most vigorous and widespread tour thus far in Jim's career. In February, Jim's week-long trek through New Mexico, Arizona, Colorado, and Texas with Johnny Cash, Ferlin Husky, and Minnie Pearl "enjoyed a bonanza," exclaimed *Billboard*. "At Odessa, Tex., the group played to nearly 10,000 people with another 2,000 turned away," the trade journal declared. "At Amarillo, Texas, they entertained over 5,000 stubholders with some 3,000 turned away." The race to greater recognition had commenced.

Shucher followed up in March with a month-long expedition for Jim and his supporting cast that began at the Norfolk Auditorium in Virginia; motored west to stops in Illinois, Kentucky, and Missouri; swerved northeast to Ontario; and then returned to the States for a March 31 show at Witsche's Arena in Providence, Rhode Island. Jim's accelerator hit the floor again in April, and he continued to tour at a breakneck pace for most of the rest of 1956. Jim's name and face became increasingly better known to the nation's country audiences, prying open markets that heretofore had only heard him perform on the radio or on records.

With Robison, Jim's route of personal appearances had been confined to a line that stretched west from Shreveport along the southwestern perimeter of states, north through California, and into the Pacific Northwest. He only made spot appearances elsewhere and never ventured east of Nashville. Now, Jim was playing dates in all corners of the country. Furthermore, when he arrived in different regions, an RCA Victor representative was usually waiting to escort him to meetings with important disc jockeys and record distributors. Jim Reeves now had first-class support behind him. Propelled by his new team members—RCA Victor, Herb Shucher, and the pickers in his band—Jim's name acquired a lustrous quality and greater currency in national circles.

8

As Jim's touring trail meandered through southern Canada and the lower forty-eight states in 1956, he observed a definite surge of energy emanating from his audiences. When he took the stage, the cheering was many decibels louder than what he had known in the Fabor Robison days. Even in the large clubs of Texas, where patrons often danced throughout a performance, the waltzing stopped and the people crowded the stage to gaze at Jim. It wasn't that he offered a particularly electrifying visual performance. Jim generally just stood, strummed, and sang, unlike many performers who might perform tricks with their instruments; or Faron Young, who hopped around like a Mexican jumping bean; or the super-charged Elvis Presley, who was storming the nation with his raucous hip jerks. Jim's reputation attracted the curious and his come-hither baritone demanded attention. The men whistled and hollered requests, while the girls chirped their admiration.

"It's hard to explain the looks on their faces," said Leo Jackson, who gawked at the stir Jim created. "It's really hard to explain. It was like they were having an orgasm or something. I was very flabbergasted with that. We'd be playing these little night clubs, and people would get up from their seats and come stand up in front and watch us. I thought, 'Wow! What is going on here?' They wouldn't just sit there like most people do. . . but they would come running up front and jockey to see who could get closest to the stage. And that happened everywhere we went. I'm talking about these clubs where people are drinking and dancing. They'd quit drinking and dancing and just stand and watch us. That really, really impressed me.

"We was out in New Mexico and Jim was singing, and this Indian woman was standing there with tears rolling from her eyes, just looking at Jim, saying, 'I love you. I love you.' About that time, this big, male Indian come up there and hit her and knocked her down, grabbed her by the hair and started pulling her away from the stage. And she's pissing on herself. You can see piss trailing after her. She's still looking up at Jim saying, 'I love you, I love you, I love you.'" Like Leo, Jim probably stood dumbfounded as he looked down on that wretched scene. From their roost on the stage, he and the Wagonmasters witnessed any number of dramas twist and turn, and a time or two, the main characters drew Jim into the plot.

"We were at Lackland [Texas] Air Force Base, playing the NCO club, and this guy kept coming up [to the stage], and he was a big, burly guy," said Leo. "Jim's singing, and this guy kept asking us for this one song, but we didn't do that song. Jim told him, 'I don't know that song.' So, Jim would be singing another song, and [the guy would] come up there hollering real loud. It was getting through the microphone." Again, Jim tersely reminded the persistent fan that the request fell outside his repertoire. Again and again, he rebuffed the man until, finally, after yet another drunken appeal for the song, Jim stepped from behind his block-like microphone and beckoned the man to him. "Jim bent over to him like he was going to whisper something to him," continued Leo, "and he had the mike in his left hand like he was singing, and he had his guitar. He took that mike and—Bomp!—hit that guy right between the eyes." The thud reverberated throughout the venue, and promptly silenced the pesky requests. "The guy went to his knees," said Leo. "You could tell the guy saw stars, and he just got up and looked at Jim and wobbled off and never came back again."

At NCO clubs or dance halls, Jim and the Wagonmasters usually appeared alone, without a supporting cast—other than the characters in the audience. They were joined by other performers only when Herb Shucher organized appearances in city arenas and school auditoriums. Then, a few other "names" had to be added to the bill to fill the venue. Throughout 1956, Jim completed short, regional tours with such *Opry* artists as Hank Locklin, Webb Pierce, Hawkshaw Hawkins, Jean Shepard, and the Carlisles. Herb and Jim also assembled a self-contained package that could pull onto a fairgrounds or carnival lot and offer nothing less than a variety show. Jim had changed the lineup of the Wagonmasters to do this, partially reassembling the contingent of musicians with whom he worked in Shreveport. Leo Jackson remained, and Jim hired fiddler Joe "Big Red" Hayes, rhythm guitarist Tommy Hill (Goldie Hill's brother and a *Hayride* performer), and pianist Floyd Cramer. He also began alternating steel guitarist Jimmy Day with Bobby Garrett. (Day's nimble, distinctive steel playing had placed him in great demand in Nashville. He played with Jim but also toured with Ray Price and Webb Pierce.)

By including Hayes, Cramer, and Hill, Jim and Herb served two purposes. Of course, the men provided top-notch backing, but they also had secured record deals of their own, thereby allowing Herb to promote a package of Jim and three other recording artists. "Big Red" (who had penned the 1955 smash "A Satisfied Mind") had a Capitol contract, Floyd was with MGM, and Tommy recorded for Roy Acuff's Hickory Records. When Reeves was the only act on the bill, each side man took the spotlight at various moments during the show. Hill led the band. "Tommy would sing a few tunes before he'd bring Jim on," said Bobby Garrett. "Then, Jim would come on, and he'd sing his first part of the show and then we'd take an intermission or a break. We'd come back and start the second half, and Tommy would bring Jim on again. It was like a two-hour show."

Comedy added a zingy flavor to the show. When appearing on the bill, Jimmy Day would perform a rube routine that traded on his lanky frame and glowing, strawberry-blond hair, and Reeves, who loved a good joke, would foist a barrage of gags onto the audience. "When I was growing up," Jim would crack, "most people had two rooms and a bath. We had one room and a path." Or, "My mother would send me down to the creek to get water. One day, I went down and saw an alligator, and I went running back to the house saying, 'Mama! Mama! There's an alligator in the creek.' She said, 'You run back down and get that water. That alligator's just as scared as you are.' I said, 'Well, if he is, that water ain't fit to drink.' "

Throughout the remainder of the 1950s, the face of the vagabond Wagonmasters stretched and contorted frantically. Artists boarded and jumped ship, and at one time or another the band featured such names as Louis Dunn, Buddy Killen, Kenny Hill (Tommy's brother), Pee Wee Kershaw, Billy Harlan, and Jack Bringle. Floyd Cramer ultimately left because he became an important part of the

One version of the Wagonmasters. Standing, from left: Joe "Big Red" Hayes and Kenny Hill. Seated, from left: Leo Jackson and Tommy Hill. (Courtesy: Richard Weize)

burgeoning Nashville studio scene as well as a top-selling artist in his own right, and others accepted better offers from competing artists ("Big Red" went to work for Ray Price, for example). A few who found Jim too frugal just refused to answer the phone when he or Herb Shucher called.

"He paid by the job," recalled Garrett, who remained with Reeves until 1959, "and sometimes if he was going to be off for the month, he would just tell us. He would disband and reorganize later. Sometimes I would go back with him. Sometimes Jimmy Day would. . . . It was a little tough at times. Fortunately, I had a job that I could just about always come back to at home." Although the per-show pay for a Wagonmaster was pretty good, Jim and Herb's penny-pinching decision to forgo paying salaries threatened the consistency and quality of his road performances. However, Jim was a top-shelf act, and uninitiated musicians could always be collected to go on the road with him.

The continually changing lineup of Jim's band surely hurt the quality of his sound on the road, and so did the burden of constant traveling. Fending off exhaustion, bad weather, and any number of obstacles in the road, the gang drove day and night, west and then east. Like some kind of wandering zephyr, they would blow into town, tote their instruments onto a teetering stage, and then dash back to the car two hours later. They were happy to get the occasional two- or three-night engagement that would keep them in one place at least for a while. Bobby Garrett recalled that in just twelve months, the 1955 Fleetwood Cadillac that carried the retinue clocked more than one hundred thousand miles. Jim had purchased the olive Caddy after RCA signed him, and he proceeded to paint the trailer that hauled the band's gear the same color. The old trailer probably needed a paint job, for it had been seemingly everywhere.

"In that '55 Fleetwood Cadillac," said Garrett, "we were up on the Pennsylvania Turnpike, and we were driving along. Tommy Hill was driving, and he looked in the rearview mirror and said, 'My God! Where's our trailer?' We turned around and went back, I guess ten miles, and there it sat over on the side of the highway, straight up. It hadn't turned around or anything. We turned around and came back, and that thing had pulled off on the shoulder of the highway and stopped. It came loose, but it came over and stopped just like somebody had parked it there. Jim had trouble with the axle on the trailer; he had to have a new one put on it several times."

Leo Jackson recalled that the trailer's tires frequently went flat and even rolled off from time to time. "One time the wheel caught on fire," said Leo. "It got hot. I guess it didn't have enough grease." The mishap occurred high in the Cascade Mountains of Oregon, which got Jim to thinking of how to dispose of the two-wheeled tagalong that had just become one-wheeled. "He'd had enough of it," said Leo. "He just unhooked it and said, 'You guys get your stuff out of there.' . . . You could see forever up there, and he kicked that damn thing off from the road, and it rolled for three hours, I bet you. He'd had enough of it. He said, 'That takes care of that.' He was real proud of that [trailer], too! When he first got it, it [cost] a huge sum at the time because he had it specially made. And then he kicked the damn thing off the mountain."

By the latter half of 1956, Jim had emerged from his fallow period, and his records were again dancing on the charts. On June 23, six months after "Yonder Comes a Sucker" faded, the wistful "My Lips Are Sealed" entered the *Billboard* charts. Shortly thereafter, the prim and fanciful "According to My Heart" checked in for a nineteen-week chart stay, and in January 1957, "Am I Losing You?," a tearful ballad that Jim penned and sang with great intimacy, began its rise to number three on the charts—his best showing since the 1954 release with Ginny Wright ("I Love You").

RCA began to discover how to best promote Jim. He seemed to succeed outside the novelty genre, and when he skimmed from his natural baritone and drew out the lyrics in an even vibrato, the records shipped from the label's warehouse in greater numbers. Steve Sholes detected crossover potential in the artist and, after picking up the option on Jim's one-year contract, began promoting him with what he called "country-bred" artists with pop appeal, acts like Elvis Presley and Chet Atkins. "Their sales in the pop field, as well as the play they get from pop deejays, are on the rise," noted *Billboard* after an interview with Sholes.

Much had changed at RCA Victor in Nashville since Jim first recorded there in 1955. Steve Sholes, just months after signing Jim, had negotiated the purchase of Elvis Presley's contract from Memphis-based Sun Records for forty thousand dollars, considered by many to be an exorbitant sum. If Presley had fizzled at RCA, the company would have tossed Sholes's career into the East River, but Presley's first outing, "Heartbreak Hotel," zoomed to the top of the charts and ignited a furor that no artist had ever experienced. In the halls of RCA, executives who had never taken seriously Sholes's work in the country and western field now accorded him a tall measure of respect for his discovery of the record company's future. Concentrating on Presley's career, he spent fewer days in Nashville and turned over to Chet Atkins more responsibility for the country sessions. Effective September 1, 1957, RCA Victor tapped Steve Sholes to manage A&R activities in the pop department, and it fell to Chet to manage the Nashville operations. Chet had operated as the de facto chief in Nashville since Elvis exploded the previous year, and he had taken over regular supervision of Jim's recordings in January 1956.

Chet Atkins had a tight bead on what Presley and the rock-and-roll sound were doing to country and western music. He had played rhythm guitar on Elvis's "Heartbreak Hotel" session in January 1956 and had seen point-blank a mixture of style, energy, and charisma that no Nashville artist could approach. Chet scanned the sales reports that quantified the teen enthusiasm for Presley's "Hound Dog," "Don't Be Cruel," and "Love Me Tender," and from his perch at 1525 McGavock Street, he watched country artists and producers bend to rock's influence. Eddy Arnold slapped on a little grease and rollicked through "The Rockin' Mockin' Bird," and the previously hitless Johnny Horton shuffled to the country Top Ten on the rock beat of "Honky Tonk Man."

Atkins saw many other examples as the urgency of Presley's voice and the slap-back beat of Elvis's bass player, Bill Black, were recreated throughout the domain of country music. "After Elvis Presley came along," Chet once told *The New York Times*, "All the country artists wanted to make pop hits. Presley almost killed country music. Every country boy thought, 'I've got to make pop records with those triplets—those little piano trills that were played behind every rock 'n' roll singer then." Of course, country music's embracement of rock was meant to win back the market share the teen audience had directed to Fabian, Dion, and Elvis—and away from Ray Price, Webb Pierce, and, yes, Jim Reeves. Even Chet Atkins, despite his comments in the *Times*, was not above wanting to incorporate the new sound. He had allowed a liberal helping of background "doo-wahs" on

Reeves's crooning hit "My Lips Are Sealed," and a little later with Don Gibson, he miked the bass drum to accentuate the beat and came up with Gibson's big pop and country hit, "Oh Lonesome Me."

Atkins knew, however, that rock and roll represented only one of many paths to a broader audience. Although the music of Frank Sinatra, Perry Como, the Four Lads, and other artists of the traditional pop genre was not as intensely popular as in previous years, it continued to sell well in the late 1950s. By exploring the easy-listening sound as well as the rock sound, Chet schemed to nudge his records over country lines into the pop arena and thereby recapture some record dollars. RCA wasn't paying Chet to preserve traditional country music. Instead, he was charged with finding ways to sell the artists in the label's country stable. The bottom line demanded that Chet compromise. He said that he intended not to make pop records but to make country records that would cross over to the pop market. In doing so, though, he stripped his artists' records of fiddles and steel guitars, and invited in the lush, decidedly un-country accompaniment of background vocalists and strings. The Anita Kerr Singers or the Jordanaires harmonized where fiddles once danced, and strings glided in place of the steel's whine.

"Rock and roll came along with the four voices, the voice backup groups," remembered steel guitarist Don Helms, who played on a few Reeves sessions. "That kind of took the place of what fiddles and steels were used to playing. Gordon Stoker [of the Jordanaires] said one time, kind of tongue in cheek, kind of gouging me up at the studio coffee shop one day, 'Well, we put you out of business, didn't we?' I said, 'Yeah, but it took four of you to do it!' . . . It did make it rough on steel players and fiddle players. It sent us on the road. [Producers] weren't using any steels or fiddles at all." The steel guitar and fiddle would occasionally gain reprieves on Jim's records after 1956, but for the most part, Chet banished the instruments from the Jim Reeves sound.

On February 7, 1957, when Jim walked into the studios for his next scheduled session, Chet awaited with a brand-new configuration of elements. Donning his lab coat for an RCA experiment, Chet barred the steel guitar and fiddle from the 7:30 P.M. session—marking the first time Jim would record without one or the other—and recruited the rich vocals of the Jordanaires, who regularly appeared on the *Grand Ole Opry* and backed Elvis Presley on virtually all his records. With simply a rhythm guitar, electric guitar, drums, bass and piano, Chet hoped to conjure an intimate atmosphere that would highlight the intimacy that Jim's voice was capable of creating. The stripped-down instrumentation and soothing background vocals, he hoped, would create the feeling of a romantic dinner for two.

The lights dimmed lower when Chet nudged Jim closer to the microphone, the surrogate lover Jim would caress. Until that session, Chet would never have dared to allow Jim or any other singer to virtually kiss the mike. Steve Sholes's favorite engineer, Jeff Miller, would jump like an attack dog if a vocalist even looked like he or she might approach within a foot of the microphone. "With me around that was impossible," bragged Miller, who feared that an errant singer would "pop a *P*," sending air through the mike and marring the recording. But Jim knew his way around a mike. Any good radio announcer has ingrained in his mind the unpleasant sound of a popped *P* over the air. After years of radio work, Jim could nuzzle up to the mike and, with the right lip, tongue, and breath control, deliver patter or a song without a single pop, bleb, or bleat. So, when Jeff Miller took what would become a permanent leave of absence in the fall of 1956, Chet Atkins played the cat and ordered Jim closer to the microphone.

First on the agenda for February 7 was a song that most likely traveled to Chet through the normal RCA channels: "Four Walls," a George Campbell-Marvin Moore ballad about a man who waits alone for the woman he idolizes. Moore wrote songs for a publishing company that Charles Grean had established with former *Billboard* Editor Joe Csida in the mid-1950s, and through Grean's contact with Steve Sholes, many of Moore's songs reached wax on the lips of RCA artists. Grean probably sold Sholes on "Four Walls," and Sholes, in turn, sent it on to Chet. Moore told writer Dorothy Horstman that George Campbell had actually come up with the idea for "Four Walls."

"My co-writer was a very busy pianist, writing by day and playing by night," Moore said, "and the song was inspired by a day-to-day observation of the marvelous manner in which his wife took the rough edges of life with no complaint. . . . Chet Atkins told me later how he happened to connect with the song. It seems Chet had a stack of material on the desk while Jim was in the room, and through some movement or other, the stack toppled into his wastebasket. Jim joined the rescue effort, putting the sheet music and demonstration records back on the desk. And while doing this, he saw the title, asked about it, listened to it, liked it, and recorded it."

Although pop singer Jim Lowe (of "Green Door" fame) recorded "Four Walls" around the same time, the song seemed tailored for Jim Reeves. At new engineer Selby Coffeen's cue, and after the gentle ringing of Chet's electric guitar intro, Jim approached the mike and delivered his most natural-sounding recording yet.

> *Out where the bright lights are glowing,*
> *you're drawn like a moth to a flame.*
> *You laugh while the wine's overflowing*
> *while I sit and whisper your name.*

Totally absent of tension, Jim's rich baritone purred in gorgeous, even resonance, and, like a bear content with his winter den, his voice reclined in its lower range where it sounded most comfortable. The delivery suggested freedom and full employment of his vocal capacity, the notes rising from the abdomen, through the throat, and unfolding in a warm bloom just inches from the microphone. And when Jim moved in slight increments to higher and lower registers within his range, he did so flawlessly, gracefully. There were no drastic changes in the vocal delivery of "Four Walls," only a seamless, entrancing feeling. Jim's voice seemed to reach the apex of an evolution, the early stages of which were so evident on the KGRI tapes and his early recordings in Houston and Dallas. Fabor Robison had added vim and flexibility to the voice but at the same time had diverted it from its natural development.

On numbers like "Mexican Joe," Fabor compromised Jim's vocal performance, pushing him into the higher range where he struggled. One could almost hear Jim wishing that he could drop to his natural, bass resonance on the Abbott hits, but he only sped ahead in elevated registers. Furthermore, he couldn't sing the words on the novelty tunes. He spoke them, poked at them, but was rarely permitted to let the lyrics sail out in his natural vibrato. On the rare occasions that Fabor allowed Jim to dwell in his most comfortable range and sing at a leisurely rate, the artist's bass-baritone voice showed evidence of improvement. It acquired depth, and by the time Jim began recording ballads in the RCA studios under the watchful eyes and ears of Steve

Sholes and Chet Atkins, the possibility of a breakthrough recording with "Four Walls" seemed at hand. "My Lips Are Sealed" and "Am I Losing You" suggested the coming of "Four Walls," and when the experimenting Atkins rearranged Jim's studio environment—altering the proximity of the mike, reducing the number of instruments, and adding the Jordanaires—Jim's voice found a comfortable room from which to project.

As the "Four Walls" session progressed from its flagship song, Jim's voice remained firmly planted in his natural range, and when Chet stepped up the tempo for Harlan Howard's "Look Behind You," Jim approached the song with the breeziness of Bing Crosby. "Okay," Jim ordered before take, "let's do it real swingified and free and easy." He swayed and swung, keeping up with the pace but not at the expense of his vocal comfort zone and vibrato. Jim groomed every word for the listener.

The "Four Walls" session on February 7, 1957, proved to be more than an anomaly. Rather, it marked a permanent shift in Jim's studio recordings. On record, he rarely strayed from his natural range again. As for "Four Walls" itself, the record's only visible country appeal was the singer's name on the label. Jim Reeves was associated with country music, but Atkins hoped that with the entirely un-country style of "Four Walls," he would find record buyers in the pop arena. With exception of the relatively quick-paced "I Know (and You Know)," written by Red Sovine, Chet had cast a pop orientation over the entire session. But when he hung up his lab coat just after midnight and headed into the darkened parking lot on McGavock Street, he could only wait and see if his Jim Reeves experiment would have any merit.

On April Fool's Day 1957, Jim and a group of RCA Victor country stars that included the Browns, Hank Locklin, Janis Martin and Del Wood flew out of New York City for a three-week tour of U.S. military bases in Germany. The stiffly named "Concert in Country Music" tour took flight with RCA dollars after the company discovered that country and western sales far outnumbered pop in the military post exchanges throughout Europe. In fact, PXes were gobbling up almost half of the country music product that RCA distributed, and furthermore, many of those records were landing in the hands of European civilians who had asked U.S. military personnel to purchase for them the latest releases by Reeves, Eddy Arnold and others.

Although the Nashville troupe would stick mainly to American military installations, RCA saw the tour as a way to raise the flag of country music in potentially lucrative foreign markets and promote the company's overall efforts to establish a presence abroad. In the years preceding 1957, RCA had slowly recruited a network of distributors and licensees around the world to make possible the simultaneous release of its records at home and abroad. Instead of watching foreign artists cover RCA hits and rake in the lion's share of the revenue, the label hoped to sell its original releases overseas through a licensee or distributor before a local performer or competing label could even think about recording cover versions.

"If you had to ship volume by boat, you were too late," explained Dick Broderick who coordinated RCA's overseas activities. "Somebody covered the record locally. Usually, they had it out in the marketplace before you had a chance." For example, in 1955, RCA watched helplessly as British trumpeter Eddie Calvert rolled up tremendous sales from his cover of "Cherry Pink and Apple Blossom White," a Perez Prado original that spent ten weeks at number one in America for RCA. The next year, British singer Jimmy Young siphoned off sales from Perry Como's "More," a Top Five release in America. Both Perez Prado and Perry Como hit the British charts with their respective versions, but since RCA released both in the U.S. first, foreign artists and labels had time to assess the potential of the songs, wax cover versions, and collect British pounds that may have been spent on the RCA originals. "For that reason," Broderick continued, "we licensed in most countries, and it worked."

The tour gave the Nashville music industry reason to pop its suspender straps. The town had certainly become the undisputed hub of country music in the United States, and now somebody wanted to shower its most-visible product on nations across the Atlantic. *Billboard* reported that a March 25 "bon voyage" fête that RCA hosted for the touring group drew some eighty country and western performers and businesspeople to Nashville's Andrew Jackson Hotel. To further hype the European trek, Jim Reeves and the gang appeared the following evening on a special *Tonight Show* broadcast that originated from Nashville. Although country music acts frequently made forays into Canada, this would be the first major overseas tour by country artists during peacetime since Gene Autry and Carson Robison performed in Europe some twenty years before.

Because Jim headlined the tour and his manager assisted with the logistics of the overseas sojourn, he brought his own band, which at the time consisted of Bobby Garrett, Leo Jackson, Louis Dunn, Billy Harlan, and Tommy Hill. The Wagonmasters also had the chore of backing the other singers on the tour, and from that perch, they saw the military boys and brass drink in the tunes from home. Germany was still in the grip of a damp, cold winter that month, when everything had begun to bloom in Nashville, but Jim and rest—including Mary, who had come along—seemed to relish all. "This is the greatest," wrote Herb Shucher to *Billboard*. "Much wine and beer, and the reception wonderful."

Not all was wine and beer, though. Almost everyone became airsick while trapped in a long holding pattern over England, and Shucher's new wife, Katherine, discovered she was pregnant in Nuremberg and remained in the city to rest until the tour ended. But such hassles aside, it was a thrill to be traveling internationally. Local girls frequently climbed up the fire escapes to catch glimpses of the boys in the band, and the dense Black Forest and endless, rolling hills of the German countryside majestically glided by the bus windows. "I guess there wasn't enough land to go around for everybody, so they had to hang it up and farm it on both sides," quipped Hank Locklin of the landscape. On a more serious note, the group's escort, Lt. Bill Kearney, revealed to the performers cities that were still in shambles from the bombs of World War II.

For Jim, the excitement of being in Europe came not from the landscape, or the hearty applause, or even the headiness of expanding the country music market for everyone back in Nashville. Instead, some news from back home pumped his spirits higher than anyone on the caravan had ever seen them go. "Four Walls," word came from RCA, was shipping out of the warehouses at a phenomenal rate, far more rapidly than "Yonder Comes a Sucker," "My Lips Are Sealed," or any other platter Jim had thus far made for the company.

"Jim loved pretty ballads," said Bobby Garrett, "but all the hits he had was these novelty tunes. All this time, he was wishing he could cut a real pretty ballad and it would be a big hit. He dreamed about that. While we were in Germany, he got the news that 'Four Walls' had sold more records than anything he had cut so far. . . . That's the

The 1957 European troupe. From left: Hank Locklin, Katherine Shucher, Herb Shucher, Louis Dunn, Dick O'Shaughnessy, Del Wood, Jim, Mary, Maxine Brown, Leo Jackson, Bonnie Brown, and Jim Ed Brown. (Courtesy: Richard Weize)

happiest I ever saw Jim. It liked to thrilled him to death to know that he finally had a big ballad hit."

A few days after the pioneering Americans returned to the States, Jim opened his April 29, 1957, *Billboard* to see that "Four Walls" had danced onto the country and pop charts. Over the next four weeks, he turned to the country charts and watched the crooning ballad vault over his own "Am I Losing You," and rock-tinged numbers such as Marty Robbins's "White Sport Coat" and Sonny James's "Young Love." During the last week of May, "Four Walls" topped the country charts (it remained at number one for eight weeks) and reached the upper echelons of the pop charts (where it peaked at number eleven), holding its own against such hits as Elvis Presley's "All Shook Up" and Johnny Mathis's "It's Not for Me to Say."

"Four Walls" was Jim Reeves's best showing since "Mexican Joe," but unlike the latter release, which would not have stood a snow cone's chance in Mazatlán on the pop charts, "Four Walls" became a legitimate pop hit. The two-pronged smash spawned cover versions by the Four Keys, Dorothy Collins, and others, but the Jim Reeves version outlasted them all. Chet Atkins and the former ballplayer from East Texas had stumbled upon a potent mixture of resonant baritone and urbane instrumentation. The combination would redefine Jim's career, carry RCA's Nashville operation into the pop arena, and—by Chet's admission—threaten to take the "country" out of country music.

With "Four Walls" blazing on the charts, Jim Reeves earned the distinction of being RCA's first Nashville artist in the newly born rock era to blister both the country and pop charts. To be sure, RCA's Eddy Arnold had pioneered country music's trail to the pop charts in the late 1940s, but by 1955—the first year of the rock genre's explosion— Eddy had moved his recording base to New York and was recording almost exclusively (and unsuccessfully) in a pop vein. When Steve Sholes passed the Nashville baton to Chet Atkins in 1956, he maintained control over Arnold's recordings. Although Eddy lived in Nashville, he was not one of RCA's Nashville artists. And although Elvis Presley had recorded first for RCA in Nashville, he too mostly lit up the studios in New York and Los Angeles.

Neither artist recorded under Chet's purview, so to find a broader audience for his artists and prove his operation's economic viability, Chet tapped those near at hand. Fortunately, he and Jim had perfected their formula. Observers would soon call Chet's reaction to rock and roll, the "Nashville Sound"—a term characterized by tight, spontaneous instrumentation and an easygoing feel. Decca's master producer, Owen Bradley, had moved with Chet toward the new sound, and other producers jumped on the bandwagon shortly after. Many producers sought to emulate the feel of "Four Walls" in their artists' performances, but Jim Reeves was the first voice of the Nashville Sound.

Immediately, RCA pounced on the chance to capitalize on the broad appeal of "Four Walls." In RCA's portfolio advertisements, Jim's face appeared next to those of established pop performers Perry Como, Dinah Shore, Lena Horne, and Hugo Winterhalter. In promotions that solely plugged Jim's music, the company took every opportunity to communicate "pop." With Jim pictured in a jacket and tie,

RCA's ads ballyhooed "Four Walls" as "BUSTIN' BIG IN POP" and touted Jim's next release, "Two Shadows on Your Mind," as "A SMASH FOLLOW-UP TO HIS POP HIT 'FOUR WALLS.'"

In 1956 portfolio advertising, the company had run a photo of a Stetson-hatted Jim next to pictures of the late Jimmie Rodgers and the country hit-making Davis Sisters, but by mid-1957, there was little indication of Jim's association with country in RCA's advertising. The ads reflected the scene in the studio, where Chet permitted little hint of Jim's country roots. Atkins and Sholes chased the pop market with albums offering Jim's velvet voice singing "Mona Lisa" and "Charmaine," and hit singles that strayed little from the "Four Walls" mold. In Chet's RCA studio, it may as well have been Columbia's Guy Mitchell behind the mike with his label mates the Four Lads singing backup, but it was Jim Reeves and the Jordanaires, and they were creeping onto Mitchell and the Lads' turf.

On the management front, Herb Shucher found that "Four Walls" had awakened the MCA talent agency and prodded it to open the mass media door wider for Jim Reeves. In 1956 Herb had helped place Jim on a syndicated television program starring *Opry* cast members, and he (and RCA) regularly booked him on local country music radio and television shows throughout the United States. The emcees of those shows, observed Leo Jackson, seemed to be in awe of the man who had made it big with "Mexican Joe." One disc jockey, Jim Pierce, was so flustered to be standing next to Jim that when he introduced the singer, he announced: "Folks, we got a famous country singer here. I'd like you to meet him. His name is Jim Pierce! Let's have a hand for him." Jim chuckled and in a gentlemanly stroke replied, "I'm sure that's a handle to be proud of, but actually my name is Jim Reeves." After "Four Walls," Jim met more seasoned personalities as he made the rounds of America's most popular television programs, including *The Steve Allen Show* on NBC and *The Jimmy Dean Show*, *The Lawrence Welk Show*, and Dick Clark's *American Bandstand*, all on ABC.

In the midst of the media's enchantment with Reeves, Shucher and MCA negotiated Jim's first regularly scheduled radio appearances outside the *Grand Ole Opry*. ABC Radio agreed to give Jim his own daily show for thirteen weeks as part of the network's revival of live musical programs, which by the late 1950s had been all but supplanted by record spinners. Throughout ABC's late-morning and early afternoon schedule, the network aired live music from stations in New York, Chicago, Los Angeles, and—from 1:00 to 2:00 P.M. Eastern time—the WSM studios in Nashville.

As with Jim's recording-studio work, nothing about *The Jim Reeves Show* suggested country music, although it was an all-Nashville production. Former WSM Program Director and Tree Publishing President Jack Stapp produced the program, and country producer Owen Bradley conducted an orchestra that created the slick, dancing strings that were so closely associated with the 1950s arrangements of Hugo Winterhalter, Ray Conniff, and other pop conductors. Regulars on the show included vocalists Buddy Hall, Dolores Watson, and the Anita Kerr Singers, who were fast rivaling the Jordanaires as the music industry's session singers of choice. To add spice to the show, guests such as the Everly Brothers, Ferlin Husky, Marty Robbins, and the Jordanaires joined the circle of regulars that surrounded Jim.

In the radio medium, Jim, of course, came across as a pro, his every line revealing the many years he had spent behind a radio mike. "When he talked on this show," recalled Anita Kerr, who arranged the songs on Jim's radio docket, "a script was written, [and] he did it so well, you never would have known that this man was reading. Whereas, when some of the other people on the show said something, you could tell that it wasn't natural, that they were reading. But with him, [the words] just fell out of his mouth."

The professional presentation wavered not one whit when Jim, his radio stint completed, jumped to weekly television appearances on ABC's *Country Music Jubilee*, a program normally hosted by Red Foley that originated from Springfield, Missouri. Foley's folksy style had helped make the program one of the top Saturday night TV choices in the Southwest and Midwest, but the "Chattanoogie Shoe Shine Boy" needed rest, so the mild-mannered—though hardly folksy—Jim Reeves got the nod to replace him for the summer of 1958. The ABC radio and television shows gave Jim unprecedented access to America, but it was worrisome to Jim, and presumably to RCA, that the exposure failed to generate the kind of success on the pop charts that he had enjoyed with "Four Walls."

Since Jim's giant hit, just three of his eight country releases had crossed over—with only modest success. "Anna Marie," a Cindy Walker composition, appeared briefly in the lower reaches of the pop charts in February 1958, and "Blue Boy," which garnered somewhat better reception, peaked at number forty-five in September. Another country hit, "Billy Bayou," surfaced on the pop charts for one week in December but quickly plunged below the 100 mark. Although almost every Jim Reeves release rocketed into the Top Ten of the country charts, it appeared that perhaps the promise of "Four Walls" had been hollow.

The Roger Miller-penned "Billy Bayou," which topped the country charts in January 1959, seems to have been an effort to temper Jim's pop efforts, as the song opened with a hearty acoustic guitar and called to mind the childishness of "Bimbo" and "Penny Candy." Chet Atkins also had Jim record "Partners," a haunting Danny Dill composition about a man who kills his gold-mining partner. That record followed the pattern of saga songs that were blanketing Nashville in 1959. Johnny Cash's "Don't Take Your Guns to Town," Johnny Horton's "The Battle of New Orleans," and Eddy Arnold's "Tennessee Stud" all had climbed high on the country charts and crossed over to the Davy Crockett-hungry, general audiences of America. "Partners," however, failed to follow Cash, Horton, and the rest to the pop charts, although it did reach number five on the country surveys.

Reeves had long since begun fretting that he would never top "Four Walls." As the ghost of the slain miner grates on his killer's nerves in "Partners," "Four Walls" became a wraith to Jim, hovering over his every recording and taunting him for failing to recapture that hit's magic. Although Herb Shucher had Jim working harder than ever—and making more money than ever—dissatisfaction steered Jim's personality. There were frequent television appearances and tours that took him into some of the nicer showrooms in Canada and Las Vegas, but Jim and the Wagonmasters still played a steady string of music ranches and musty dance halls that were unlikely venues for someone marketed as a pop singer.

"He was very serious," said Bobby Garrett of his boss's demeanor. "He seemed to have a built-in fear of not making it big like he wanted to. I don't think anybody understands where that fear came from because he always did [make it big]. After 'Four Walls,' I remember he was so afraid that he wasn't going to be able to cut another big hit ballad. He seemed to have a constant fear of not being able to go into the studio and record things that would become a hit."

In the fading glow of "Four Walls," the explosiveness that Jim had exhibited as a child on the school playground and in the studio with Fabor Robison began stinging those around him from time to time. The man who marveled at the new geography that touring revealed to him and was the "happy, happy man" that "Little Red" Hayes had observed in 1953 became impatient and intransigent at times. Buddy Killen, in his autobiography, chalked up to depression Jim's personality swings and recalled that the singer had begun to see a psychologist. Counseling, though, seemed to have little impact on the graceless side of Jim. If Bobby Garrett or Leo Jackson botched a lick on stage, Jim would lash out with a sharp reprimand that the audience could hear clearly.

"He had chewed out one of us right on the bandstand in the microphone," recalled Garrett. "And I said, 'Jim. Why would you do something like that?' He said, 'I have to keep you guys in line.' I said, 'Jim, I don't know about everybody else, but I know for myself that I could play you a better job if I could just relax and play it.' He said, 'No. I got to keep you on your toes.' That was his answer to my question.

"Jim and I had a big argument one time," continued Garrett, "and I told Mary, his wife, 'Mary, I don't know why Jim has [to be this way]. . . . She said, 'Jim is afraid that he's not going to be able to accomplish what he wants to accomplish. He's afraid he's going to fall short. That puts a burr under his saddle.' He sometimes would be nearly impossible to get along with, and she said that was because of his fear of not being able to accomplish what he wanted."

Jim hurled criticisms more freely than ever before, and the unyielding perfectionist in him burst forth more frequently, but his heart had not turned completely black. It was only that the elusive follow-up to "Four Walls" seemed unattainable, and that dogged him and frayed his nerves. On good days—and most of them were—Jim could still be the congenial guy who sat on the Alexandria Aces bus on the way to Thibodaux. "You could be going down the road," observed Bobby Garrett, "and there might not be anybody saying a word for several miles. He had a natural knack for coming up with something funny to get everybody laughing and in a better mood."

Jim played benefit performances, met with youth groups in the cities he played, and appeared on public service programs for the armed forces and various charitable organizations. He retained his fatherly attitude as well. Jim continued to put up Leo Jackson in

A sporty Jim Reeves on the Grand Ole Opry. *Don Helms plays steel, and Buddy Killen thumps the bass. (Courtesy: Richard Weize)*

his home after the youngster moved to Nashville, and when Uncle Sam drafted Leo in October 1957, Jim held open the guitarist's spot in the Wagonmasters until he returned in July 1959. Jim brightened in the midst of children and spoke often of his desire to have some of his own. In a 1958 letter that Jim hand wrote to friends who had just had a baby girl, he only half-kiddingly suggested that he and Mary take on one of their boys. "Mary says now that you have Cheryl Ann, one of the boys can live with us—*permanently*?"

In the studio, Jim was fully capable of hurling an icy response toward Chet or the studio musicians, but in almost the next instant, he could exhibit a countervailing warmth. Velma Williams Smith, one of the few female session musicians in Nashville at that time, saw the cool turn to warm at a September 4, 1958, session at which Jim recorded a list of sacred songs such as "In the Garden," "Whispering Hope," and "Precious Memories." "That was the first time that I had met him," recalled Smith. "When I walked in with two guitars in my hand, there was no one in the studio at the time but he and I.

I introduced myself and said, 'I'm your rhythm guitar player for the day.' You could almost read that he thought, 'Yeah. Well I can see that this is going to be great.' When we got into the first rundown, he came and put his arms around my shoulders, and he said, 'I can see that we're going to get along just fine.' I said, 'That's all I need to hear, and if I do something you don't like, tell me, and I will rectify it.'"

Out of the studio and on the road, observed Leo Jackson, "Gentleman Jim" was almost as likely to be in the house as the man who berated his band in front of the audience. "Jim got on my ass, but let me tell you, I earned it when he did. Jim took care of us. He would give us anything that we needed. We'd work places, and the club owner or the booking agent would come and say, 'Man, we lost money on this. I don't know what I'm going to do.' I saw Jim turn around and give him the money back, [but] he still paid us. Jim had expenses coming out, and he would turn around and give the money back to the booking agent or the club owner. Now that didn't happen just one time. That's just the kind of man he was."

9

Jim began changing the composition of his road band in 1959 to more closely mirror the sound he and Chet Atkins produced in the studio. In 1957, to distance himself from the country appellation, Jim had released the band name "Wagonmasters" to Porter Wagoner (who Herb Shucher also managed for a time) and dropped the fiddle from his background accompaniment. And although he continued to use the steel guitar on the road to fill in where the Jordanaires or a piano could be heard on record, by 1959 Jim was ready to do away with that instrument, too. In the interim, Jim had employed Bobby Garrett on steel guitar, and when Bobby was on the road with George Jones, Jimmy Day often took over.

According to Garrett, the steel's swan song with Jim occurred in November 1959 during an engagement at the Showboat Hotel in Las Vegas. After the shows there, Jim planned to spend the holidays with Mary in Texas before heading out on a tour arranged by Harry "Hap" Peebles. This one was to begin in Sioux City, Iowa, then whip through Nebraska and Kansas. As usual, Jim announced that he would break up the band at the conclusion of the Showboat dates. But for Bobby Garrett, that was the last straw. "I had been through that a number of times before. I told him that time, 'I can't keep doing this anymore. Consider this my last job. He said, 'Okay.' I left, and I didn't go back."

Animosity had been building between Garrett and Reeves on the tour leading up to the Vegas shows, stoked by Garrett's refusal to take Jim's guff and their conflicting philosophies regarding the steel guitar. "He wouldn't let me perform like I would have liked to have performed on his tunes," complained Garrett. "Instead of just hitting little old simple slides—the simplest you could play—I wanted to do some things that I thought were good, that sounded good to me, that he wouldn't allow." But Jim hired musicians to complement him, and since the fans flocked to see and listen to him, it was entirely understandable that he muted the backup instrumentalists. Garrett grumbled nonetheless and recalled that the two were edging toward blows in Las Vegas before Mary interceded. As the curtain fell on one of the Showboat performances, the two became embroiled in a "hot and heavy" argument over something that had happened during the show. Garrett recalled that as tensions increased and the discourse became more inflamed, Mary quickly descended a flight of stairs leading to the stage and exclaimed, "Hey you guys! The mike's still on!" The audience had heard every word.

After Garrett stated his intention not to return to the band, Jim never again used a steel guitar on the road. Garrett played behind Jim only one more time, on a January 1960 session after the Peebles tour. For an RCA budget album, Jim and Chet had slated four songs that required a soft rhythm punctuated by a tinging steel guitar. Chet knew that Jim, with his journeyman efficiency, could croon through the numbers in less than the allotted three hours, so he made room for Eddy Arnold, who needed a few minutes to record one track, "Texarkana Baby," for an album.

"I wanted to redo something, and Jim wouldn't let me," said Garrett of the rushed session. "He said we didn't have time. I hit a chime lick on one of [the songs], and he said, 'That sounded like a wild turkey gobblin'.' I said, 'Well, let me do it over.' He said, 'No, we don't have time.' I wanted to please him. I wanted to make him happy with whatever he did." Jim scooted off the studio floor to make room for Eddy Arnold, and although Eddy too had said good-bye to the steel guitar, he was struggling in 1960 and had resorted to rehashing his old, steel-tinged material to sell records. Floyd Cramer, drummer Buddy Harman, and bass player Bob Moore stuck around for "Texarkana Baby," but when Eddy asked to use Bobby Garrett and Leo Jackson—both of whom Jim had specifically recruited for his session—Reeves refused. The competitor in Jim never liked to share his band and its accompanying sound with fellow performers. "That kind of hurt my feelings," said Garrett.

Leo, who had remained nimble in the army by playing with the Special Services' Circle A Wranglers and had frequently returned to

Nashville at Jim's behest for important dates, received his discharge in July 1959 and immediately fell in with the band again. He was the core around which Jim would build his new band. During Jim's ream of shows in Las Vegas that November, he had become reacquainted with pianist Dean Manuel, who, according to Bobby Garrett, had met and sat in with Jim on the 1957 European tour. Manuel, recalled Garrett, had been playing with a military band in Europe, and by the time Jim met him again, he was pounding the ivories for country-rockabilly singer Bob Luman at the Showboat. While in Vegas, Jim had offered Dean a job in his evolving band, but Dean had refused. A few days later, however, Bob Luman received word that Uncle Sam wanted his services for the next two years. The draft had dealt a new band into Jim's hands. Reeves hired the newly unemployed pianist and two other Luman regulars: bass player James Kirkland and drummer Mel Rogers. Guitar impresario James Burton had filled out the Luman band, but Jim already had a guitar player. Kirkland and Burton had rocked behind Ricky Nelson in the late '50s before their stint with Luman—dubious, tainted credentials, as far as Jim was concerned.

"I don't want any rock and rollers," he impressed on Dean when the pianist told him about Kirkland.

"No," replied Manuel. "He's not rock and roll."

In Nashville, Reeves introduced Leo to his new, untainted band mates—Manuel, Kirkland, and Rogers—and began rehearsing them in the basement of his and Mary's newly built, rambling brick house in the Nashville suburb of Madison. "When they got there, we went down in Jim's office and knocked [band] names around," said Leo. "Jim said, 'I got this record, "Blue Boy." What do you think of that?' We said, 'Sounds great.'" According to Leo, the newly formed Blue Boys hit the road with Jim in January 1960. They set out together—in a bus now—probably in late January for a swing through Texas, some two weeks after Jim's tour for Hap Peebles ended in Kansas City, Kansas.

Jim had shuffled more than his road band by the time he greeted 1960. When he and the Blue Boys hit the road for the Lone Star State, Hal Smith of Nashville's Curtis Artists Productions (and part owner with Ray Price of Pamper Music) had arranged the bookings instead of Herb Shucher. In early November 1959, Jim had announced the end of his almost four-year relationship with Shucher and added that he planned to buy out the manager's half interest in their Open Road Music. Shucher had just helped Jim negotiate a renewal of his RCA contract, but according to Shucher's wife, Katherine, Jim felt that he no longer needed Herb's help.

"My husband said Jim had told him that he didn't need a manager anymore; he could manage himself," said Katherine Shucher. "He was a little on the frugal side." Herb had recently signed the Browns and that may have aggravated Jim's jealous streak and fractured the relationship. Shucher continued for a short time with the Browns and exclusively booked Bill Anderson, Roger Miller, and the Louvin Brothers. Later, he moved with his wife back to the Northeast to run an educational recordings business in New York City. (Sadly, Herb developed lymphoma and melanoma and died in 1975 at the age of forty-four.)

Jim, true to his plan, never acquired another manager. Mary and secretary Joyce Gray ran the Jim Reeves office, which was located in his Madison home, and later Jim later hired a former San Antonio and Nashville disc jockey named Ray Baker to operate Open Road and another publishing firm Jim had established, Tuckahoe Music.

In the studio, Jim still searched for that perfect song that would be "Four Walls II." He saw the eerie "Partners" and its flip side, the wistful "I'm Beginning to Forget You," stop well short of smash status, and, perhaps out of bewilderment, he remained absent from the studio from the June 9, 1959, "Partners" session until October 15, 1959. By 1959, Chet Atkins had used the "Four Walls" formula with other of RCA's Nashville artists and had produced several hits that soared up the country and pop charts on the strength of the tight, easygoing Nashville Sound that had first found its voice in Jim Reeves. Deep country acts like Johnnie and Jack and Porter Wagoner seldom made any concessions to pop, and Chet never tinkered much with their sound, but in the late 1950s Atkins's finely tuned approach gave many other artists that RCA called "country" a scythe to clear a path to the pop market.

In 1958 the label's Don Gibson launched "Oh Lonesome Me" to the top of the country charts for an eight-week stay and also placed the song in the Top Ten on the pop charts. Gibson and Chet repeatedly emulated that performance throughout the late '50s. Eddy Arnold, in search of a hit, any kind of hit, returned to RCA's Nashville

The Blue Boys. From left: Dean Manuel, Leo Jackson, Mel Rogers, and James Kirkland. (Courtesy: Richard Weize)

studios and, with Chet, came up with two 1959 country hits—Arnold's first in almost two years—that crossed over to the pop side. Amazingly, Jim Ed Brown and the Browns even rang the top of both charts in 1959 with "The Three Bells." That feat had never been accomplished by an RCA country act and surely widened some envious eyes in Chet's stable. Over the course of the next year, the retiring producer would crack the pop charts with Floyd Cramer, Skeeter Davis, and even "Singing Ranger" Hank Snow.

Nothing in Nashville buzzed with as much efficiency as Chet Atkins's recording operation. Although country music was entering wider markets with increasing regularity as the 1960s dawned, no label made the transition with its artists more often than did RCA Victor. Columbia's Johnny Cash, Marty Robbins, and Johnny Horton, and Decca's Patsy Cline gathered wide audiences with their rock and pop effects, but they bowed to the towering RCA and its thriving roster of singers. A combination of factors, beginning with Steve Sholes's commitment to country music in the 1940s, had lifted RCA to preeminence in the recording industry of the late 1950s. The label had finally moved from its rented space on McGavock Street in 1957 to a new building of its own at 1610 Hawkins Street, and while the compact studio there could become cramped with a bevy of backup singers and session musicians, there was an acoustical ambiance that contrasted with a specious sound that some say McGavock Street produced.

The new, sound-friendly walls of the Hawkins Street studios reverberated with an aggregation of people who worked with Chet to produce his interpretation of the Nashville Sound. There was a core of session musicians that most often included bass player Bob Moore, pianist Floyd Cramer, drummer Buddy Harman, and guitarist Hank Garland, a group that had worked so many sessions for Chet and other producers that they were synchronized like pistons in a pleasantly humming engine. The Jordanaires embedded RCA's recordings with their soft, vibrant background vocals, and as the 1960s approached, they alternated with increasing frequency with the Anita Kerr Singers, the quartet comprised of two men and two women that had performed on Jim Reeves's ABC radio show. Of all those Chet gathered around him, it could well be argued that Anita Kerr herself was the most important.

A native Memphian, Anita began playing piano at a young age, and in 1948, decided to pursue a full-time musical career in Nashville, where she initially picked up work playing and singing at dances and in clubs. After too many nights of such employment, she took a staff pianist position with WMAK Radio and in her spare time assembled a quartet that sang for fun—no money—on WLAC.

"Then Jack Stapp at WSM heard about me and the vocal group," recounted Kerr. "So, then he called me and asked me to talk with him. . . . I went to WSM, and he hired me to direct this eight-voice choir which was on a regional network [show] there. It was called *Sunday Down South*, with Snooky Lanson. I started writing and conducting and singing with this eight-voice choir, and the A&R man from Decca Records, Paul Cohen, was in and out of WSM all the time because that was really the beginning of all the recording in Nashville. (There was always an A&R man from somewhere.) Paul would come in and he heard the group, and he wanted a choir on a

religious song that Red Foley was doing. He asked me if I would write
the arrangement and have the choir sing with Red on it. That was the
beginning. He was really the one who gave us the name 'The Anita
Kerr Singers' We had no name; we were just the choir on that show.
He asked me, after we recorded, 'What do you want me to call you?'
I said, 'I don't know. I haven't even thought about it.' He said, 'Your
name's Anita Kerr. How about The Anita Kerr Singers?' "

Paul Cohen soon began employing Kerr's octet on Decca sessions
with Burl Ives and even Ernest Tubb. In 1957, after a winning appearance on *Arthur Godfrey's Talent Scouts* in New York, the "Old Red-
head" hired the Kerrs to sing as regulars on his show. Godfrey asked
Anita to pare the group to a foursome, and hence, the Anita Kerr
Singers became Dottie Dillard, Louis Nunley, Gil Wright, and, of
course, Anita K.

"After that," continued Kerr, "we were going back and forth from
Nashville for five or six years. There would be two weeks in New
York and then four in Nashville. [The Godfrey show was] another
thing that made our work pick up considerably. It got to the point,
when we were home, we were offered more sessions than we could
do. I had to refuse some of them because we were always booked."

When Atkins could, he gobbled up Anita's time, hiring the singers
and recruiting her to write arrangements. Although Nashville's studio
musicians prided themselves on their ability to produce the tight
rhythms and delicious fills without sheet music or formal arrangements, Chet nonetheless hired Anita to write chord sheets for them.
Before session day, she would sit down with the singer and his
grocery list of songs in order to set the appropriate keys. At home, she
would then sketch out the arrangement for each song, and when
she returned to Hawkins Street for the session, she would bring in the
chord sheets and instructions indicating where each musician and
vocal group should come in with their improvised fills. Chet and
Anita could rely on the backup pickers and vocalists to improvise
when, during the song, the recording artist concluded a verse or
chorus and made way for a break or a bridge. They only had to know
when to come in, and Anita's simple arrangements told them.

Anita Kerr and her singers had worked about half of Jim Reeves's
sessions since the "Four Walls" date in 1957, and as often as possible, Chet used Kerr's arrangements when Jim went into the studio.
She even mapped out songs for Jim when Chet opted for the more

masculine sound of the Jordanaires instead of the Kerr Singers. As usual, when Anita arranged the music for one of Jim's sessions, she met with him prior to the date.

"Chet was usually there, too," said Kerr. "So, it was the three of us talking about how the song should be treated. Once I went home and wrote it and got back the next day—Chet didn't ever give me too much notice—[Jim] would just breeze right through them. He always knew his songs very well and had wonderful vocal control. He sang really good, I thought.

"I would say that Jim, when it came to singing a song, it was very simple the way he sang it. Very smooth. I don't want to say no emotion, but he never changed. It was just the same all the way through the song, whereas Eddy [Arnold] would go up and down—he would have a little more emotion in his singing. But then, on the other hand, I always felt Eddy sounded still somewhat country, whereas I thought Jim had gone further away from country in his sound. But Jim, when he really killed me was when he would narrate something. That I really loved."

Anita, in fact, once arranged and appeared on an album that contained virtually nothing but Jim's virile recitations. On *Talkin' to Your Heart*, which was released in 1961, she adapted to music the writings of Robert Service and Edgar Allen Poe, and came up with the numbers "(Far Away Feeling) The Spell of the Yukon" (based on Service's work) and "Annabel Lee" (based on Poe's). Jim's fans surely stained the album's glossy cover with dozens of tears after listening to him earnestly recite Anita's adaptations as well as Hank Williams's composition "Men with Broken Hearts" and "Old Tige," a story about a dog's loyalty.

From 1959 to 1964, the Anita Kerr Singers—more often than the Jordanaires—got the nod from Chet to appear on Reeves's sessions. According to Kerr, her group's sound created a feeling that was more akin to pop, and since she was doing much of the arranging it only made sense to bring along Dottie, Louis, and Gil. "The Jordanaires couldn't read music at all," posited Kerr, "and we could. So, I'm sure if I was hired to write the arrangement and they say, 'Bring your singers,' they knew if I wrote it, the singers could read it. I think the things we did were closer to pop because we could read [music], whereas the Jordanaires, most of their sessions were faked." Although the Jordanaires had bolstered "Four Walls" in 1957, Anita

Kerr and her singers became a more important component of Jim's sound as his music entered the 1960s.

Jim, cognizant of what Anita could help him achieve in the pop arena, kept her and the singers close at hand and never, according to Kerr, alienated them with the histrionics that many saw Jim unleash in the studio. In fact, contrary to others' observations, Kerr has claimed that she never saw Reeves misbehave in the studio. "He was always very nice to work with, extremely quiet. He was a quiet man; he sang very softly, and he did demand quietness in the studio. He didn't like it if people were noisy. Maybe it messed up his concentration. He was always nice about it. I can't think of one time that I've ever heard him raise his voice or look like he was going to."

However, Louis Nunley of the Kerr Singers was often the source of just the kind of noise of which Kerr spoke. "I always had a reputation of being a laugher," said Nunley. "I laughed on sessions." Nunley could be counted on to meet everyone at the door with a joke and keep the humor flowing throughout the session. Not so on Jim's sessions. Reeves instructed Louis to clam up or leave. "He thought I was laughing at him, which I wasn't," Nunley explained.

"He was a very introverted person," said Kerr of Jim's disposition in the studio. "He wasn't really outgoing. He wasn't the kind who would come up and hit you on the shoulder and say, 'Hey, that was really great!' He would come up and say in a very quiet way, 'That was good'—because he was a quiet man and introverted. Eddy [Arnold] would come up and laugh and slap you on the back and say, 'Hey, that was something.' And Jim was just the opposite."

Similar to what Anita Kerr experienced, the captain of all these studio machinations managed to maintain a respectful, though hardly brotherly, partnership with Jim in the studio. The relationship between Jim Reeves and Chet Atkins was, for the most part, anathema to the Reeves-Fabor Robison antagonism at Abbott Records. "It was the exact opposite," confirmed Leo Jackson. "Chet would approve [a song Jim wanted to record], but more than likely if Jim liked it, Chet liked it. Or if Chet liked it, Jim liked it. There was a mutual respect."

Chet—going back to his experience in Shorty Thompson's band and probably before—had come to know the ways of stars. Most had egos made of nitroglycerin. Like his mentor Steve Sholes, Chet never jostled the nitro or played studio czar. He allowed the creative flow to wend where it might, gently interceding when he saw the need to erect a dam or channel the flow into another direction.

Since 1955, Chet had observed that Jim had definite ideas about what songs to record and how to record them, and he indulged the artist. And Jim, as Leo Jackson suggested, acknowledged that Chet knew something about producing hit records and accepted it when the gravely voice from the control room asked for another take or suggested that Jim change the rate of his delivery. Chet called the shots in Nashville for the suits back in New York, so Jim avoided clashing directly with Chet or even Chet's right-hand woman, Anita Kerr. However, as former RCA engineer Bill Porter told historian John Rumble, Chet did fear that the infamous Reeves temper would flare in his direction.

"To a certain extent, Jim Reeves dictated more to Chet than most people," said Porter. "[Chet] seemed to be sort of apprehensive when [Jim] was around—pins and needles a little bit. Not that [Chet] would be intimidated by him, but he didn't seem to want to get into a controversial argument, so he kept things even as much as he could, because Reeves was doing the right thing. He had chart records going and picked the right material, so why's Chet gonna suddenly interfere?"

Such was the scene in Jim Reeves's studio world. He worked in concert with a diplomatic producer who, though malleable, pushed for innovation and fostered a studio environment that allowed other creative minds—not just his own—to achieve it. There was, in Anita Kerr, a pop-thinking arranger who could marshal her singers and the studio musicians into a format that appealed to wider audiences. And then there was rock-solid floor of it all—the seasoned fraternity of background instrumentalists and vocalists who had helped transform Nashville into a recording center that rivaled New York and Los Angeles. Their tight yet breezy sound meshed beautifully with Jim's sincere, straight-ahead vocal delivery that, with less-skilled accompaniment, may have seemed somewhat unemotional.

In his autobiography, Buddy Killen recalled Jim agonizing over whether he should record a song that Columbia Records had released in 1959 by a relatively obscure artist named Billy Brown. "He'll Have to Go" was written by Joe Allison, a Los Angeles disc jockey, and his wife, Audrey. They built the song from the phrase "Put your mouth closer to the phone"—something Joe often had to say as he strained to hear his willowy voiced wife on the telephone. It was a close cousin to "Four Walls" in that the lyrics paint the portrait of a man who is trying to keep from losing his woman to someone else.

From Killen's perspective, it appeared that Jim was hesitant to bring it into the Hawkins Street studio. "He was skeptical about 'covering' a song by another artist so close to its release date," wrote Killen. However, Billy Brown's version appeared destined for obscurity, which finally prompted Jim to record it.

What RCA's Nashville scene had done for the Browns and Don Gibson—raising their hits higher on the pop charts than "Four Walls" had reached and arranging longer stays at number one on the country charts—was about to happen for Jim Reeves. The team's recording of "He'll Have to Go" would result in a remarkably significant country-pop hit and finally deliver to Jim the long-awaited follow-up to "Four Walls." Anita Kerr wrote a quiet arrangement, but from what engineer Bill Porter has told John Rumble, Jim appeared to have well-developed notions about how the song should be recorded.

"When we did 'He'll Have to Go,'" said Porter, "it was Jim's idea to bring in [Bob Moore] to play bass on that. [It was] my first time to really do a good electric bass on a recording of any consequence. And that didn't normally happen [with most artists]. It was Reeves's idea to use electric bass, because Chet didn't normally think that way."

Perhaps Jim heard in Moore's electric bass a whispering, vibrating hum that complemented his deep inflections. Instrumentally, though, it would be the pulsating vibraphone of Nashville veteran Marvin Hughes that underscored Jim's vocals best. The shimmering sound opened "He'll Have to Go," and whether it was Jim's, Anita's, or Chet's idea to use the vibes, it proved to be an appropriate partner to Jim's voice throughout the number. The instrument suggested welling tears, an emotional act that Jim chose not to recreate in his voice on that day. Jim's purring voice competently conveys the intimacy of speaking with a loved one on the phone, but in "He'll Have to Go" there is a mysterious third party sitting near the girl. The man must plead for her attention, but Jim's delivery completely ignored that aspect of the song and treated "He'll Have to Go" as strictly a romantic ballad. The vibes cried the necessary tears, and even the Anita Kerr Singers boo-hooed, but Jim seemed to concentrate on honing the low, sexy quality of his voice.

According to Bill Porter, Jim focused on diving deep into the lower registers of his bass-baritone voice, particularly when he asked the barman in the song to turn the jukebox music "way down low." "He went an octave lower," Porter told John Rumble. "I think he added that himself, 'cause I think the first time he sang it up [high], and he didn't like it, so he put the low part in the second time we did it. During the recording session *per se*, nothing was unusual there except Jim did it over and over until he got his bass voice the way he wanted it."

Although Jim's interpretation of "He'll Have to Go" lacked vulnerability—communicating instead only the warmth of a cozy phone conversation—his voice was utterly appealing and could easily make a listener forget that the singer had partially missed the song's point. "I was amazed at how well he sang it," said Anita Kerr. "It really showed off his voice because when he sang low it was absolutely beautiful." It took the totality of Chet's studio corps, though, to communicate the full meaning of "He'll Have to Go." In "Four Walls," Jim's voice had borne the weight of a man's insecurity over a woman, but even though he failed to do that again on the October 15, 1959, session, sales of "He'll Have to Go" significantly outpaced those of "Four Walls." Backed with the catchy "In a Mansion Stands My Love" from the same session, "He'll Have to Go" bustled out of the RCA warehouses like an East Texas quail flushed from the brush. In early December 1959, as Jim and Mary made arrangements to return to East Texas for the Christmas holidays, the song appeared on the country charts, and later in the month, it slipped onto the pop charts.

"He'll Have to Go" percolated up the country charts among a variety of styles: the rocking of Ray Price's "The Same Old Me" and Webb Pierce's "I Ain't Never," and the sagas of Marty Robbins's "El Paso" and Johnny Cash's "I Got Stripes," for example. The Browns' glossy version of "Scarlet Ribbons" probably represented the best that the country charts could offer in the way of the middle-of-the-road pop sound in late 1959, but the styling of "He'll Have to Go" soon became the archetype of how country could emulate such pop headliners as Como and Sinatra. In fact, in the pop arena, Jim Reeves and "He'll Have to Go" easily surpassed Perry Como's hits at the time ("Delaware" and "I Know What God Is") as well as those of another soft music star, Andy Williams ("The Village of St. Bernadette" and "Wake Me When It's Over").

Jim climbed over Frank Sinatra, Johnny Mathis, Bobby Darin, and other stalwarts as "He'll Have to Go" rose steadily on the pop charts during February and seemed destined to reach number one. But the week of February 21, Percy Faith's dreamy "Theme from *A Summer Place*" slipped into the top spot for a nine-week stay, leaving "He'll Have to Go" to languish for three weeks at number two before yielding to Dion's "Wild One" in March. "He'll Have to Go" garnered perhaps its highest accolades when country comedians Homer and Jethro parodied it and Jeanne Black rushed out the answer "He'll Have to Stay," a Top Ten country and pop hit conceived by Steve Sholes's former associate, Charles Grean. Jim's chrome-detailed song also marked his debut on Britain's *Record Mirror* charts, where it remained for four months, peaking at number eleven.

The hit confirmed in regal fashion that Chet Atkins—with a cast of fine lead vocalists and stellar studio talent—had helped make Nashville a relevant hub in the eyes of the American music industry. It was no longer a sub-section of the New York scene but an independent, viable source of million-selling records. Jim, of course, probably saw his hit's impact differently. "He'll Have to Go"—at least temporarily—allayed his fears of failure, proving his ability to thrive once again in the uptown-country genre to which he loved to apply his voice. It was his brightest moment in ten years of recording, and on April 23, 1960, in the middle of a *Grand Ole Opry* program at the Ryman Auditorium, Chet presented Jim with a gold record for "He'll Have to Go."

To say that Jim Reeves's tremendous appeal to such large and diverse audiences was merely a result of his velvet-smooth voice and Chet's varnished approach to recording country acts is to ignore a major part of the story. The success of "He'll Have to Go" had a great deal to do with RCA Victor's massive and highly organized sales and promotion efforts. Certainly, Steve Sholes had identified Reeves as having major crossover potential as early as 1957 when "Four Walls" began making inroads on the pop charts, and he began marketing Jim in that direction. In fact, former RCA Vice President Jack Burgess, who had dabbled in A&R but concentrated on sales, recalled flying Jim on the wings of "Four Walls" to meet a gathering of writers, northeastern record distributors, and RCA brass at the Concord Hotel in the middle of the Catskill Mountains' "Borsht Belt."

On the Opry *stage, Chet Atkins presents Jim with a gold record for "He'll Have to Go." (Courtesy: Richard Weize)*

"We had a limo pick him up in Newark," said Burgess of what was possibly Reeves's first encounter with RCA's northeastern representatives . "He arrived [at the Concord] about midnight or thereabouts, hungry as a bear. I made arrangements to have some of the chefs stay around to feed him. I remember Jim sitting down asking if we could have a bite to eat. Here we are at the Concord, and he just sits back and relaxes and says, 'Oh it's just good to sit down and relax. Nothing would taste better than a nice mess of ham and eggs.' I looked at him, and the waiter sort of did a double take. I said, 'Jim, how would you settle for a nice filet—good steak and eggs?' He says, 'Hey! That might do it.' I covered him pretty fast that way. I chuckled and the waiter looked at me with a nod and everything was fine. After the waiter was gone, we were sitting there talking for a minute [and] I said, 'I just want you to know while you're here, they follow the [Jewish] dietary laws.' He had no idea what I was talking about, so I had to explain it to him." By 1960, Jim, of course, had become more familiar with the ways of the Northeast and meetings with corporate big-wigs were passé.

RCA Victor had placed reasonable emphasis on promoting country talent since the 1940s, but the big promotional money was always earmarked for the pop artists, who could attract far wider sales. Only Eddy Arnold really had warranted high-level attention from the promotion department—until Jim Reeves came into the picture. In "He'll Have to Go," the RCA sales and promotion staff saw an opportunity to "break" the record in the pop-buying markets of America, the markets that generally spent the most money on albums and singles. Pop records rarely moved in sufficient numbers in the South (Dallas and Atlanta were the primary exceptions), so the markets RCA concentrated on were primarily northern and only marginally interested in country music. "He'll Have to Go" had none of the traditional country markings, so the sales and promotion people took a look at Jim Reeves, who had crossed over before. Since RCA released dozens of singles every month, the sellers and pluggers had to concentrate on the records that had potential to break big. "He'll Have to Go" was nominated.

While other large labels often relied on distributors to promote their records, RCA Victor's distributors also had to move the parent corporation's so-called "white goods": refrigerators, washers, stereos. They could supply stacks of records to local retailers, but they were

terrible at sparking initial interest in a particular song. It was like the
Maytag repairman trying to sell Elvis Presley's latest platter—a bad
match. To remedy the situation, the label placed promotion men in
eight regions of the nation to fill a record-plugging void that RCA's
cumbersome distribution network could not. In late 1959 and early
1960, the eight-man promotion corps hit the streets in such cities as
Philadelphia, Chicago, Cleveland, Detroit, Los Angeles, and Washington, D.C., carrying copies of "He'll Have to Go."

Gordin Bossin, an eager promotion man who covered Michigan
and Ohio, dropped copies of the record in his brief case and visited
disc jockeys such as "Bobbin'" Robin Seymour at WKMH in Dear-
born, Michigan, and Don McLeod at WJBK and Ed McKenzie (a.k.a.
Jack the Bellboy) at WXYZ, both in Detroit. Bossin showed up at the
stations with pizza at night and doughnuts in the morning, looking
for that chance to talk up Jim Reeves.

"Detroit was a hotbed for breaking artists of all types," he
recalled. "You had three or four competitive radio stations working
hard against each other to get the number-one ratings, so the playing
of a new record first was always an important factor. Disc jockeys
liked to get on the air and say, 'Now, for the first time in the metro-
politan area, here's Jim Reeves's new hit.' Breaking records was something that the disc jockey took a lot of pride in, and did to help build
ratings. . . . [It was] the same in Chicago and Cleveland and New
York, Dallas, Los Angeles, Philadelphia. I think that competition
with two and three top radio stations in each of those markets, playing the same kind of music, created that kind of enthusiasm and
excitement. It was just a time period when, if you took an artist
around or even if you took his new record out on a Monday morning,
by the time Tuesday evening rolled around, you had dropped the
record off to about twenty-five different disc jockeys in different time
slots on the air. That second or third day, you'd come back into your
office and the sales manager would say, 'We're getting calls.' You
could break a record in three or four days."

Throughout the nation, RCA's promotion men followed Bossin's
regimen and flooded their respective markets with "He'll Have to
Go." In New York, Johnny Rosica urged the pop-oriented WABC to
give the song a spin, and in Washington, D.C., Auggie "the Doggie"
Blume massaged WWDC's disc jockey Fred Fiske. Jim Reeves
worked the street as well. He chatted with disc jockeys when he and

the Blue Boys pulled into a city, and he even made special trips to promote the record. Bossin recalled bringing Jim over the border from Michigan to Windsor, Ontario, to push the song on Bud Davies's record hop on CKLW Radio.

"If you wanted to work into the night and get up four hours later, he was ready to go," observed Bossin of Reeves's "He'll Have to Go"-inspired work ethic. "He was most cooperative. Most of the country artists were. They were always appreciative of everything you did." Thanks, in part, to the RCA promotional effort, Jim's sweet-sounding record racked up stronger sales than anything he had previously recorded.

"We exposed Jim to everybody, the best we could," summed up the label's vice president of sales, Jack Burgess. "It took a while for people to come around to the conclusion that he was not purely a country artist. That was the general reaction, initially. It took a while, and I don't say it ever really hit full blast. He was never accepted in the pure, so-called pop sense of that period. As a crossover, he was accepted, but he was never classified as a pure pop performer." Although Jim would never be noted as strictly a pop artist, he had recorded and sold a recording that would be remembered as one of the big pop hits of 1960.

10

The success of "He'll Have to Go," revitalized Jim's sagging pop image in the eyes of the public and RCA Victor. RCA's promotional engine now treated almost every Reeves release as a potential "He'll Have to Go" and splashed high-toned advertisements for his records in magazines throughout the nation. Jim was Nashville's ambassador to the mass markets of America, and his record sales illustrated the success of his diplomacy. Of the nine singles that Jim placed on the country charts in the two years following "He'll Have to Go," only one, "Stand at Your Window," lacked the verve to make the *Billboard* Hot 100 pop rankings. His albums also regularly penetrated the pop charts, and there was a dramatic resurgence in the number of invitations to appear on television. Among shows beckoning Jim to appear were Dick Clark's *American Bandstand*, Red Foley's *Jubilee U.S.A.*, and *Today on the Farm*, an NBC program hosted by Eddy Arnold.

In addition to the TV appearances, in 1960 and '61, Jim and the Blue Boys breathlessly raced to play engagements that, naturally, had piled up. Jim dressed Leo, Dean, Mel, and James in tuxedo-cut jackets, bow ties, and slacks, and tried to recreate a quasi-Vegas showroom presentation. For the opening thirty minutes of each show, Leo's guitar work led the Blue Boys through "Yakety Axe," "Poor People of Paris," and "Clarinet Polka," and then tall Texan James Kirkland would step to the mike and introduced Jim. It was all very dignified and about as far from Fabor Robison's String Music Show as Jim could imagine.

But Jim wasn't stupid. He knew that the many fans in Lawton, Texas, and Sidney, Nebraska, and every other city and town remembered "Mexican Joe" and "Bimbo," and connected the songs with Jim Reeves "the country singer." He included an ample serving of the unvarnished songs in his shows, and worked with the Blue Boys to develop some rube humor that the country audiences always seemed to welcome. In the tradition of the Duke of Paducah (Whitey Ford), Rod Brasfield, Stringbean (David Akeman), Lonzo and Oscar, and other country comedians, the Blue Boys became the Lump Lump Boys for a few minutes during Jim's shows. Jim apparently co-opted the name and concept from his memory of the *Louisiana Hayride* house band (Buddy Attaway, Soko Sokolosky, and the Lump Lump Boys), who had dressed in grass skirts, sombreros, and sailor hats, and served as Horace Logan's comic relief.

Art, Mart, Bart, and Fargo—egged on by Jim—garnered gales of laughter that contrasted with the serious tone of Jim's love songs. "When we went into the comedy routine," recalled James Kirkland, "all four of us just laid down our instruments and walked off and just left him. Jim would do 'Streets of Laredo' or 'Scarlet Ribbons,' just him and his guitar." The boys hurried backstage and threw on overalls, straw hats, and checkered shirts—the Lump Lump garb—and waited while Jim's hushed voice closed "Scarlet Ribbons." Then, whatever atmosphere of solemnity that Jim had created was completely shattered as the boys lumbered on stage, carrying instruments that were clearly not in Blue Boy fashion.

"I would play banjo," said Leo Jackson, "and Dean would play fiddle, and Mel would play bass, and [James] would try to play piano. We sounded awful, but that's what Jim wanted." The Lump Lumps frolicked and joked with hillbilly hysteria as Jim played the straight man, and toward the end of the routine—while Dean, Mel, and Leo left to shed their gear—James Kirkland would grab an old liquor jug and trade insults with Jim, a sure catharsis for James if he happened to be angry with his boss.

In general, Jim maintained a breezy pace throughout his concerts. During the course of the night, he bundled his hits into snappy medleys, effortlessly floated his baritone into the audience, and cracked corny jokes. He could play the show—from opening number to closing—with great confidence, largely because the Blue Boys were reliable and could anticipate almost every direction he took. Jim, though, rarely strayed from the routine that he and the band had repeatedly rehearsed.

"At the time," claimed James Kirkland, "we had the best touring group in Nashville, as far as being able to project and sell our show or dance job. We rehearsed. If we got in [to Nashville] at daylight some morning, that would give us time to sleep, get up, and take care of our business. And that night, we'd be back at Jim's house, in the basement, running over stuff that we had been doing for two months, working [on] new stuff, and [for the] the comedy group, . . . we would run over jokes."

Reeves expected a precision performance, and if something behind him went awry, the prickly grouch inside Jim would awaken and bite the Blue Boys—just as it had when the Wagonmasters backed him on stage. "He fired the drummer once," recalled Leo. "Mel had been out drinking the night before. Jim said, 'The people paid their money to get in here. We're going to give them what they paid for. Let's do the best we can.' Mel Rogers wasn't doing that this time. He was looking out there at a girl, and his beat was slowing down. And Jim reached [his foot] back there to pick up the tempo, and it knocked the drum off the stage. It kind of rolled out in the audience. It was really funny, but Jim fired Mel. But he hired him back the next day because Mel had got drunk. He was in terrible shape." Nobody could criticize Jim for demanding the best from the Blue Boys, but for Mel and the rest of the guys, drinking became a sticky, smelly by-product of the unrelenting schedule that Reeves pressed upon himself and the band.

Jim seemed haunted by the specter of anonymity and refused to keep his bus off the road for very long for fear that the record-buying public would forget his name. So, he took whatever dates Hal Smith could book for him and in 1961 tackled what was probably the most hectic touring schedule of his career. During the first six months of the year, Jim and the Blue Boys visited at least sixteen states, and in the latter half of '61, they added nine more states to their road diary and also mounted two treks to Canada. The winding circuit surely drained Jim, but it absolutely kicked the Blue Boys into delirium. The band members took turns driving the bus, and they often had to ply the highways while Jim flew to a date. And when Chet called Jim back Nashville to do a session, the artist frequently took off a few days while the Blue Boys battled monotony on the road.

"He'd catch a plane while we was on the road between dates," said Kirkland, "and he'd go back to Nashville, record, and then he'd

With the Blue Boys at Baltimore's Gwynn Oak Park in August 1961. (Photo by Myrna Ellis)

get on another plane, and we'd pick him up at the next show date on the bus. He would pitch us a tape and say, 'There it is.' And four pieces of us had to duplicate everything on that tape, the background singing and the music. We were always able to do that."

The work and travel were fused together in an unending reel during 1961, and everyone gave up a pound of flesh. Jim had to break away for interviews, RCA-arranged visits to distributors and disc jockeys, and the occasional recording session, while the Blue Boys increasingly turned to alcohol and amphetamines in order to cope. "Bennies" (Benzedrine) were popular among traveling musicians for their eye-peeling abilities, and among the Blue Boys, they had become something akin to vitamins. The pep pills helped to bridge the long miles between towns, as did reading, joke-telling, songwriting, liquor, and poker. "Jim loved poker," said Leo Jackson. "He was kind of stingy. He didn't lose much, but he liked to play."

Liquor, however, appeared to be the drug of choice and seemed to offer a way to lessen the heavy toll that life on the road took on a Blue Boy. "One time we finished up in El Paso," recalled Leo. "So, we'd go across the [Mexico] line to Juarez. We were allowed [to bring back] two quarts of liquor apiece. So, that's eight quarts of liquor. (Jim

On stage in Phoenix. (Photo by Johnny Franklin; courtesy: Frank Anderson)

"Put your sweet lips a little closer . . ." (Photo by Johnny Franklin; courtesy: Frank Anderson)

Jim and Mel Rogers switch jobs. (Photo by Johnny Franklin; courtesy: Frank Anderson)

James Kirkland in Lump Lump costume, clowning with his boss. (Photo by Johnny Franklin; courtesy: Frank Anderson)

The Blue Boys do the Lump Lump Boys. (Photo by Johnny Franklin; courtesy: Frank Anderson)

wasn't with us. He flew back.) By the time we got home—we drove from El Paso to Nashville—all eight quarts of that tequila was gone. We drank all eight quarts in a day and a half."

Bass player and emcee James Kirkland was the first to succumb to the rigors of the road. During the 1961 marathon of engagements, "I went from 180 pounds down to 120," he remembered. "I sung two hours a night. I took care of all the records and the photo albums [that Jim sold], plus I did 90 percent of the bus driving. I got to drinking and doping pretty heavy, and it wasn't because I wanted to do that. I had talked to Jim about getting a bus driver, and I told him, 'I'm killing myself.' He had a word or two of sarcasm to say. . . . We were in Canada at the time that it happened, and we got to where we were going and we were unloading everything, and he apologized. He said, 'I want to do something that I've never done in my life. I want to apologize. I was out of line.' I said, 'If you're man enough to apologize, I'll be man enough to accept it and go on.' But after that, it never was the same." Physical exhaustion and a growing resentment of Reeves led Kirkland down the steps of the touring bus and back to a day job in Texas.

"Jim was from the old school," Kirkland continued. "He thought if he paid you just enough to exist on, he could depend on you. And that really wasn't so. I told him one time, 'You got an exceptional group of musicians. Every time we walk out on the stage, we got one thing in mind, and that's to make you look as good as we can make you look, and nobody is trying to take anything away from you. We work for you, and we work with you, and in making you look good, we make ourselves look good. You really need to appreciate us just a little bit more than you do.' It wasn't long after that till I left."

James Kirkland bid adios to the Blue Boys in early 1962, just in time to miss the international segment of Reeves's jam-packed touring itinerary. The favorable reception abroad of "He'll Have to Go" had confirmed for RCA Victor's management that Jim could indeed build markets for the company in foreign countries, particularly European countries. However, it was becoming apparent to the label that Jim had another nation to conquer via personal appearances, a nation with many people of European descent but which lay thousands of miles from Europe. That nation was South Africa.

In the spring of 1962, Bob Yorke, RCA's head of A&R, had met a South African at the opening of the company's studios in Rome and received an earful about his standard-bearing Nashville artist, Jim Reeves. Gerald McGrath, who manufactured and released RCA's product in South Africa (via Teal Records), buttonholed Yorke and asked when Reeves, as well as Chet Atkins and Floyd Cramer, would be touring his country. In its recounting of the meeting, *Billboard* wrote that McGrath "was anxious to have Atkins, Reeves, and Cramer perform in person because they are highly popular in South Africa." Reeves, according to *Billboard*, had sold more records in that country than Elvis Presley. Yorke immediately tapped Dick Broderick in RCA's international division to arrange with Teal Records a tour of South Africa featuring Reeves, Atkins, and Cramer.

It would be one of the first tours by American country artists to bypass American military bases abroad and play strictly the civilian market, or the "economy," as the RCA executives termed it. For many South Africans, the tour would intensify the love they carried for Jim Reeves and his music. Atkins, Cramer, and American artists from other labels, such as Frankie Laine and Dinah Shore, also had racked up significant sales in South Africa, but Jim's popularity there outshone them all.

American record companies had long shown interest in South Africa, and when *Billboard* reported in 1956 that an average hit in that nation sold between sixty thousand and seventy thousand copies, it was evident that the labels were making remarkable inroads there. Still, there was much more gold to be mined from the record-buying market, which, according to *Billboard*, included two and a half million white buyers and one million black buyers. The possibilities in South Africa had attracted Columbia, Decca, and Mercury, but no label seemed to be doing as well as RCA with its lustrous roster that featured Jim Reeves and Elvis Presley (not to mention Chet Atkins and Floyd Cramer).

Country and western music appealed to many South Africans because its themes of frontiers and rural living were a very real part of South Africa's corner of the world. Jim Reeves's popularity most likely stemmed from his virile voice, which, among the nation's men, may have conjured images of the ideal South African male who could face life in a rugged country, and among the women, perhaps invoked dreams of the man they longed to marry. There were probably countless reasons for his appeal in South Africa, but it was singularly evident that among many people there—black and white—Jim Reeves was virtually worshipped. "If the population of this country could have produced a singer of their own," remarked one South African, "that's who they would have produced." For proof of that phenomenon, one need only to have observed the reception that Jim and the troupe received upon their arrival in Johannesburg.

Jim, Chet, Floyd, the Blue Boys (who now featured Bobby Dyson on bass), and comedian Dick O'Shaunessy (a veteran of the 1957 European tour) left Nashville for South Africa on August 16, 1962, and after stops in New York and Rome, they landed in Johannesburg on August 21. As the RCA caravan's aircraft taxied off the runway at Jan Smuts Airport, Jim and the rest peered out the windows to see a crowd that could only be likened to those Elvis Presley had confronted in the U.S. in the 1950s. According to press reports, some three thousand people had thronged to the fringes of the tarmac to greet the Americans, and young and old, black and white, they "outscreamed the screaming engines of the Boeing jet."

Jim, Chet, and Floyd, feeling good about stretching their legs, lumbered down the steps into mass confusion. They were introduced to the fans over loudspeakers and then were hustled into the terminal for a press conference. As the trio spoke to reporters inside, the crowd outside virtually surrounded the building and clogged the path from the door to a line of waiting cars that included a red Cadillac convertible. When the meeting with reporters concluded, it took a phalanx of armed policemen to clear a way to the cars for Jim and the rest.

"We made it to the cars," said Leo Jackson, "and all the way— it was about four or five miles—to the hotel, people were lined up." Amid three policemen on motorcycles and an ad hoc swarm of teenage motorcyclists, the cars—led by the red Caddy—snaked through the streets, determined to reach the hotel on Eloff Street in Johannesburg. Hundreds of cars tailed Jim, according to the press, and at a busy intersection, a group of "screamagers" flooded into the road to halt the cars and demand autographs. The Americans had never witnessed such pandemonium. They could only lurch through the human roadblock and hope nobody would be hurt. There was no escape, it seemed, as the chain of wildly enthusiastic fans stretched all the way to the hotel, where hundreds more were waiting to attack Jim and the rest.

"When we got to the hotel," continued Jackson, "[and were] try-ing to get out of the car . . . they were grabbing at us, at our clothes, and they tore some of our clothes. Jim, he had on this nice Italian-cut suit [with a] red lining inside, and they just tore it, ripped it." The fans surged forward, and as the musicians tumbled into the revolving doors of the hotel, the frenetic crowd trapped them between the tall glass panes. "We did make it inside, and Floyd, he was really shook up. He took his sunglasses and threw them to the floor. . . . You could tell that the [hotel management] people had talked to the help in the hotel and told them not to bother us because it looked like they were scared to death when we walked into the lobby. But when Floyd threw his sunglasses onto the floor and they broke, this girl couldn't contain herself. She ran out from behind the counter and picked up the pieces: 'Oh please! I've got to have this. I've got to have this.' So, Floyd let her keep them, but he was that shook up that it scared the hell out of him."

The performers all dashed to their rooms, to safety. Like Floyd, Jim also had obviously been spooked. Blood ran from his hand, the result of his worshippers' efforts to strip a ring from his finger. "I never expected anything like this," he told a reporter later. "I only managed to keep my ring by clenching my fist." Even in the rooms, however, Jim felt as if there were no escape. Like a crowd of revolu-tionaries demanding to see their leader, the South Africans clamored for Jim from the street. "Jim Reeves! Jim Reeves!" They were adamant and carried on until Jim relented. "He seemed reluctant," wrote a reporter on the scene, "but eventually obliged, waving and blowing kisses at the crowd. They responded with hysterical screams. Then, apparently satisfied, they dispersed."

The "hysterical screams" rarely abated as the RCA team flew on a small Viking airplane to the South African cities of Pretoria, Dur-ban, Port Elizabeth, Capetown, Bloemfontien, Kimberley, Nelspruit, and Salisbury. "People just flocked to see Jim," recalled Leo. "He was like a god in South Africa [to] blacks, not only whites." In fact, from Cape Agulhas to the Limpopo River, the Americans were treated like royalty wherever they traveled. And the arrangements the tour plan-ners and promoters had made were like nothing the artists had ex-perienced in America. Leo, who was accustomed to setting up and breaking down his own equipment, sat back and enjoyed while oth-ers handled the chore. "They had big [trucks] carrying all this stuff.

We had private planes to fly us everywhere. I saw the guitar when I
went on stage. I would tune it, and when we got through, I'd set the
guitar down and that's the last time I'd see it until the next show.
That was great. We'd go off stage and have beer, girls, and food."

On stage, Jim received enthusiastic ovations. But on sporadic
occasions, the applause Chet Atkins attracted dwarfed Jim's. In
Port Elizabeth, reviewers crowned Chet king of the show. "I think
he got more applause and louder applause than the number-one
billing, Mr. Reeves," observed one reviewer. "There is no doubt
that this moon-faced Texan knows how to sing, but he lacked
showmanship sparkle that a person expects from a top entertainer.
After the gigantic programme build-up, it was an anti-climax when
he walked on to the stage." Another reviewer who attended the
same show agreed that Jim lacked stage presence, but he seemed to
think that was a trivial deficit. "He . . . showed that he is no great
shakes as a showman. But who needs to be a showman when he
has a baritone voice so mellow, soothing and round. The tweetalige Texan warmed the hearts of his admirers with two Afrikaans
songs, 'Ou Kalahari' and 'Ek Verlang na Jou.'" (Jim's pronunciation
of the foreign lyrics was virtually perfect.)

During down times, the tour organizers arranged for the performers to see slices of South African landscape and culture, and on
one such excursion, Jim, Floyd, and Chet received a scare that surpassed the frightful pandemonium that greeted them on their arrival
in Johannesburg. Their pilot, Bill De Meillon, had flown the trio to a
rugby match, but later, as they were preparing to fly to an evening
concert in Cape Town, news of bad weather blew in. Cape Town airport was closed, but De Meillon was concerned about the lost revenue and disappointed fans if Jim and his companions missed the
date. He faced a quandary: Should he attempt to fly to Cape Town
despite the foul weather or ground his plane and force cancellation
of the show? De Meillon chose to go and received special clearance
to land in Cape Town.

The old plane's fuselage was made of wood and canvas. (It had
appeared so rickety to Jim at the outset of the tour that he exclaimed,
"We're going in that?") De Meillon took off in reasonably good
weather, but as the Viking aircraft approached Cape Town, he
encountered the worst weather he had ever seen from the cockpit. As
the plane shook in the rough air, he looked to his left and right and

saw ice—a potential kiss of death—building on the wings. To evade
the turbulence and dangerous icing, he climbed seventeen thousand
feet—too high, really, for the unpressurized plane. Telling everyone
to remain still, he leapfrogged over the weather and executed a sharp,
rattling descent into the Cape Town airport. Everyone was shaken,
particularly Jim and Floyd Cramer, but they made the concert. "I'm
still blue with cold," Jim told the audience that night.

Despite such extraordinary events, and the lukewarm reception
in Port Elizabeth, the South African tour further solidified Jim's following there. Jim had penetrated the lucrative market far more
deeply than any other American artist, a situation that would benefit
him and his record label. He departed in early September, promising
to return. Upon his arrival back in the United States, Jim recorded a
handful of songs in the Afrikaans language (they appeared with material performed by Chet and Floyd on the South African-released
album *In Suid Afrika*), and he entertained an offer to play the lead in
a South African film production. If there had been any question
before the South Africa trek, there was little doubt afterward that Jim
Reeves was indeed an international star.

For Jim, there was more to life than chasing hits and playing
concert dates from Port Elizabeth, South Africa, to Port Arthur,
Texas. He was a man who enjoyed outdoor activities such as golf
and hunting, and although those diversions may not have relieved
the stress that discolored his personality, he at least could leave his
work behind occasionally to pursue other interests. The fields and
forests of Panola County had provided sustenance to the Reeves
family in the 1920s and '30s, and they also revealed to Jim the plea-
sures that could be found in the Great Outdoors. As a child, he had
fished in Socagee Creek and hunted small game with his older
brothers; as an adult, Jim continued to fish and hunt, but for sport
rather than necessity.

Those who knew Jim during his Shreveport days knew that fishing ran a close second to music in his life, and his former Henderson
Oilers teammate Leo Ferguson (who had steered Jim to KGRI)
recalled fishing and hunting trips in East Texas with Jim long after he
exited baseball. "One time we was going to go fishing [on the] Sabine
River," said Ferguson of one such trip. "We was going to set out trot-
lines and squirrel hunt. Well, we got down on them oil field roads,

and it rained. We got stuck before we got to the river. We dug and we did everything we could to get out, and we couldn't get out. I said, 'Hell, let's just go to sleep.' You get in the backseat, and I'll get in the front seat. We ain't wet a hook, and we ain't killed a squirrel.' Finally, an oil field man came down through there the next morning and pulled us out, and we just came on home.

"We went squirrel hunting," continued Ferguson, describing another botched trip, "and he had an automatic .22. We walked and walked and hadn't seen no squirrels. We finally seen this tree, and it was just running wild with gray squirrels. He shot one time and killed a squirrel, and his gun jammed. He couldn't shoot anymore the rest of the day. He got a little disturbed then, I'll tell you." In hunting, as in baseball and singing, some outings are better than others. Even during the seemingly endless tours that followed the release of "He'll Have to Go," Jim managed to escape to the wilds of East Texas to hunt turkey and deer, or to the pristine beauty of Table Rock Lake in southern Missouri to angle for bass. For less involved excursions, Jim would head for Nashville's golf courses with Mary or a regular RCA Victor contingent that included Chet Atkins and Eddy Arnold.

One of Jim's constant companions in pursuit of game during the 1960s was songwriter Alex Zanetis. A former operatic performer and the son of an Illinois oilman, Zanetis had exactly one country hit under his composing belt (Faron Young's 1961 recording of "Backtrack") when he brought Jim Reeves the song "I'm Gonna Change Everything." Recorded with a cha-cha beat, the song reached number two on the country charts in late 1962 and crossed over to the pop charts for two weeks. It was the usual routine for a Reeves hit: climb high on the country charts and then jump into the pop Hot 100. What was unusual about "I'm Gonna Change Everything" was Zanetis's presentation of the tune to Jim. Alex was living in Illinois at the time, and while sitting around with a Nashville guitarist, he came up with a composition that seemed suited to Jim Reeves. The guitarist, Max Powell (who would later play for and manage Webb Pierce), tried to reach Jim in Nashville by telephone to pitch the song, but he learned that Reeves and the Blue Boys were in Indianapolis. A call to Curtis Artists Productions pinpointed Jim's hotel. Zanetis was a pilot and owned a plane, so he, Powell, and another picker who was hanging around hopped into the aircraft for the short flight to Naptown, arriving in the wee hours before dawn.

From that point, Zanetis's pitching methods became, well, unconventional. "I went up to the motel room and knocked the door in," recalled Zanetis. "[Jim] grabbed the telephone, and I said if he touched that telephone, I'd break his arm. He was still in bed, and he said, 'Take whatever you want. Just don't hurt me.' I said, 'I'm not going to hurt you. You're going to listen to five songs. Four ain't going to be any good, but you're going to record one, and it's going to be a number-one song.' (And he's still under the covers, just shaking.) I sang three songs and segued into 'I'm Gonna Change Everything.' He crawled from the side of the bed and said, 'Jesus Christ, Ricky Nelson would give his left nut for that song!' From that day on, we were the best of friends."

They did indeed become friends, and Zanetis began writing for Jim's publishing companies. Within eighteen months of Jim's recording of "I'm Gonna Change Everything" in June of 1962, he waxed four Zanetis songs in the RCA Victor studios, including the 1963 country-pop hit "Guilty." When the songwriter moved to Nashville, he frequently stayed with Jim and Mary, and often set out with Jim on his sporting adventures. They often winged their way to fishing and hunting locations in Wisconsin, Florida, Kentucky, and other spots where boys could be boys.

In Florida, Zanetis recalled, a day of deep-sea fishing would often conclude in a bar, and the songwriter would typically saunter over to the piano to bang out his compositions. One evening, however, a female admirer plopped down on the bench with him and proceeded to take his mind off the music. "Then, she reached over and gave me a great big kiss," recalled Zanetis. "She said, 'I'm so sorry. I'm sorry, but I don't know what the aroma is. It just drove me crazy.' I said, 'That's just aftershave lotion.' She said, 'I'm sorry . . . sorry . . . sorry.' Jim's just standing there, and his eyes are going out of his head. This good-looking gal's just making all over me. Jim was a woman chaser himself, and so, Jim came over and said, 'What's the trouble?' She said, 'I just couldn't help myself. This aftershave he's wearing—what is it?' I said, 'Aqua Velva.' So, she just apologized and it all passed.

"A month later, I'm landing a plane [near] Kentucky Lake, on a private little airstrip. [Jim and I] got a cabin rented for a week. We got a plane packed with stacks of groceries, which we had paid for fifty-fifty. When we got to the cabin, we're unloading all the goodies, putting them on a shelf. Suddenly, Jim grabs a packet and puts it behind his back. I said, 'What's that?' He said, 'What?' 'What you're hiding behind your back?' He said, 'Nothing,' I said, 'It came out of the sack.' He said, 'It's nothing!' I said, 'Look, we're fifty-fifty. I paid for half of the groceries. Now, whatever you got is half mine. What do you got behind your back?' He slowly brought around a bottle of Aqua Velva aftershave."

Before Zanetis landed that grocery-laden plane near Kentucky Lake, chances are that at various points during the flight, Jim had taken a turn at the controls. After so many flights on Zanetis's plane to hunting and fishing spots, Jim had begun to get the bug to fly. It was a new dimension to outdoor life, offering a feeling of dominion over the sky. Jim thirsted to join his friend in the ranks of the airborne. Zanetis had earned his pilot's license in the 1950s and evidently had influenced others to learn to fly once he appeared on the Nashville scene in 1962.

"Guys in the band, guys in the studio, all started flying," said Zanetis. He panicked when word reached him that his first interpreter, Faron Young, had taken a notion to try his hand at flying. "I said, 'Faron, somebody told me you're going to go out and buy a plane tomorrow.' He said, 'You know I wouldn't do that without asking you, Alex.' I said, 'I hope not.' He hadn't even started flying yet. Well, the next morning, he had a check . . . burning in his pocket, and he went out and bought a plane. He started flying and taking passengers." A cockiness suffused Faron that Zanetis feared would bring an unpleasant end to the flying career of the "Singing Sheriff." Although Young never crashed his plane, Patsy Cline, Cowboy Copas, and Hawkshaw Hawkins all would die in a plane crash on March 5, 1963. Cline's manager, Randy Hughes, also died in the mishap. He had been at the controls of the Piper Comanche, which, according to Alex Zanetis, Hughes had purchased from him just thirty days before.

Had Jim decided to take up flying after the Cline crash, Zanetis may have protested adamantly. He doubted Jim's ability to manage the intricacies of flying. "When I would fly him," said Zanetis, "he would want to take the wheel, like a little kid wants to take the wheel from daddy. He was very skittish and nervous. One time when I had the plane in a slow descent, I was looking at a map and let him have the wheel. And I heard him just grunt and moan. I looked over, and he was staring straight ahead. I looked where he was staring and there was a big ole four-engine plane coming right up at us. I took the wheel away from him and turned it off course. He was just petrified. He was the kind of pilot that—if I let him land it—if he bounced [the plane on the runway] once, he'd brood for two days because he bounced it. He had no business flying." Nevertheless, Jim began taking lessons, and appropriating the controls from Zanetis more often. "He didn't have the mind for flying. Some kids got all the guts, and they know the front end of the plane and the back end of the plane and the guts of the plane. They're mechanically minded. He was not. He was not plane-minded, but he still wanted to do it."

Zanetis, though, grew more worried about Jim's skyward aspirations upon discovering that the aeronautical licensing authorities required only a few hours of practice "under the hood" (an opaque shield that instructors place over the cockpit windows to train neophyte pilots how to navigate solely by instruments). "I was very much against that ruling because . . . the six hours gave them a [false sense of security]. They could fly [by instruments only] because they did it going around the airport with an instructor with them."

With diversions such as flying and hunting, as well as the affirming success of "He'll Have to Go," the brisk sales of subsequent releases, and his expanding international acclaim, one perhaps would have expected Jim to curb his intransigence and white-hot temper. If anything, though, he became more temperamental and inscrutable. "He'll Have to Go," South Africa, and his pleasure trips with Alex Zanetis failed to permanently brighten his demeanor and quell his insecurities. He seemed incapable of truly relaxing. "[Jim] was not one to nap in the sun very much," said Zanetis. "He got out on the boat, and he loved it, but I don't think he ever really unwound."

One evening while traveling between concert dates, Jim reclined amidst the steady droning of his tour bus, nipped at a bottle, and gave voice to his uncertainties. "I don't know what it is," he blurted out to the band members. "I can't sing. What is it about me that they like? I can't sing." Leo Jackson and the guys laughed uneasily, marveling at Jim's atypical display of weakness. However, he appeared to them to be sincere.

"Jim," reassured Leo, "you can sing. You got that thing that people relate to."

"Well, I don't know what it is."

It was apparent that Jim was still searching for the next step in his career. After posting pop hits, playing concert halls, and appearing on such mainstream television programs as *American Bandstand* and *The Ed Sullivan Show*, Jim Reeves and the Blue Boys still performed on the midways of amusement parks, on the dusty stages of county fairs, and in the dank dance halls of Texas. When he and the Blue Boys played swanky venues, he felt naked, like a parvenu, unable to truly satisfy the audience. He seemed to be embarrassed by his country side when his schedule brought him to upscale engagements. On such occasions, he hired old standby comedian Dick O'Shaugnessy to embellish the show, and in 1962, for a two-week engagement at the posh Caves Theatre and Restaurant in Vancouver, British Columbia, Jim stretched to take the act uptown. He adorned the Blue Boys in real tuxedos (instead of the usual tuxedo-cut suits), and to the band's amazement, hired a choreographer to teach them a dance routine. "The choreography didn't do shit because nobody could dance and play," recalled Leo. "I couldn't. I could move around a little—a few steps here, a few steps there. Nobody else could either. Mel Rogers, he tried to dance and the beat went to hell. Jim gave up on that."

"He always felt like he wasn't a showman," continued Jackson. "He was one of those that wanted to do a real show. He didn't want to just stand there and sing, which was the norm for country artists at the time. That's why he would make us do funny things. . . . Jim always felt like we had to give people more than him just singing. He just didn't feel like that was enough. He was wrong, of course. People were very happy to stand there and hear him sing."

Jim Reeves was a perfectionist and understandably sought the best presentation possible onstage and on record. But his character could not just be defined by a simple blue-collar determination to exceed his expectations and what he perceived as the expectations of others. Jim could be more clearly understood in the context of his lifelong desire to get what he wanted, which perhaps was fed by the indulgence he had received as a child and then exacerbated by the shining allure of baseball and then music. Jim's unmitigated drive, though, became a witch's brew when his haunting fear of failure raised its head. Then, his insecurity manifested itself not only in tinkering with his stage act or quiet admissions of inadequacy, but also in venomous attacks on those with whom he worked. He at various times appeared to be rude, ungracious, cranky, or even possessed by demons. Of course, the sum of Jim's character included more than those ugly traits, but his insecurities, his drive to outdo himself, and the indulgence he received as a youngster and later as a star snowballed, making many of those around him wish for a different kind of Jim Reeves.

RCA engineer Bill Porter, who had worked the "He'll Have to Go" session and many others for Chet and Jim, had often witnessed the storm that Jim's temper could unleash. As Porter told John Rumble of the Country Music Foundation, the storm turned in his direction during a 1962 studio date. It would be the engineer's last session with the volatile singer.

"Jim's attitude was somewhat arrogant, somewhat hard," Porter told Rumble. "We had one session I remember; Jim called the session for Sunday afternoon. Chet didn't want to come and I didn't want to come because of the crazy hours we were both working. [Jim] had heard a drummer down in Printer's Alley [a dining and entertainment district in Nashville] that he really liked, a guy about seventeen years old, so he wanted to book this session and use this drummer. The kid came in and he was scared to death. Here's all these pro musicians, and he couldn't get it together. Chet and I were kind of angry about the whole thing anyway, but I was angrier than Chet was because I was working more hours than Chet at that time. So, finally I pushed the talk-back button. I said, "Jim Reeves, leave the drummer alone. He's doing the best he can." Oh, he freaked out! He come flying into the control room. He says to Chet, "You tell your engineer to shut up! This is *my* session, not his!" So we went into it, we really did. As a result of that, I didn't work any more Jim Reeves sessions. It was not quite a physical battle, but close to it.

Chet Atkins, too, weathered the explosions, although Jim generally reserved them for those who he considered to be underlings. But, nonetheless, Alex Zanetis once saw his pal absolutely manhandle the producer over the composition "Guilty," which became a country-pop hit for Jim in late 1963. "I had pitched that song for two and a half years," explained Zanetis. "Faron called it a piece of shit. Owen Bradley [of] Decca was in my living room in Florida, and I played it for him. He shook it off. Down in Panama City [with Jim], I went over to the piano in a piano bar in the middle of the afternoon and started messing around and got to playing 'Guilty.' Jim was sitting next to the bar and said, 'What's that?' I said, 'That's a favorite little song of mine, and I'm the only fan it's got.' He said, 'Let me hear some more.' And I played it, and he walked over and he said, 'I want to record that.' I couldn't believe it, but he did. He did it against Chet Atkins's approval."

On February 27, 1963, Jim recorded "Guilty" in Nashville, and the song exceeded three minutes in length, which was unusual as most A&R men assumed that disc jockeys ignored songs that were so long. Jim, in fact, had recorded few songs over three minutes in his entire career. "A couple of months later," continued Zanetis, "we were on another trip, and I heard him on the phone with Chet. He said, 'Look, you son of a bitch, put the song out.' That's pretty rough language. Chet is no slouch; he's a gentleman's gentleman. To hear him on the phone talking like that! 'I don't give a shit if it's eleven minutes and three seconds long, put it out!' I knew that 'Guilty' was three minutes and eleven seconds.* At that time anything over three minutes was kind of a no-no."

Zanetis noted that, despite Reeves's volatile nature, Jim could comport himself as a perfect gentleman at times. He was exceedingly gracious around Alex's wife and children, and the searing flame of Jim's temper never blazed toward Zanetis himself. Still, Zanetis seems to have been around for more than one of Jim's tirades. "One time they were having a birthday party for him at his home, and Chet Atkins was there and several other people of that caliber. [Jim] snapped at his wife and humiliated her just awful. He had a violent temper, I remember."

What Zanetis witnessed was not an anomaly; many visitors to the Reeves's Madison home noted that Mary generally remained hushed around Jim and flourished when he left the house. Clearly, his quick temper leached into his personal life and tested the patience and dignity of Mary, in particular. She had devoted her life and work to supporting Jim, and she tolerated his unfaithfulness. Part of the package also involved withstanding his outbursts, as she did during the birthday party.

"She would just cower," remembered Zanetis. "She was quite a nice lady, quite a fine lady. But she just couldn't handle him [that

---

*"Guilty" actually clocked in at three minutes and nine seconds.

night] because he was in a frenzy. He was very violent, and he was very demanding. She just cowered back up in a corner and just took it. She didn't fire back; she had no defense. It was just a shame and an embarrassment in front of everyone. When they were alone, I don't know what she might have said to him, but my expectations are it wasn't a hell of a lot because he was so dominating."

11

Jim's career crossed into a new dimension in 1963. There were already so many dimensions—country music star, pop star, television personality, international star—but film star would be the latest sobriquet applied to the mercurial performer. Jamie Uys Film Productions of South Africa signed Jim to star in *Kimberley Jim*, a tale of an American gambler, Jim Madison, who wins a South African diamond mine in a crooked card game. Originally titled *Strike It Rich*, the movie's name was changed to emphasize Reeves's connection with the production. *Kimberley Jim* followed a formulaic plot—plenty of fights, girls, and pauses to allow Jim's singing—but in South Africa, it may as well have been *Gone with the Wind*. Jim Reeves was South Africa's favorite entertainer, and enthusiastic audiences anxiously awaited him in cinemas across the nation. Filming was to begin in March, and the visit would also include a few concert appearances in the African nation.

After a tour of the American Midwest that confined Jim to the road for most of February, plus three days of recording in late February and early March, Jim and the Blue Boys (who would also star in the production) departed Nashville for Johannesburg on March 7, 1963. As Jim winged his way across the Atlantic, his single "Is This Me?" (written by ambitious young songwriter and Starday recording artist Dottie West) was climbing high on the country charts but struggling to make the pop charts. His past few country hits, in fact, had barely penetrated the pop listings, falling far short of the precedent set by "He'll Have to Go." Returning home as a film star, Jim perhaps hoped, would place him more securely in the category of popular music. "The movie," Mary Reeves told interviewer Dixie Deen, "was just another of the goals which Jim had in the back of his mind, just like the big records." *Kimberley Jim* was scheduled for release in America in 1964, after its debut in South Africa.

The crew arrived in Johannesburg on March 11, and almost immediately, the RCA licensee in South Africa, Teal Records, ushered Jim into a studio there to record. During his visit, Jim was slated to record several numbers for the *Kimberley Jim* soundtrack, but the hurried first session was unscheduled and designed to capitalize on the American success of Ned Miller's "From a Jack to a King"—which, interestingly, had been released on Fabor Records. Miller's hit had made it into the Top Ten on the American country and pop charts in early 1963 and in March had begun a swift rise on the British charts. It was only a matter of weeks, perhaps, until "From a Jack to a King" crossed the South African border, so RCA had prodded Teal to wax a version by Jim when he arrived in Johannesburg. It was felt that a cover version of the song by Reeves could conceivably blunt Miller's potential in South Africa.

Although RCA often had been victimized by foreign labels that piggybacked on its American hits, it was apparent that it too thwarted the foreign potential of songs produced by competing labels. The company tipped off its licensees about popular American songs and urged them to produce covers for their local markets. The practice accorded RCA no financial profit, but if the recommended song became a hit, it enhanced the prestige of the licensee, which in turn benefited RCA. For Jim's part, he probably was delighted to take part in the scheme to foil Fabor Robison in South Africa.

In Johannesburg, Teal brought Jim into the Electrical and Musical Industries (EMI) studio, where he would be working with Bill Walker, Teal's musical director. Walker, an Australian who had attended the Sydney Conservatory of Music, had worked with Jim, Chet, and Floyd on the 1962 tour and was tapped to write the arrangements and conduct the orchestra on "From a Jack to a King," as well as on all the movie music. Walker would also conduct the orchestra that was slated to appear behind Jim and the Blue Boys on the South African concerts. A major portion of Bill Walker's duties with Teal, however, involved recording American or European hits for the South African market. "I would copy arrangements, go in the studio and record it, and get it released before [the competing] record was out," said Walker.

In March 1963, he found Jim a very willing conspirator in the
plot against Miller and Robison's "From a Jack to a King." "He
thought it would be fun," recalled Walker. "We went in, we recorded,
and in two weeks we had a national hit. . . . He thought I was the best
thing since toilet paper." "From a Jack to a King," which seemed ide-
ally suited to Reeves, acquired the brilliance of South African gold
and became one of the nation's top-selling recordings that year.

More important than underscoring Jim's following in South
Africa, "From a Jack to a King" unveiled a slightly altered vocal
delivery that was perhaps inspired by the grand, expansive arrangements that Walker had penned for the *Kimberley Jim* soundtrack. In
his performance of "From a Jack to a King," Jim moved closer to a
classically styled pronunciation that was more reminiscent of a
Broadway singer than a Nashville warbler. When Reeves and Walker
turned to material for the movie soundtrack, the change was more
evident still. On such songs as "Born to Be Lucky," "Diamonds in the
Sand," "Roving Gambler," and others, Jim—probably with Walker's
coaching—eschewed the traditional rock-country emphasis on consonants and caressed the vowels of the songs. For example, in his
rendition of the lovely ballad "Is This Me?" (the hit on the American
charts when he departed in March), Jim rushed through words like
"leaving" and "thinking" and dwelled on the ending "ng" sounds.

There was nothing unusual about that styling in Nashville or in
other studios where rock and country singers recorded. However, a
"higher-toned" singer would never think of lingering on the conso-
nant sounds, and in South Africa, Jim took on the coloring of such a
singer. On "Diamonds in the Sand," he drew out the "saaa" in the
lyric "sand" rather than skating to the "nd" as his normal approach
dictated. "He moved into another idiom," recalled Walker. "He
moved it up to off-Broadway." The alteration seemed insignificant to
the ear because, as usual, Jim's pleasing bass-baritone voice was the
songs' drawing card. Nonetheless, the new styling traveled back to
the United States with Jim after the movie's completion.

On the celluloid side of Jim's work in South Africa, he appeared
to adapt to the role of film star easily, although the acting itself presented more of a challenge to him. Jim's co-star, Clive Parnell, who
played the gambler's impish sidekick, observed a big-name entertainer who, naturally, felt nervous and uneasy in (and was perhaps
unimpressed by) his first acting role. The English-born Parnell had

acted on the stage but was making his film debut also. "He was a lit-tle unsure with dialog," recalled Parnell. "He had difficulty learning dialog. He was getting bored with having to learn it all, so I would take a bit more of his [lines] because I didn't have a problem learning dialog." The hurry-up-and-wait tedium of movie work, as well as his shaky footing as an actor, frustrated Jim. But when it was time to do his singing scenes, he flourished.

"He got impatient, and he got a little flustered," said Parnell of Jim's introduction to acting. "You know what it's like on a movie set. When the lights are up, you tend to sweat anyway, but when you're nervous and a little unsure, you actually look like you've been standing in a shower. Of course, he wore a hairpiece, which took quite a bit of looking after under those circumstances. But in the bits that led into the songs, he seemed to sort of gain confidence from the fact that, immediately after what he was about to say, he would get to sing. Because as soon as he got to sing, he was a different personality altogether."

According to Parnell, Jim also became a "different personality" when producer-director Emil Nofal ordered take after take in order to correct mistakes that the other actors or extras had made. This threw Jim into fits and often put Parnell in the role of mediator between his co-star and Nofal. And it wasn't just the multiple retakes that angered Jim, according to Parnell.

"When we first went to the outdoor set, we walked into [Jim's] caravan and, of course, the fridge wasn't plugged in because they hadn't worked out a way to get the generator close enough to plug the fridge in so [it] would work," he recalled. "Jim Reeves walked in, and I walked behind him, and he walked around the caravan and he opened the fridge and he turned and walked back out. I followed him, and we walked back to the limo, got in the limo, and everybody was absolutely agog. And he said to the driver, 'Would you take me back to the hotel, please?' He hadn't said [another] word. [Emil Nofal] came up and said, 'What's going on here?' Jim said, 'I'll come back when the fridge is plugged in and when it's fully stocked.' (I think it was Seagram's V.O. he drank.) We just drove off the set, and I thought it was just the most remarkable thing."

Nofal, a dashing director who resembled a cross between Errol Flynn and Clark Gable, was a twenty-five-year veteran of the South African film industry and was hardly accustomed to such impudence

Looking on with actress June Neethling, who played Elize in Kimberley Jim. (Courtesy: Frank Anderson)

Jim Madison and Gerry Bates (played by Clive Parnell) hawk their wares. (Courtesy: Frank Anderson)

Jim Reeves as Jim Madison in Kimberley Jim. *That's bass player Bobby Dyson behind Jim. (Courtesy: Frank Anderson)*

from his actors. But the magnitude of Jim's popularity was unmatched by that of any actor with whom he had previously worked. For Nofal, landing Jim Reeves for the starring role in the South African production of *Kimberley Jim* was akin to a Hollywood producer signing mega-star Cary Grant to appear in a film of *Ben Hur*-like proportions.

"Emil was a pretty glamorous-looking guy," said Clive Parnell, "and he used to smoke cigarettes in a cigarette holder. He had that kind of old-style movie producer/director/magnate look about him. Of course, he was always used to all the ladies freaking out to get into his movies. And all us actors were really quite keen to be in his movies as well. He was used to being treated with the utmost respect, whereas Jim treated him as kind of a [regular] guy. Emil had to try to treat Jim differently than us. But Jim saw what was going down, and he absolutely insisted that I be treated exactly the way that he was treated, which was very wonderful for the six weeks that he was here. But then I had to finish the picture. After he'd gone, I was given the most unbelievable riot because I lived like a star for six weeks, and now it was time to bring me down to earth."

The shooting schedule for *Kimberley Jim* had been arranged so that Jim's parts would be filmed first, allowing him to head back to the U.S. and leaving Nofal and the crew to splice together the rest of the production. Few people, except perhaps for Clive, waved wistfully when Jim exited the set. "I think everybody was hugely amazed that this gentleman who sang with such a wonderfully tender voice could turn into a bit of monster," said Parnell. "But [the explosions weren't] ever in front of a big enough crowd for it to have any impact on [his] image." In fact, many South Africans mobbed Jim just as they had in 1962, and every day outside the set, hundreds of gasping fans jockeyed for a glimpse of their American idol.

If word of Jim's moody tantrums leaked from the set, it wasn't evident in his worshippers' faces. They loved him, and when "From a Jack to a King" earned Jim a gold record while he was filming in South Africa, the song's burgeoning sales confirmed their adoration. Reeves performed his cover version in concert at the University of Pretoria on April 3, and a reviewer commented that the crowd's response was so enthusiastic, it shook the venue. "The crowd went fairly mad," wrote the *Pretoria News*, "and never has the campus echoed to such shrill whistles and prolonged shouts. Jim sounds real good when he sings so confidingly of moving from loneliness to a wedding ring—'I played an ace and won a queen'—that [it] won the girls and set them off on their 'We want Jim' chant."

A few nights later, on the eve of his departure from South Africa, Jim performed the song again at the University of Witwatersrand. Clive Parnell attended the farewell concert and learned a striking lesson in the art of manufacturing pseudo-events. "It was an amazing evening because 'From a Jack to a King' had just gone gold. But we had known for some time that it had gone gold. . . . I'll never forget that we were sitting having dinner [with a Teal representative] one night about three nights before the concert. . . . The guy told Jim that [the record] had gone gold in South Africa, and we would announce it on the Saturday night of the concert at the university. I was still fairly naive in those days [and] didn't understand the workings of record companies and recording stars. . . . This guy rushed onto the stage halfway through the concert and stopped the whole concert cold, and he said he had this incredible announcement to make. He stopped the band and he stopped Jim and he made the announcement that 'From a Jack to a King' had just gone gold. Jim broke down emotionally. He was very moved by this announcement that he'd gone gold—which I found very peculiar because he'd [heard about it] the Wednesday before. . . . I thought that was the best performance he'd given for a few days."

On the *Kimberley Jim* set, despite his frequent detonations, Jim delivered a very respectable acting job. "Reeves is pliable and likable, and his songs are intro'd naturally," commented *Variety* in a review. Sure, Jim appeared stiff at times, even bored, but the jitters Clive Parnell had observed on the set never came through on the screen. Like his early singing performances on the Macy's label all those years before in Houston, he appeared somewhat one-dimensional in his first acting appearance. But he also demonstrated an identifiable potential to succeed as an actor. Jim's singing parts flowed as freely as winds across the platteland, and he filled the screen in a way that commanded attention. The Jamie Uys company clearly planned *Kimberley Jim* as a vehicle to showcase Jim's singing as well as Jim himself. His mere presence on the screen, although rather minimal, was the film's primary attraction.

As Parnell indicated, Jim had given away some of his lines, but he really never had that many lines to begin with. Emil Nofal cast him as a minstrel who commented in song on the movie's various themes: diamond mining, relationships, and gambling. It was Parnell, playing Jim's cohort Gerry Bates, who received most of the screen time and kept the plot moving with his crackpot schemes to hoodwink various townspeople. Jim arguably was not even accorded sex-symbol status in the movie. That fell on two virile figures (played by Dawid Van Der Walt and Vonk De Ridder) who worked in the diamond fields that Jim and Gerry won in the card game. Instead, Jim played a minstrel who became a fatherly figure to various characters. In a role for which his affection for young people had prepared him, Jim touchingly serenaded a group of schoolchildren, scolded his young comrade for his devilish ways, and helped reconcile a disappointed child with his father. "Everybody's father is special," Jim explained to the boy in his best paternal tones.

Although Reeves's performance in *Kimberley Jim* will never be considered anything close to Oscar caliber, he nonetheless acquitted himself admirably in a new genre. A few country music personalities had appeared in Hollywood productions (Faron Young, Marty Robbins, Johnny Cash, Eddy Arnold), but none had claimed a regular spot in the cinematic world. With a little coaching, Jim appeared qualified to make the attempt. He left South Africa in April 1963 amidst talk that he might return for another movie production in 1964.

When they stepped off the plane in Nashville, Jim Reeves and the Blue Boys had a May's worth of dates in the Pacific Northwest to fulfill. Then, before their jet lag had dissipated, they were back in the air, heading for a spate of performances in Ireland and England during late May and early June. In Ireland, Jim would play to the citizenry, but in England, where union restrictions prohibited American musicians from playing concerts unless an equal number of British performers were playing dates in the States, Jim would only be appearing on television and in private clubs.*

In those pre-British invasion days, the union rule had kept many American performers from touching Britons in live performances, despite the enormity of their hits in the U.S. RCA, for instance, had released Jim's "Welcome to My World" in Britain during June, and

---

*Ireland's union probably opened the country's stages to Jim and the Blue Boys when Jim agreed to include Irish bands on his bills.

although it performed enviably on the charts there, Jim was denied the chance to further fuel its sales with live appearances. At least he would be able to play to audiences in Ireland, where fans adored Reeves with as much ardor as the British and snatched up so many copies of "Welcome to My World" that the song became that country's third-most popular recording of 1963. In the end, though, Jim would wish that he had never set foot on the enchanting Emerald Isle.

His road through the Irish cities and villages was pocked with inconveniences, an unethical promoter, and broken-down pianos. By the time Jim landed in Ireland on his Irish International Airlines flight, he was a certifiable international star who had been accorded royal treatment on his two most recent trips abroad. To him, Ireland must have seemed a royal letdown. The narrow roads clogged with herds of dingy white sheep and the ballrooms that seemed little more than grange halls must have brought to Jim's mind images of East Texas in the 1930s. The star in Jim Reeves probably longed for a more smoothly paved thoroughfare on his tour. After all, back home—no matter how tiring and grubby things were on the road—he had the relative comfort of the bus, wide-open roads, and the option to fly home if he so desired. In Ireland, however, there were no such escapes. It was as if Fabor Robison had yanked him back to 1953 and forced him to play a circuit of rural Texas honky-tonks.

Even worse than the inconveniences was the performance schedule that confronted Jim and the Blue Boys. Unbeknownst to Reeves, the promoter had booked two and sometimes three shows for a single evening—at different venues. It was a devilish effort on the part of the promoter to milk Jim's visit to Ireland for everything he possibly could. The patrons in the various ballrooms would have to be satisfied with seeing the great American singer perform just seven or eight songs before he rushed from the stage to another engagement that often was fifty or sixty miles away. The evening lineup of gigs, according to Leo Jackson, was nearly impossible to fulfill.

"The first show would be like 7:00 P.M.," he said. "We were supposed to do another show at 10:00 or 11:00 somewhere else. But you can't get there on those roads. It's impossible. We would get there at 1:00 in the morning for this 11:00 show, and then we had another show that we were supposed to do at midnight. We would get there at 4:00 in the morning to do that show. If there was a cart or herd of sheep in the road, there was no way to get around it. You had to follow that until this guy got to where he was going, and then we could go. That happened all night long. It kept on happening."

One could well imagine that Jim refused to take the promoter's deception with a smile on his face. The Tennessee hero hunkered down and resolved to finish the tour, but he did so in a most uncooperative manner, a manner that would give rise to the legendary tale of Jim Reeves's visit to Ireland. It would be a story that in certain Irish towns would be told over and over, almost as frequently as the tales of banshees and leprechauns.

Dilapidated pianos became part of the legend. In the ballrooms of the Irish hinterlands, Jim and the Blue Boys found pianos that seemingly had survived Oliver Cromwell's pillaging of the island in the seventeenth century. Keys sat in jagged rows, and the sounding wires inside the instruments drooped from years of abuse and disuse. Jim's pianist, Dean Manuel, carried pliers to restore proper tension to the wires, but in many cases, it was hopeless to expect anything more than a high-pitched wheeze from the pianos. In the 1950s, a wrecked piano or a piano in any condition meant nothing to Reeves, but in the post-"He'll Have to Go" era, he relied on Manuel's playing to anchor his sound. In Cork, during the tour, Jim let fly his objections to a reporter: "The pianos in many of the ballrooms I've sung in were in a terrible condition. In some places they had to borrow the instrument from a private house. My act depends on the piano as the Blue Boys are only a quartet, and I cannot put on a really good show without one."

Leo Jackson recalled that on one cool, late-spring night in Ireland, the piano to be used for the show—the finale of the evening's pair of engagements—was crumbled almost beyond recognition. "We got there—and Jim's contract clearly states for the venue to have a piano to be tuned to A [440]—and there's this damn ole upright piano. Hasn't been played in years. Half the keys are missing. The white keys are black because the ivory's gone from them. The strings were broke and wrapped around other strings. So, Jim said, 'Dean, see if you can play that thing. See if it's playable.' Dean sat down there, and there wasn't no way—and Dean could play anything. It didn't matter if a couple of strings were broken or it was out of tune, Dean would make it sound presentable. He said, 'Jim there's just no way.' He said, 'Okay, boys, pack 'em up.'" Throughout the tour, Jim protested the rickety pianos and unrealistic schedules by refusing to play the gigs or sharply pruning his performance program.

By Friday, June 7, a couple of weeks into the tour, Jim had so soured on his Irish experience that he made little effort to project his Gentleman Jim image to the audiences. The tour's bookers and promoters had deceived him, and all of Ireland seemed to be at fault. The events of June 7 were the seed from which the lore of Jim Reeves's visit to Ireland would grow. At 10:30 that evening, Jim and Blue Boys were to play the utilitarian Pavesi Ballroom in the far northwestern city of Donegal. Word of Jim's appearance had stirred up Donegal, for rarely did such a celebrated act pass through town. An artist of Jim Reeves's caliber might play Dublin or Belfast but would never think of venturing into the rural west of Ireland. "They didn't go to Donegal, and they certainly didn't go to a ballroom that was made of breeze blocks," said Jerry Rice, whose band, the Witnesses, played for the Pavesi dancers that night. "This was just a long ballroom with a stage at one end and a cafe at the other."

Jim was scheduled to appear later that night some thirty miles away in Lifford, near the border with Northern Ireland, so when he and the Blue Boys approached the stage door of the Pavesi that night, he was in no mood to tarry. "All these kids had gathered with bits of paper and cigarette packets to get his autograph," recalled Rice. "And he got out of the car and waded through them. He wouldn't even look at them. I'm talking about a dozen or more kids, that's all. When I say kids, I mean school kids, from ten to twelve years old. 'Mr. Reeves would you give us an autograph?' And he just pushed them away."

Inside, Jim again rebuffed autograph seekers and, according to Rice, just waited for his cue inside a toilet stall in the ballroom's small dressing room. "He went on that night," recounted Rice, "and he was very rude to his own band. He [also] made some crack about a guy who was a photographer in the hall that night. This guy had a hump in his back, and he actually referred to him as being ugly. That was really awful."

After a brisk set of some thirty to forty minutes, Jim and the Blue Boys packed up and rolled out of Donegal to the Orchid Ballroom in Lifford, a venue that hardly resembled its florid name. Instead, like the other cookie-cutter ballrooms throughout the Irish countryside, its cinder-block walls and high ceiling suggested a medium-size airplane hangar. The Orchid, like the Pavesi, had been built for a singular purpose: dancing. Forget the amenities. Jim and the Blue Boys walked into a building with four walls, a ceiling, and a maple dance floor that was packed with people jumping to the music of the Mighty Avons showband. The dancers had paid ten shillings to see Jim, and when the star took the stage around 12:30, they forgot their dancing and went to fetch their money's worth by crowding as close to the stage as possible. Jim looked over a mass of awed and adoring faces, but the sight made little impression on him.

"He was in very, very bad humor," observed Peter Smith of the Mighty Avons, "with the result that he went on and he sang a medley of a few of his songs. He turned around to the piano player, and he said, 'That goddamn piano is not in tune.' . . . He gave them a signal. He threw a white hankie across his shoulder, and pushed a lot of songs into a medley." At the conclusion of the neutered "He'll Have to Go," "Four Walls," and other hits, Jim exited the stage. "He never said anything to the people about whether he [was going] to come back again. He went down to the dressing room. He got his coat, went out to his limousine, and disappeared."

Ten shillings represented a sizable portion of an Irishman's weekly budget, and the crowd wanted to hear considerably more of Jim's warm, resonant voice. "The velvet in the man's voice, even over the P.A. that night, was gorgeous," marveled Smith. It was as if somebody had stripped the patrons' blankets from them during a warm, dreamy slumber on a cold, damp night. They wanted Jim Reeves back on stage. "They were very, very disappointed," said Rice, "and there was nearly a riot at the end when he went off. The people shouted 'More, more, more.' He wasn't coming back. The promoter even left, and we had to go back on and try to soothe them."

Tempers flared and angry shouting filled the Orchid, but there was no use protesting; Jim had left the building. Smith remembered that it fell to his band mate Larry Cunningham to fill the void by doing a musical imitation of Reeves. "People wanted their money back, and the booing started. But we were lucky enough that it made [our reputation] in Donegal at the time. We were only starting to make headway. . . . We went on, and we started playing and Larry started singing the Reeves songs. We softened the crowd down." Mopping up for Jim was as good as a hit record in Donegal. Newspapers reported the next day that the Mighty Avons had saved the day for Jim Reeves.

Across Ireland, news spread of Jim's abrupt abandonment of the stages. And behind him, he left a trail of disappointed fans. Although the fans could sympathize with Jim's displeasure regarding the chicanery of the bookers and the awful-sounding pianos, they thought that a country gentleman should treat his fans with more respect. The voice that suggested a gentle, thoughtful man had misled them. At every corner, it seemed, Jim took the opportunity to sabotage the efforts of the promoters, not realizing or caring that in doing so, he was damaging his reputation among the Irish people.

Billy Livingstone was an emcee from Northern Ireland who the tour promoters had hired to appear on Jim's dates in Northern Ireland and the larger southern towns of Dublin, Cork, and Limerick. The promoters also asked Livingstone to try to make Jim happy when the singer's obstinacy or frustration flared. For Livingstone, the job seemed more like that of a circus ringmaster, both on stage and off. In Belfast, recalled Livingstone, Reeves walked off the stage after performing only a handful of numbers and left the emcee to improvise a comedy routine for the riotous crowd.

In the Northern Ireland town of Derry, claimed Livingstone, Jim repeated the disappearing act. "The place was packed to suffocation. The walls were bulging. He walks on the stage and he says, 'Nice to be here. Thank you very much.' In that velvety voice, . . . he [sings], 'Put your sweet lips a little closer to the phone.' Pulled the house down. Then he says, 'Can I have an A on the piano.' He fiddled with his guitar, and he sang another number. Then he said, 'Thank you folks. I'll be back in a minute.' Walked out, and did the same again. . . . Into the car and away to the hotel. He leaves you stuck. He did about three songs, and [the fans] expected about at least seven or eight songs.

"Then we got to Limerick," continued Livingstone, "and all the press were there. His first time down in the south of Ireland, and he was in the VIP room. There was maybe twenty or thirty of the press from all over Ireland, because Ireland just loved him. They loved him in Ireland. Somebody said [to Jim], 'You better go out and just say hello to these people.' . . . The press waited for about an hour in the press room, and he wouldn't come out of his bloody VIP room. He said, 'Nah. Nah. I don't want to talk to anyone.' So, I went in and said, 'Just go out and say, "Hello. It's great to be here. I'm looking forward to the show. Lovely to be in your country. I must go and have a coffee. I haven't got a coffee." Make any excuse! It all will take about two or three minutes.' We couldn't have dragged him out. So, the press slayed him for not showing his face."

To mollify Jim and perhaps soften his demeanor in the public's eye, Livingstone said that he suggested horseback riding, sightseeing, and golf. He claimed even to have recruited a professional escort for Jim, but nothing took the glare from Jim's eyes. "A most odd character," said Livingstone. "I tried everything."

Jim had every right to lash out at the promoters (for whom Livingstone worked) who had led him to believe that two shows a night meant two shows in the same venue, but he protested in a way that alienated his fans. To risk estranging potential record buyers was foolish. From the outset, Jim should have dealt with the issues in the way that he would ultimately seek recompense from the Irish promoters: through the courts. Still, for some, Jim left some lush impressions in Ireland. His concerts in Dublin's International Arena sent many audience members home aglow, and as reporter Peter Clerk observed, he gave a brilliant performance in the southern coastal city of Youghal. "He had the audience in the palm of his hand from his opening number," wrote Clark. "He proved himself a superb showman as well as being the singer with possibly the most pleasant voice in the musical business."

12

Jim Reeves would never return to Ireland, but RCA Records did intend to dispatch him to Europe for an April 1964 tour of Germany, Austria, Denmark, Sweden, Norway, the Netherlands, and Belgium. Although RCA commissioned the tour to expand the international country market, demand for Jim abroad was already superseding demand for him in the United States. In Great Britain, for example, RCA plucked from the *Gentleman Jim* album the number "I Love You Because," released it as a single, and watched it settle in for a lengthy stay on that nation's pop charts starting in March 1964. In America, RCA designated the *Gentleman Jim* tracks strictly for the album market, doubting the potential of "I Love You Because," an old country song written by Leon Payne, a blind musician from Alba, Texas.

During the first half of 1964, Reeves and his hits duked it out on the British pop charts with burgeoning bands like the Beatles, Rolling Stones, and Dave Clark Five, but back at home, his releases were becoming lost in the shuffle among pop audiences. RCA released "Welcome to My World" in the States in January 1964, but—even with a healthy dose of strings and other pop embellishments—it foundered in the pop arena, although the ever-faithful country music fans pushed the single to number two on the country charts. The previous year, "Welcome to My World" had climbed into the Top Ten on the British charts. Fans overseas seemed to be embracing Jim Reeves's singles and albums with greater relish than were Americans.

Certainly, Jim was in no danger of falling from the marquee of American entertainment, but in pop markets, he was becoming

overshadowed by the dazzle of the British invasion, which represented the most exciting new wave in pop music since the emer-
gence of Elvis Presley. On the country side, Jim, who had turned
forty in 1963, surrendered some of his territory to a legion of
promising artists in their twenties and thirties who had come along
just after him. Many, like Porter Wagoner, Buck Owens, and
Stonewall Jackson, rolled up sales with their unvarnished honky-
tonk brand of country music, while others, including Bill Anderson
and Roger Miller, were having success with a style that appeared to
owe something to Reeves and his progenitor, Eddy Arnold. Jim still
had his place on the contemporary scene in America; however, it
had just become more difficult to conjure up a powerful hit of the
"He'll Have to Go" variety.

Jim knew that he had accomplished just about everything a boy
from Carthage, Texas, could hope for, and, besides, if the walls fell in
on his music career, he had income streaming in from a portfolio of
investments that included ownership of his old radio station KGRI, a
few Texas oil wells, a small record company, and three music publishing companies. Perhaps that had a calming effect on him—or perhaps it fueled the raw frustration he often exhibited and pushed him
to seek more. John White, Jim's brother-in-law, recalled collecting the
performer from the Houston airport during Christmas 1963. Jim had
returned home to Texas with Mary for the holidays, and as the three
made their way through travelers who seemed not to recognize the
celebrated musician, the subject of Jim's career arose. "I've accomplished everything in life," Jim told White, "more than I ever
dreamed I would. I don't know where to go from here."

On New Year's Day 1964, Jim and Mary returned to Nashville
from their beloved East Texas, and on January 2, Jim played a Country Music Association-sponsored engagement at the Hillwood Country Club in Nashville. From there, it was back on the road for an
especially grueling February and March. In February, Jim and the
Blue Boys trudged through the winter cold of Minnesota, North
Dakota, Wisconsin, Illinois, and Indiana, and then, in March, dropped
south to warm themselves on a hop-scotching tour of the Texas club
and dance hall scene. Throughout the trek, Jim pulled his bus off the
road to visit with old friends, and he often spotted familiar faces in
the audiences. Texas was always a homecoming for Jim.

When Shep Baron, Jim's roommate from the Alexandria Aces, saw that his buddy was booked into a Beaumont, Texas, club, he hoped to find him in a mood to reminisce, but all he found was a former pitcher who had tired of the road and tired of the nightclub dates. A girl sat in the back of the hall, popping pictures with a flash camera. "Get that damn flicker out of my eyes. You're blinding me, girl," Shep recalled Jim demanding. Rudely, the woman refused to let up, so Jim shouted over the audience to the club manager, "Would you please get this damn camera stopped over here? She's about to blind me!" At the break, Jim appeared flustered to Shep—flustered and fed up. "I'm gonna tell my manager not to book me in any more of these damn nightclubs," he told his old teammate. "We got three more weeks of this bullshit." Indeed, Jim had three more weeks, but Curtis Artists Productions also had booked another string of Texas club dates for June, after he returned from Europe.

When Jim repaired to Nashville after the hard winter tour, he had little more than a week to rest and prepare for the European excursion RCA had arranged. With Jim on the bills abroad would be the Anita Kerr Singers, Chet Atkins, and Bobby Bare, who had raised an excited clamor in the States and abroad with his hits "Detroit City" and "500 Miles Away from Home." In a rare instance, Jim would not be bringing a full complement of Blue Boys. Only Leo Jackson and Dean Manuel would accompany him, as drummer Mel Rogers had been drafted and bass man Bobby Dyson had chosen to leave the band to work in the publishing business. Bass player Henry Strzelecki and drummer Kenneth Buttrey, who had backed Jim in the studio and occasionally played live gigs with Chet Atkins, came along and worked behind Jim and Chet. It was unusual for Jim to allow musicians in his employ to back other stars, but on this tour, Leo and Dean also played behind the Kerrs, Chet, and Bobby Bare.

With *Billboard* trumpeting that the tour showcased "Nashville as a talent and music center of international importance," Jim took off on another crusade to spread the gospel of country music. And it was almost as if Jim and the troupe were doing missionary work, because their pay dipped well below their usual fees and the shows were packed so closely together that there was little time to breathe between them. "You're asking [them] to go overseas and play two weeks for a total of maybe fifteen hundred dollars and everything paid," explained Dick Broderick, the coordinator of the tour for RCA. "In other words, no big dollars. But you pay your dues, and it's going to work out eventually in [record] sales. . . . The artists would say, 'I can go out and play Tulsa, Oklahoma, and Des Moines, and a gig in Corpus Christi, Texas, and I can make fifteen thousand dollars with all expenses. Now you're telling me to go over to these countries where I can make fifteen hundred? What do I do that for?' The answer is, 'You do it.' "

These were the wobbly early days of country music's push into international markets, but the work of Broderick, his RCA artists, and RCA's foreign licensees and distributors would give the genre solid footing abroad for many years to come. Jim, especially, carried the banner for country music in foreign markets. Just as he had been the voice of Chet Atkins's Nashville Sound, he also became America's emissary of country music. "More so than anyone," remarked Broderick, "he was perfect to present country to the Europeans. . . . He was a gentleman, the old 'Gentleman Jim' Reeves."

RCA placed extraordinary emphasis on the tour because, for the first time, its country artists would be playing live shows primarily to the continental European "economy," the civilians. Jim and the rest would also play a few military bases, but RCA had designed the junket to energize sales of records in Europe's civilian market. So, on April 2, the RCA gang jetted out of New York on a Lufthansa flight for Hamburg, West Germany. On the trip over, Jim sat next to Louis Nunley, the Kerr vocalist whose continual joking during recording sessions so agitated Jim. On the flight, though, Jim shed his problems with the background singer and joined in the frivolity. "All night the old jokes [flew]," remembered Nunley. "We sat and just had a marvelous time on the way over there. Everything was just beautiful after that."

Upon their arrival, the reception in Hamburg was far more subdued than in South Africa but no less remarkable. The reception's organizers boarded the jet and—as if they were Hawaiians doling out leis—passed out cowboy hats to the performers. "To the Germans, we were supposed to be cowboys," said bass player Henry Strzelecki. "They gave us all hats, and we had to wear them when we got off the plane. . . . They gave us neckerchiefs, so we put those on and we got off the plane. . . . They really expected to see [cowboy actor] Hoot Gibson. That was their mentality of what country and western performers are: 'They're country and western, like cowboys.' When we got off the plane, these Clydesdale horses were pulling a real beer coach with kegs of beer on it—I mean *gigantic* kegs. . . . There were two guys up there driving the horses. One of the guys fell off, and the wagon rolled over his leg. They had to amputate his leg, right there. We sent him flowers the next day."

From there, the days degenerated into a long, hazy streak. Feeling like those Clydesdales under a whip, they traveled from city to city and country to country. "We were up at 5:00," recounted Strzelecki, "on the plane by 7:00 or 8:00, got to the next city and set up in time to do the show. We did the show, and had a press conference every night after the shows. . . . We never left before 1:00 or 2:00; it was just a blitz." On consecutive nights, the troupe played Hamburg, Munich, Vienna, Hanover, Essen, and Berlin, and after a night off on April 12, resumed the frenzied pace, fulfilling another spate of performances that lasted until the artists departed Europe.

The tour was an unrealistic zigzag through Europe that RCA never should have allowed, no matter how many new record buyers it generated. The unrelenting circuit frazzled Jim, Chet, Bobby Bare, and the Kerr Singers, and it indirectly created a public relations flap that threatened to overshadow the goodwill the tour seemed to be building on the continent. Mustering every ounce of gentlemanly reserve available, Jim made a point of criticizing the tour logistics in almost every interview he gave. "We have been getting an average of three hours sleep during the tour," he complained to a *Billboard* correspondent in Oslo. "This tires the members of the troupe, and we all are not at top form when we perform. I'd rather not repeat a promotion tour like this."

A few days later, during a taped conversation with singer and radio host Kitty Prins at the Hotel Amigo in Brussels, Jim again hinted at his dissatisfaction: "It's been a very difficult tour; it's been a tiring one. We're traveling quite a lot, a different country almost every day. In spite of that, we had the chance to meet some of the people that we've written to a long time, and a lot of people who've made us feel quite at home." Jim's words sounded as if they had run a gauntlet of clenched teeth. In reality, only the ill-fated swing through Ireland had been a worse touring experience for him. In Berlin, a suitcase containing Jim's hairpiece had been filched from outside the hotel, and worse still, harsh articles about the troupe's shows at military bases had painted a nasty face on the tour.

According to a military newspaper, Jim had stormed off the stage of the Capri Enlisted Mens Club in Friedberg after telling some rowdy GIs to "shut up." Earlier in the evening, Bobby Bare had brought to mind visions of home for the soldiers with his hits "Detroit City" and "500 Miles Away from Home," so, understandably, Bare's was a tough act to follow. "Atkins followed," the paper reported, "but got a cooler reception from the crowd. Then Reeves came on stage and, as he looked around the cheering audience, apparently felt there was too much noise to suit him." When Jim tried to silence the revelers, shouts of "We want Bobby Bare" arose amid a clatter of glasses hitting tables and feet stomping on the floor. "Reeves," the report continued, "turned abruptly and walked off stage in a huff followed by hoots of derision." A few nights later, according to the paper, Jim refused to appear before a military audience in Munich—forcing cancellation of the show—and then he did the same in Gelnhausen.

Talk of lawsuits, blackballing Jim Reeves from military installations, and banning his records from the post exchanges enlivened newspaper accounts of the controversy. But more damaging than anything else, perhaps, was the charge that Jim had called the Friedberg audience of enlisted men "animals." It was as if Communist premier Nikita Kruschev himself had slammed his shoe down on the Army's collective head. "When you get too big for the people that made you, buddy, you're finished," raged an Armed Forces Network disc jockey in the papers. "I don't think any of our boys deserves to be called an animal."

According to Leo Jackson, Chet Atkins had used the term "animals" when he had found it difficult to get through his Friedberg set after Bobby Bare's appearance. "It wasn't Jim," claimed Jackson. "It was Chet Atkins, and that surprised me because Chet is so easy going. He says, 'We came here to play for you. You won't even let us play. You act like a bunch of animals. Act like Americans.' . . . They were rowdy. You might as well have not been up there." Still, the "animal" remark remained linked to Jim, and when he flew home to the States, it seemed that the American soldiers in Europe had impaled his name with a bayonet. It would take a few months for the flak from the U.S. military to fade.

Fortunately, Jim Reeves had left behind a far more appealing legacy of his European tour: a televised concert in Oslo, Norway. The cameras on April 15 documented Jim and his band in top condition.

While in Oslo, the artist had grumbled to *Billboard* about the European tour, but that evening, only the desire to please the audience seemed to be on Jim's mind. Jim performed at his most fluid, swaying joyfully to every song and leading the band with his vigorous guitar strumming. Perhaps the erect and subdued Norwegian audience challenged him, or maybe it was the thought of the extensive television audience. He poured onto the men and women tenderness from "Adios Amigo" and "Four Walls," and when Henry Strzelecki stepped up to harmonize on the chorus of "Bimbo," Jim looked to be as happy as a pitcher on a strikeout spree. He almost flirted with Strzelecki. Viewers in the modern hall and those who watched from home later experienced a quintessential Jim Reeves presentation. His baritone empathized with the message of every song, and his face and body glowed with the gentlemanly comportment that his voice communicated. When he slid into "Blue Canadian Rockies" from "Four Walls" and then mistakenly slipped back into "Four Walls," he handled it with sheepish self-deprecation. "I pulled a boo-boo," he admitted with a grin.

Of course, no quintessential Jim Reeves presentation would be complete without a dash of bad manners. As he drank in the applause for "Adios Amigo," a Norwegian disc jockey emerged from backstage to present him with a silver disc commemorating the twenty-five thousand copies of "Adios Amigo" sold in Norway. "Thank you. Thank you," Jim responded. "That's nice. If it's really silver, I'm going to melt it down when I get home."

The Anita Kerr Singers, who also appeared with Jim that night, couldn't believe their ears, but, after all, the remark had come from Jim. "I remember us thinking that wasn't too nice of a thing," Kerr said. "He, like everybody else, could have his bad moments." Despite the insensitive joke, Jim bestowed a pleasing performance on his audience that evening, confirming that, although the military bases had developed a stronger taste for Bobby Bare, Jim Reeves's voice still rang truest in Europe.

During the interview in Brussels when Jim complained about the European tour, the Belgian interviewer also queried the American star about the direction his career would be taking. There seemed to be no certain path, and as Jim had told his brother-in-law at Christmas, he knew not what would come later. "I kind of let someone else do the leading," he answered. The interviewer didn't comment. Was Reeves referring to his faith in God? He must have been because Jim definitely called most of the shots with regard to his career. Why else had he fired Herb Shucher? "I'll continue recording, of course, as long as RCA will let me," Reeves went on. "And I guess I'll go back to South Africa sometime before too long and make another picture. And . . . oh, I don't know . . . just stay in Tennessee and Texas as much as possible and go wherever else I have to."

Although Jim's long-term goals, as he articulated them, seemed somewhat ill-defined, he appeared to be planning to transform his stage and record productions into something akin to the concert-like pop stylings of his *Kimberley Jim* soundtrack performances: grand and sophisticated. To achieve that, Jim had invited Bill Walker to leave South Africa and serve as his musical director in the United States. "Bill was going to come over and work with the Blue Boys," surmised Leo Jackson. "He was going to teach us stage things, like production numbers. Jim was wanting us to go in that direction." According to Walker, there was also talk of a network television show on which the Australian would coordinate the music.

A recording session probably ranked fairly high on Jim's list of goals to accomplish once he returned to Nashville. He had not tickled a microphone on Hawkins Street since December 1963, when he had waxed the final tracks for the album *Moonlight and Roses*. So, on May 18, Jim joined Chet Atkins to record five songs. Included on the docket were "I Guess I'm Crazy," which was slated for July release, and "This Is It," a tune penned by well-known Texas songwriter Cindy Walker, whose work regularly attracted Jim's attention. There was no respite from touring, either, after Jim returned from Europe. Incredibly, between his arrival back in America and the May 18 RCA session, Jim and the Blue Boys sprinted through a nine-day tour of the Pacific Northwest. Then, a few weeks after the recording date, Reeves found himself in Texas for a series of dreaded nightclub appearances (which included a date with Dottie West at the Longhorn Ranch in Dallas).

The American tours and international junkets clearly had siphoned off much of Jim's interest in his work. The road had lost its sparkling appeal and promise of new adventures, so Jim appeared to be planning to enjoy life at home for a while. He could perhaps use some down time to regroup and focus on the future. "I've come to the conclusion that it's impossible to buy happiness," Reeves told a British disc jockey who visited with him after the European tour. "And there's certainly no fun in touring around, living in planes and hotels, until you drop. I have this lovely home here in Madison, and when I'm away, my thoughts are forever returning to it. Ironically I've scarcely had the opportunity of living in it or enjoying it, so I've decided to take it easy and relax a little. I've been lucky enough to make a few dollars, and I don't intend to knock myself out adding to my bank balance. I'm gonna rest up for a while."

And rest he did—for a while. For much of July, Jim vacationed with Mary and concentrated on his golf game, stopping only for a session on July 2 and some demo work later in the month. Engineer Chuck Seitz, who worked the July 2 RCA session, watched Jim rush into the bathroom before the 1:30 studio date and change from his golf clothes into street attire. Inside the studio, Jim was scheduled to cut several tunes for an album of romantic songs, so Chet had scheduled two sessions for the day. The first concluded at 4:30 P.M., and by 10:00 the session congregation was back at it.

Joining Chet at the production helm for the second installment was Bob Ferguson, the former manager of Ferlin Husky and a recent addition to Chet's A&R staff in Nashville. With his thick-framed glasses and receding hairline, Ferguson easily could have faded into the background of an insurance company office, but instead he provided an element of contrast in a recording studio full of toupees and pompadours. Ferguson was at the session because Chet was looking to delegate a few of the responsibilities he had accumulated since RCA's Nashville operation had rocketed into the mainstream of American recording. Perhaps Ferguson could bring some fresh ideas to Jim's overall production, or perhaps take over supervision of Jim's album recordings while Chet continued to steer the recordings for single release. In any case, Chet asked Bob to join him on the evening of July 2.

"Part way into that session," recalled Ferguson, "Chet closed up his briefcase and said, 'I believe I'll head home.' I was dumbfounded. He said, 'It's going to be all yours.' And his eyes got that twinkle in them that they would get when he was pulling something like that. He said, 'Jim's got the songs and you know what to do.' So, he just walked out the door. The engineer . . . looked at me and he was grinning, too. He said, 'Well, chief, what next?" I said, 'Well, I guess we better do the next song.' He said, 'I guess so.' I walked in there, and it was pretty clear to me that Chet and Jim had [decided I would produce], and it was okay with Jim. Because Jim was the consummate master performer, he said, 'Well, let's get the next song ready.'

"Actually, Chet and Jim had planned out the recording, . . . so I wasn't producer in the sense that I worked out the songs with the musicians and all the things that you do when you do a full production. They had done that. We went through a rehearsal, and Jim said, 'Are you ready?' I said, 'I believe we're ready.' And he turned around and stepped to the microphone and sang it without a hitch. He was great at that. What we were doing was making an album, and the album had been named, or at least the idea for it was fairly well progressed. So, it wasn't like a critical single would hang on to this thing. It would have been hard for me to mess it up." Ferguson's presence in the studio that day was actually a test to see whether he and the temperamental performer could get along. Quite independently, Jim selected some material written by Cindy Walker and waxed melting interpretations of her "In the Misty Moonlight" and "Maureen." He also tackled "Missing You," which had hit for Webb Pierce in 1957.

Jim entered a recording studio just once more during July 1964, gathering the Blue Boys and pianist Bill Pursell at the Nugget studios in the Nashville suburb of Goodlettsville to test some songs that Jim said had come from friend who was imprisoned in Texas.* Nugget belonged to the country comedy duo Lonzo and Oscar, and Jack Logan, whose brother Bud had become the Blue Boys' full-time bass man. According to Pursell, who was a member of Nashville's elite session corps and had appeared on the July 2 RCA sessions, the Nugget date was considerably stormier than the session earlier in the month had been.

"Somewhere during the middle of the afternoon, Jim—looking towards Bud Logan—said, 'Uh-uh-uh.' I looked up, trying to figure what was going on, and I saw him looking directly at Logan, and Logan was looking down. I don't know to this day what the heck he was talking about or what he was doing. It was sort of like a father

---

*Reeves was probably referring to his old friend Rusty Courtney, who served time in Louisiana's Angola State Penitentiary.

Bass player Bud Logan, left, joins Jim and Leo. (Courtesy: Frank Anderson)

talking to his six-year-old child. We finished the whole afternoon, and Dean Manuel was sitting on one side of me and Jim was on the other, and, of course, we were working out these tunes. Finally, afterwards, I signed the [time] card and said good-bye. I went outside and got up to my car. I had a Buick Wildcat in those days. I got into the car, and it was the strangest thing. I was pulling away from the studio, and I had the impression of something like a black cloud over the roof of that darned [building]. It was weird. I remember getting into that car and taking off down that road like a bat out of hell."

With some time to kill before a scheduled August-September tour, Jim decided to fly to Batesville, Arkansas, to look at some property in the area, which at the time was becoming a popular resort. Accompanying him would be Dean Manuel, who had grown up in that area. The pair planned to rent a plane at Berry Field, Nashville's main airport, on Thursday, July 30, then fly to Arkansas, spend the

night, and return home the next day. On the morning of their departure, Jim received a phone call from Bill Walker, who had arrived in
New York and was preparing to make the final leg of his journey to
Nashville, where he would join Jim. First, though, Walker wanted to
see the Broadway production of *Oliver!* (he had conducted the
orchestra for a British touring-company production of the musical in
South Africa). "Stay in New York," urged Jim. "Steve Sholes will get
you tickets."

After the telephone conversation, Jim and Dean headed for the
airport, stopping briefly at a local bank to withdraw money for the
trip and chatting with Nugget's Jack Logan, who they saw in the teller
line. After Jim secured a four-seat Beechcraft Debonair from South-
eastern Beechcraft Company at Berry Field, the duo sped down the
runway and, with the summer day's heat building on their brows,
took off over the dark green, bulbous hills encircling Nashville. The
day before, a freak thunderstorm had caused flooding in areas of the
city, but as Jim and Dean took to the air that late-July morning, they
saw only blue skies. The pair spent Thursday examining land in
northern Arkansas, and early the next afternoon, after Jim checked
with authorities at Walnut Ridge, Arkansas, about weather conditions between Batesville and Nashville, they started for home.

Back in Nashville, life was proceeding at its normal midsummer pace. Mary was playing in a golf tournament. Leo Jackson was
at his home in Hendersonville. The Jim Reeves single "I Guess I'm
Crazy" was climbing the country charts. And at the Hawkins Street
studios, Jim's most recent producer, Bob Ferguson, had begun final-
izing plans for a Chet Atkins session that was slated for 6:00 that
evening. Only the rumblings of afternoon thunderstorms threatened
to mar the day.

At about 4:45 P.M., as Jim began his approach into Nashville from
the southwest, he contacted the Berry Field control tower, giving his
plane's serial number—N8972M—and requesting clearance to land.
He also reported that he and Dean were flying into heavy rain that
had drifted into the area per the weathermen's predictions. The air
traffic controller on duty offered to vector Reeves around the bad
weather, but Jim chose to press forward through the storm in a
straight line toward Berry Field. It was a foolish move on Jim's part,
as he would need to rely on his instruments to navigate in the low-
visibility conditions. Unfortunately, he was accustomed to flying

primarily by sight and was not in the habit of depending on his instruments for direction.

Minutes later, the Nashville tower again made contact with Jim, asking if he had punched through to calmer conditions. "Negat . . . ," was all the controller heard as Jim's response was chopped off. And then, at 4:52 P.M., the Beechcraft disappeared from area radar screens. The tower tried again and again to contact Reeves by radio, but no response crackled back. There was no way for the tower to know for sure what had happened. Had Jim's radio been damaged during an improvised landing in some pasture? Or had he and Dean spiraled out of the sky to their deaths? Within minutes, the airport authorities in Nashville ordered planes to crisscross the area around the suburban community of Brentwood where the plane appeared to have vanished.

Meanwhile, as the aviation authorities investigated their suspicions, pianist Bill Pursell, who lived in Crieve Hall near Brentwood, jumped into his Buick to head for Chet Atkins's session in town. "I was running late, and it was about 5:35 in the afternoon, and as I came out of my door, heading over to my car, I looked over to the right, and right in that field there was an electrical plant and a grove of trees. I looked directly at a black cloud, and I remember thinking to myself—because we were all flying a lot and [were] weather conscious—"I wouldn't fly through that cloud if you paid me." Pursell motored into Nashville, only to find that Chet had decided to forgo using a piano on the session, so he took a seat in the control room with producer Bob Ferguson.

Some two hours into the session, around 8:00, the phone rang at Hawkins Street. It was the airport authorities, asking if anyone knew Jim's whereabouts. Bob Ferguson got on the phone and said that Reeves had not come in the studio at all and that Chet was recording at the moment. "We were taking a break," the producer recalled, "and Chet was somewhere else. I said [to Bill Pursell], 'I just got a funny call.' . . . Bill looked at me and said, 'Who was it?' I said, 'Airport people.' He said, 'You know, we need to call back.'" Immediately, Ferguson and Pursell began making calls and found that Jim's plane was long overdue and that authorities suspected he and Manuel had gone down. Ferguson returned to the session, but since there was no confirmation that Jim had crashed, he decided not to tell Chet and ruin the session. "I thought, 'I'm not going to tell

Chet. We got a wonderful session going.' It was really cooking. As soon as it was over, I called him into the booth and said, 'Chet, Jim's plane is missing.' He said, 'Oh no, not Jim!' "

Mary Reeves first heard about the possibility that her husband's plane had gone down when she arrived home from her golf outing and switched on the television news. She initially refused to conclude that Jim had died, but drawing on the practicality of her rural upbringing and the years of supporting the business of Jim Reeves, she stoically set about making preparations in the event that Jim and Dean had died. While remaining in contact with search parties around Brentwood, she picked up the phone and asked Leo Jackson to stay with Dean's wife and two daughters while the story developed, and then, as Mary told reporter Dixie Deen, she "prepared for the final things." "That night," she explained to Deen, "after it was confirmed that they were down, I sat up a while, listening to the news, then I decided I had better try to get some sleep, because I knew that the next day would be a big one. That's what I did, and of course, the next day was . . . big."

While Mary followed Friday evening's events, Jim's soon-to-be musical director took in the Broadway production of *Oliver!* at New York's Majestic Theater, comparing the American performance to the British one. "When I came out of the show that night," recounted Walker, "Steve [Sholes] was waiting for me in the lobby. He said, 'Look, Jim's plane's gone missing. You better get on down to Nashville.' I called Mary. She said, 'Come on down.' "

Despite the ominous loss of radio contact, the bad weather, and the plans Mary had begun making on Friday night, nobody knew for sure whether Jim and Dean had perished. Despite Brentwood's close proximity to Nashville, the area was largely rural and a downed plane could easily be lying far from a regularly traveled area. A few Brentwood-area residents who lived near Franklin Road, the main southern route into Nashville, told reporters and investigators that they had heard noises ranging from sputtering to a crash. "I heard the plane's engine sputter out and then I heard a thump," one resident told *The Tennessean.* "It sounded like it went down in one of the several hills behind my home."

But there was still no sign of the plane despite a frantic search being conducted by rescue workers. The scene resembled military maneuvers as a pair of National Guard helicopters with powerful searchlights swooped low across the Brentwood pastures and woods throughout Friday night, and an army of jeeps and other vehicles darted in and out of the small roads and country lanes that snaked through the area. The number of searchers grew by the minute, and some remained in the primary search area throughout Friday night. But neither they, nor the jeeps, nor the helicopters, nor the planes spotted any wreckage.

At sunrise on Saturday, the air search resumed and masses of people, including Boy Scout troops and equestrian clubs, combed the land. John White, Mary's brother, flew in from Texas to join the search, and Eddy Arnold, Chet Atkins, Bill Pursell, and other performers joined in as well. "Once the word got out that it was Jim Reeves, there were literally hundreds of people," recalled Jerry Thompson, who covered the events for *The Tennessean.* "The roads were lined on the sides [with cars.] People would just pull the car off on the side of the road and park and get out and start walking. At the height of the search, on Saturday morning, there were several thousand people in that area. They were combing the fields. They were combing the woods. They had aerial searches going on." The rumble of four-wheel-drive vehicles was incessant as rescuers traversed the landscape. "They made their own roads," noted Thompson. "If they came to a gate, they just opened the gate and went on anybody's property. There was a real concentrated effort to find this plane."

Authorities chased leads miles away in Franklin, Hendersonville, and in Maury County, where on Friday a pilot had landed in a farmer's field and asked for directions to Nashville. However, not a single lead panned out. All through Saturday, as temperatures soared into the nineties and the air became thick with humidity, the sweltering searchers trudged through the dense woods, hoping to find Reeves and his pianist alive and well, or perhaps injured and trapped in their plane but alive nonetheless. But they saw not a single glint of the plane's wreckage.

Back in Madison, Mary calmly turned her thoughts to possible postmortem proceedings. "I began to think about where to have the ceremonies and what kind to have; then, where I was going to bury him?" she told Dixie Deen. "We didn't have anyplace. Then, if I chose here, someplace, what reaction would that cause ten years from now? You have to think about a lot of things, not just like an ordinary man, you see." By Sunday morning, August 2, Mary still

Authorities and rescue workers descend on the Jim Reeves crash site, August 2, 1964. (Courtesy: University of Maryland)

had received no word about Jim and Dean's whereabouts, and rescue authorities could not tell her when they would have word.

Bob Newton, a member of one of the official rescue teams, spent his Sunday morning talking to residents along the Old Hickory Boulevard thoroughfare just north of Brentwood. One man with whom Newton spoke claimed that he saw the plane circle over his home on Friday and then chug off toward a nearby lake. Newton, who in World War II had gone down in a plane crash himself, took out a map, drew a straight line from the man's home on Old Hickory Boulevard to the lake, and then began to walk along the route. Newton's projected flight path took him across a small road where he found people who said they had heard a crash nearby on Friday. Newton pressed on, sticking to his line through a wooded area and then into a small clearing—where he saw the tail portion of a plane. He approached, seeing mangled folds of debris hanging from tree branches and lying on the ground. It was as if the plane had simply been blown apart by a bomb, not pulled to earth by gravity. Worst of all, as Newton probed closer, he saw the gruesome, dismembered remains of human beings. He backed off quickly and called for help.

Newton had found the wreckage only five hundred yards from the point where the search had begun on Friday evening. The owner of the land on which Newton located the craft had not been home at the time of the crash. When investigators and rescue workers arrived, they saw complete devastation. "It's just a mess," one Tennessee State Trooper told journalists. "It looked like somebody had gone out there and dumped some debris and trash." The crash, according to newspaper reports, threw one passenger thirty feet from the plane's point of impact, while the other passenger's body remained in the cabin and had been burned by a fire that apparently started when the plane slammed into the ground.

When word spread that the crash site had been located, many dashed to the area seeking to satisfy their curiosity or remove a souvenir. Eddy Arnold, who had searched the area by air and on land, was among the first to arrive and waded through the swarm of onlookers to join the investigators and police who had gathered. Arnold was able to identify the passenger that had been hurled from the plane, and a driver's license in the victim's wallet confirmed Arnold's identification of the body. Media reports soon announced to the world that country music star "*Gentleman Jim*" Reeves had died in a plane crash near Nashville, Tennessee, shortly before 5:00 P.M. on Friday, July 31, 1964.

Epilogue

The federal Civil Aeronautics Board (CAB) concluded that Jim Reeves had ignored control tower warnings and proceeded into "adverse weather conditions" that he attempted to negotiate by sight, rather than instruments. Alex Zanetis, Jim's flying compadre, surmised that Jim became disoriented when he lost sight of the horizon in the middle of the storm, and when the inexperienced pilot consulted his instrument readings, they were fluctuating wildly. In an effort to stabilize the aircraft, Jim overcompensated with the controls, first in one direction and then another, Zanetis theorized, and then perhaps the plane stalled. "When you stall out, you spin in," he said. The CAB reported that Jim lost control and the aircraft plunged into an "uncontrolled descent." The Beechcraft speared through a dense patch of trees that would hide the wreckage for forty-four hours until Bob Newton came upon it.

Jim Reeves died as he had lived, trying to do things his way. In the studio or on the road, Jim's persistence at molding the world according to his vision had alienated associates and cost him a fan or two, but in the air on July 31, 1964, his obstinacy had cost two lives: his own and that of Dean Manuel.

When Mary finally received confirmation that her husband had died, she methodically activated the contingency plans she had made during the search for Jim. "When we found out they were killed," she told Dixie Deen, "that put into motion all of these things that I had been thinking about. It was a blessing in one sense, because it gave me time to think more clearly and prepare." The challenges of her East Texas childhood, and then the rigors of her marriage to Jim and his career, had trained her for that day. In a businesslike manner, Mary scheduled a memorial service in Nashville for Tuesday, August 3, so that the country music industry and the city could pay their respects to the entertainer, and then she arranged for her husband's body to be transported to East Texas.

Along U.S. 79 between DeBerry and Carthage, on a plot of land that Jim had passed countless times on his way to and from high school, Mary secured a burial site. In time, a handsome statue of the singer would be erected above his grave, overlooking the busy road. The small patch of ground has become a shrine for his fans and stands as a reminder to Panola County that, more so than cotton or oil, or Tex Ritter, Jim Reeves remains its best-known export.

The legacy-building would not stop with the statue in Panola County. RCA resumed issuing Jim Reeves material soon after his death, capitalizing on the robust career he had in life and the esteem many people held him in following his passing. At the moment Jim's plane plummeted from the sky on July 31, 1964, his records were again ascending the charts around the world. His album *Moonlight and Roses* had waltzed to number one on the *Billboard* country LP charts and carved a niche in the trade magazine's list of top pop albums. "I Guess I'm Crazy," which Jim recorded in May, had climbed into the country Top Ten and was "bubbling under" the pop charts, and his duet with Dottie West, "Love Is No Excuse," still lingered on the country charts after almost twenty weeks. Internationally, the strangely appropriate "I Won't Forget You" had begun to climb the listings in Ireland and the United Kingdom, and would surely catch on in other nations.

Without question, Jim Reeves had perished while virtually at the top of his form. His was not an over-the-hill career brought back to life by sentiment spawned by an untimely death. Instead, the plane crash that claimed Jim Reeves's life froze him near the pinnacle of his considerable talent, providing a strong platform from which Mary Reeves and RCA would launch the artist's postmortem career. Jim's career continued after only a slight pause—and then the only part missing from the Jim Reeves promotional engine was Jim Reeves himself.

RCA continued to mine the Reeves song catalog, a collection that was vastly supplemented by the reels of songs Jim had taped in other studios and in his basement. Mary would often say that those demo recordings were Jim's life insurance policy. Songs like "Distant Drums" from Reeves's home collection, in fact, paid far more handsomely than an insurance policy. According to Cindy Walker, who wrote "Distant Drums," Reeves wanted to record the ballad about a soldier leaving his girl, but Chet Atkins thought the song too suggestive of war for Jim's audiences. Walker frequently brought her best material to Jim, so, as a favor to her, Jim recorded a demo version of "Distant Drums." "There," he told her. "It should be easy to get the song recorded now." But Cindy Walker refused to take the demo.

A year or so after Reeves's death, Mary called the songwriter to RCA's Nashville studios to hear Jim's haunting voice singing "Distant Drums" over new background instrumentation. Walker broke down crying, and "Distant Drums" broke the charts. The song became one of the biggest smashes of Reeves's second career, topping *Billboard*'s country chart for four weeks in 1966 and cracking the Top Fifty of the pop listings. In the United Kingdom, fans made "Distant Drums" the top song of 1966, and it performed similarly in other nations around the world.

Throughout the remainder of the 1960s, the late Jim Reeves scaled the country charts with songs like "This Is It," "Blue Side of Lonesome," and "I Won't Come In While He's Here." The hits, many of which made the Top Ten, continued to accumulate in the 1970s, and in 1981, an electronically engineered duet with the late Patsy Cline—"Have You Ever Been Lonely (Have You Ever Been Blue)"— sailed to number five on the country charts. Three years later, in 1984, as the country music environment became more hostile to such veteran performers as Eddy Arnold, Hank Snow, and Johnny Cash, Jim's "The Image of Me" struggled to number seventy on the country charts. Reeves's name has yet to resurface on the American singles charts; nonetheless, sales of his recordings remain healthy in the United States and abroad. As late as Christmas 1996, an album of Jim Reeves hits appeared on the British charts.

Incredibly, though, Jim Reeves remained a force on the record charts for twenty years after his death, tallying sales on a par with those of Arnold, Snow, Cash, and other artists who could promote their records with interviews and personal appearances. But Jim's postmortem career had something that others lacked: Mary Reeves. She hired former RCA executive Harry Jenkins to direct the business of Jim Reeves, then tirelessly promoted her husband's name and music around the world. Mary appeared at annual fan club conventions in the U.S. and abroad, gave countless interviews, and, with secretary Joyce (Gray) Jackson, answered stacks of fan mail that accumulated in the Madison office. Even after she remarried a few years after Reeves's death, her marketing of the country troubadour continued with zest. Mary opened the Jim Reeves Museum outside Nashville to keep the legacy alive, and she continued to beat the promotional drum into the 1990s for "Gentleman Jim" around the world, as if she were a publicity agent and Jim Reeves was expected in town in a day or two.

The "Gentleman Jim" image, of course, helped immensely as Mary promoted the Jim Reeves product. In public, she portrayed him as a kind husband, refusing to scratch the veneer of a reputation that many believed reflected the tenderness of his singing voice. It was helpful to say that the gentle, romantic voice emanated from a man whose character exhibited similar characteristics. But, in recent years, Mary began to talk about Reeves's infamous temper, and in Buddy Killen's 1993 autobiography, she is quoted as urging Killen to recount in his book Jim's dalliances with women. Over the years, others who knew and worked with Jim Reeves anted up tales of his troubled side until that side became yet another dimension of the "Gentleman Jim" persona. In an age of kiss-and-tell exposés, it was inevitable that accounts of Reeves's ungraciousness would leak out to sully the Gentleman Jim mystique.

It was just as inevitable that Reeves would display ungraciousness during his lifetime. As a doted-upon, last-born child who later pitched his high school team into two state championship games, he had become used to accolades and was encouraged to go after what he wanted. First, he aspired to be a professional baseball player but failed. Then, he wanted to become a professional country music singer, and when he had established himself as such, he exerted himself in all ways to become the best and to stay the best. Such drive, coupled with feelings of insecurity that he could fail—as he had in baseball—could ignite an emotional outburst as dark and forbidding as an East Texas twister. Reeves simply lashed out at any impediments that obstructed his road to success, whether those impediments were an out-of-tune piano, a drummer's straying rhythm, or a storm cloud.

The Jim Reeves Memorial outside Carthage, Texas. (Photo by Michael Streissguth)

It is certainly ironic that a singer who marketed himself as a gentleman was frequently anything but genteel, but it is also important to note Reeves's capacity for generosity. As bedeviled as his demeanor might be at times, Jim Reeves was not a devil. Although his tantrums and occasional disregard for others' feelings left an indelible impression on those around him—and probably most accurately defined his personality—Reeves never completely unraveled nor was his behavior always caustic. He held an affection for the East Texas of his youth and frequently returned to the area to visit family and friends.

Many mark Jim's character by his love for children, and clear recollections of Jim's kindness percolate with modest frequency. Country singer James O'Gwynn credits Jim for persuading the *Grand Ole Opry* to sign him, and the late Dottie West often said that Jim steered her toward Chet Atkins and an RCA recording contract. "I lived with him for nearly five years," exclaimed Leo Jackson. "Would anybody that's a mean-spirited person take care of somebody like that? No!" Jackson recalled that Jim often shelled out a few bucks to hungry men, and both Leo and fellow Blue Boy James Kirkland saw Jim on several occasions return the band's performance fee to help out a struggling club owner.

Kirkland recalled one such desperate proprietor who met Jim's bus when it pulled up in front of a club in Austin, Texas. "He came out, and he told Jim, 'Before you ever unload, I want to apologize to you. You won't have a crowd tonight.' Jim said, 'What makes you think so?' He said, 'Well, I put out some publicity in the newspaper and television on you. Every time I did this, it was agreed upon . . . that they would hold the checks on the advertisements until after you came to town. Then, I could pay them. All the sudden, they run those checks through, and they bounced. I'm on a shoestring [budget], and this one was going to make it for me. But let me tell you, I still want you to play, and I've got enough cash money in my pocket to pay you. But I'm just going to tell you that you're not going to have a crowd.'"

To the contrary, recalled Kirkland, fans packed the club, forcing the proprietor to turn would-be patrons away. "When it was over, after we loaded everything up, we came back into the bar, and this guy looked at Jim and sort of grinned. He counted his money out for Jim and laid it up there to him. Jim looked out [as if to be thinking], and he knew what the [motel] rooms were for that night, and he knew how much diesel that the [bus] took. It's like he took a hundred bucks, and he shoved the rest of it back. He told this guy, 'Maybe this will help you get started.' . . . This guy just gave us magnum after magnum of pink champagne and a whole case of long-stem champagne glasses. He said, 'I don't want you to use one twice. Every time you pour one, when you get through drinking out of that, I want you to throw it out the window of that bus and get you a new one.'"

No matter how many recollections, flattering or unflattering, come to the fore about Jim Reeves's personality, it is his remarkable singing voice that will remain at the core of his legacy. The world has remembered—and will continue to remember—Jim Reeves for the velvety, purring bass-baritone voice that he summoned on "Four Walls," "He'll Have to Go," and so many other hits that caressed the ears and imaginations of listeners whose preferences encompassed many musical genres. Although Jim's career remains filed in the country music category, his voice defied classification, soaring over political and cultural boundaries to draw in listeners from all walks of life. From New York to Johannesburg to London to Oslo, his fans cared little whether his records came from the country music capital of Nashville or the wilds of Siberia, it was Jim Reeves's voice that mattered. It massaged, delighted, and brought to mind an ideal of manhood that was both strong and sensitive.

Reeves's resonant voice, with its widespread natural appeal, also helped broaden the market for country music at a time when the economic viability of the genre was seriously being threatened by the rise of rock and roll. Turning onto the inroads that Eddy Arnold had paved for country music into urban markets, Jim proffered a decidedly un-country style that could still attract buyers in the country market yet also ring up sales in markets that were traditionally hostile to country music. Jim spawned a new breed of Nashville performer, "country-based" rather than "country." After Jim Reeves, it became generally acceptable in Nashville for a performer to sound like a pop singer as long as that person associated himself or herself with the country music scene. One could be a "country Como" as long as one maintained a presence on the *Opry*, paid the usual dues by playing a round of fairs and country music package shows, and maintained a base in Nashville. Eddy Arnold had stepped out of that mold, and the country market scorned him for doing so.

While Jim Reeves took the Eddy Arnold approach to singing—sweet and unadorned—he retained many other markings of a country singer. All that pop music fans heard, however, was a great voice, and they bought Reeves's records because of that. As a result of Jim's pioneering efforts in new musical markets, RCA's Nashville operation ultimately became remarkably profitable in the late 1950s and 1960s, and Chet Atkins's tight, pleasant "Nashville Sound" became a style to be emulated. Following in the lingering refrains of "Four Walls," the Browns, Skeeter Davis, Don Gibson, and a rejuvenated Eddy Arnold found sweeping acceptance among country fans, and their recordings regularly crossed over into the pop markets.

Not only did Jim Reeves cross the boundaries between musical genres, he also was instrumental in helping country music cross the Atlantic and open up lucrative markets in Europe and South Africa. Reeves's stock began to rise in America at a time when RCA was aggressively seeking to promote its various lines of music overseas. Jim had proven his viability in different markets within the United States, so he became a natural choice to represent RCA's country product in foreign countries during the early 1960s. The label's promotion of Jim Reeves in foreign lands proved to be immensely valuable as it generated considerable sales of country music product and opened the door for other country acts to tour abroad. In 1998, thanks in large part to Jim Reeves, sales of American country music artists' recordings and concert tickets continue to soar in overseas markets.

Because Jim Reeves died just twenty days shy of his forty-first birthday, there is much speculation about what he would have achieved had he lived. Since recordings bearing his name continued to reach the American charts as late as the 1980s—and sales of those records faltered only when most of his living contemporaries began to falter—we have a fairly accurate picture of the course his singing career might have taken. Reeves probably would have made more movies and toured Asia, and his records almost certainly would have continued to top the charts in America and abroad for the remainder of the 1960s before his popularity waned in the 1970s and '80s as younger artists took their turns on the country music carousel.

However, before he passed on, Jim Reeves made a long lifetime's worth of contributions to the musical landscape, and those contributions—perhaps more than anything he might have accomplished after July 31, 1964—stand as his greatest legacy. Jim Reeves will ultimately be remembered for expanding country music's influence and stimulating people's imaginations—which, in the final analysis, is what good singing should do.

Bibliography

GENERAL

Aircraft accident report. File 2-0613. Federal Aviation Administration.

Billboard magazine, 1949–1964.

Broadcasting Yearbook. Washington, D.C.: Broadcasting Publications, 1950–1952.

Certificate of Birth. James Travis Reeves. Texas Department of Health, Bureau of Vital Statistics.

Panola Watchman newspaper (Carthage, Texas) 1923–1942.

Radio Annual-Television Yearbook. New York: Radio Daily Corporation, 1948–1960.

RCA Records. Recording Sheets 1955–1964. Unpublished. Courtesy of Bertelsmann Music Group.

Weize, Richard, Arie den Dulk and Kurt Rokitta. Jim Reeves discography in *Jim Reeves: Welcome to My World.* Hambergen, Germany: Bear Family Records, 1994.

REFERENCE MATERIAL

Bashe, Philip. *Teenage Idol, Travelin' Man: The Complete Biography of Rick Nelson.* New York: Hyperion, 1992.

Bufwack, Mary A. and Robert K. Oermann. *Finding Her Voice: The Saga of Women in Country Music.* New York: Crown, 1993.

Cooper, Daniel. *Lefty Frizzell: The Honky-tonk Life of Country Music's Greatest Singer.* Little, Brown, 1995.

Delmore, Alton. *The Delmore Brothers: Truth Is Stranger Than Publicity*, 2nd ed. Nashville: Country Music Foundation Press, 1995.

Eberly, Philip K. *Music in the Air: America's Changing Tastes in Popular Music, 1920–1980.* New York: Hastings House, 1982.

Eng, Steve. *A Satisfied Mind: The Country Music Life of Porter Wagoner.* Nashville: Rutledge Hill Press, 1992.

Escott, Colin with George Merritt and William MacEwen. *Hank Williams: The Biography.* Boston: Little, Brown, 1994.

Escott, Colin. Liner notes to *Jim Reeves: Welcome to My World.* Hambergen, Germany: Bear Family Records, 1994.

Escott, Colin. *Tattooed on Their Tongues: A Journey Through the Backrooms of American Music.* New York: Schirmer, 1996.

Federal Writers' Project of the Works Projects Administration for the State of Texas. *Texas: A Guide to the Lone Star State.* New York: Hastings House, 1940.

Federal Writers' Project of the Works Projects Administration for the State of Louisiana. *Louisiana: A Guide to the State*. New York: Hastings House, 5th ed., 1959.

Federal Writers' Project of the Works Projects Administration for the State of Virginia. *Virginia: A Guide to the Old Dominion*. New York: Oxford University Press, 6th ed., 1956.

Federal Writers' Project of the Works Projects Administration for the State of Mississippi. *Mississippi: A Guide to the Magnolia State*. New York: Hastings House, 5th ed., 1959.

Filichia, Peter. *Professional Baseball Franchises: From the Abbeville Athletics to the Zanesville Indians*. New York: Facts On File, 1993.

Foster, R.F., ed. *The Oxford History of Ireland*. Oxford: Oxford University Press, 1989.

Guralnick, Peter. *Last Train to Memphis: The Rise of Elvis Presley*. Little, Brown: 1994.

Hall, Wade. *Hell-Bent for Music: The Life of Pee Wee King*. Lexington: University of Kentucky Press, 1996.

Hoffman, Frank and George Albert. *The Cashbox Album Charts, 1955–1974*. Metuchen, N.J.: The Scarecrow Press, Inc., 1988.

Hurst, Jack. *Nashville's Grand Ole Opry*. New York: Harry N. Abrams, 1975.

Jasper, Tony. *The Top Twenty Book: The Official British Record Charts, 1955–1993*. London: Blandford, 1994.

Johnson, Lloyd and Miles Wolff. *The Encyclopedia of Minor League Baseball: The Official Record of Minor League Baseball*. Durham, N.C.: Baseball America, 1993.

Jones, Margaret. *Patsy: The Life and Times of Patsy Cline*. New York: HarperCollins, 1994.

Kingsbury, Paul. *The Grand Ole Opry History of Country Music*. New York: Villard, 1995.

Larkin, Colin, ed. *The Guiness Encyclopedia of Popular Music*. Middlesex, England: Guiness, 1992.

Malone, Bill C. and Judith McCulloh, eds. *Stars of Country Music: Uncle Dave Macon to Johnny Rodriguez*. Urbana: University of Illinois Press, 1975.

Malone, Bill C. *Country Music USA*, 2nd ed. Austin, Tex.: University of Texas Press, 1985.

McCloud, Barry and contributing writers. *Definitive Country: The Ultimate Encyclopedia of Country Music and Its Performers*. New York: Perigee, 1995.

Obojski, Robert. Bush League: A History of Minor League Baseball. New York: Macmillan, 1975.

Sanjak, Russell. Updated by David Sanjak. *Pennies from Heaven: The American Popular Music Business in the Twentieth Century*. New York: Da Capo, 1996.

Shestack, Melvin. *The Country Music Encyclopedia*. New York: Thomas Y. Crowell, 1974

Tindall, George Brown. *America: A Narrative History*, Vols. 1 and 2. New York: Norton, 1984.

Whitburn, Joel. *Pop Memories 1890–1954*. Menomonee Falls, Wis.: Record Research, 1986.

Whitburn, Joel. *Top Country Singles 1944–1993*. Menomonee Falls, Wis.: Record Research, 1994.

Whitburn, Joel. *Top Pop Albums 1955–1992*. Menomonee Falls, Wis.: Record Research, 1993.

Whitburn, Joel. *Top Pop Singles 1955–1993*. Menomonee Falls, Wis.: Record Research, 1994.

Whitburn, Joel. *Top R&B Singles 1942–1988*. Menomonee Falls, Wis.: Record Research, 1988.

Willoughby, Larry. *Texas Rhythm, Texas Rhyme: A Pictorial History of Texas Music*. Austin, Tex.: Texas Monthly Press, 1984.

Wilson, Monica and Leonard Thompson, eds. *The Oxford History of South Africa*, Vols. 1 and 2. Oxford: Oxford University Press, 1969.

Preface

Schone, Mark. "Lord Jim: The African Diaspora Loves the Mellow Crooner." *Village Voice*, January 16, 1996.

Chapter One

"A Feed Crop an Imperative Necessity." *Panola (Tex.) Watchman*, March 5, 1930.

"Cotton Report." *Panola (Tex.) Watchman*, December 31, 1930.

"Five Thousand Bales Short of 1928." *Panola (Tex.) Watchman*, December 4, 1929.

Forer, Lucille with Henry Still. *The Birth Order Factor: How Your Personality is Influenced By Your Place in the Family*. New York: David McKay Company, Inc., 1976.

"Hard Times Relief." *Panola (Tex.) Watchman*, September 3, 1930.

Jordan, Terry G. *Trails to Texas: Southern Roots of Western Cattle Ranching*. Lincoln, Neb.: University of Nebraska Press, 1981.

LaGrone, Leila B. *History of Panola County, Texas, 1819–1978, Part I*. Carthage, Tex.: Panola County Historical Commission, 1979.

Leman, Kevin. *The Birth Order Book: Why You Are the Way You Are*. Old Tappan, N.J.: Fleming H. Revell Company, 1984.

Reeves, Emma Barrett. "Reeves Review." Self-published, c. 1982.

"Restriction of Acreage." *Panola (Tex.) Watchman*, September 24, 1930.

Richardson, Rupert N., Ernest Wallace, and Adrian Anderson. *Texas: The Lone Star State*. Englewood Cliffs, N.J.: Prentice Hall, 1981.

Rutherford, Hugh. Genealogy of Lorenzo Harris Adams. Unpublished, 1996.

Sharp, Lawrence R. "History of Panola County, Texas to 1860." Diss. University of Texas, 1940.

"Six Stills Are Taken in Panola County." *Panola (Tex.) Watchman*, August 29, 1923.

Sulloway, Frank J. *Born to Rebel: Birth Order, Family Dynamics, and Creative Lives*. New York: Pantheon Books, 1996.

Veach, Damon. "Louisiana Ancestors: Wyatt Woodruff Adams." *Baton Rouge Advocate*, undated.

White, John A. "In Spite of It All." Self-published, 1997.

Wilson, Bradford and George Edington. *First Child, Second Child . . . : Your Birth Order Profile*. New York: McGraw-Hill, 1981.

Author Interviews: Louie (Reeves) McNeese, Margaret (Barnett) Reeves, Virgie (Reeves) Thomas, Marvin Walker, Mary Walker, John White.

Chapter Two
Boatright, Mody C. and William A. Owens. *Tales from the Derrick Floor: A People's History of the Oil Industry.* Garden City, N.Y.: Doubleday, 1970.
"Bulldogs Open Season at Nacogdoches." *Panola (Tex.) Watchman*, March 13, 1941.
"Carthage Baseball Club to Play in Dallas for Title." *Panola (Tex.) Watchman*, May 15, 1941.
"Carthage Beats Yearlings, 3–1." *Panola (Tex.) Watchman*, April 16, 1942.
"Carthage Bulldogs Trims Tatum 17–1 Here Thursday." *Panola (Tex.) Watchman*, March 28, 1940.
"Carthage High Exercises Set for June 1." *Panola (Tex.) Watchman*, May 21, 1942.
"Carthage in Finals After No-Hit Game." *Houston Post*, May 23, 1942.
"Dallas Adamson Cops Diamond Title." *Houston Post*, May 24, 1942.
Finch, Robert L. Letter to June Graves, March 30, 1942.
Frantz, Joe B. *Texas: A Bicentennial History.* New York: W.W. Norton, 1976.
"Graves Reports to Houston Team; Morrison Enters Army Service." *Panola (Tex.) Watchman*, May 28, 1942.
Graves, June. Interview with Cody Pierce. *Loblolly* (Gary, Tex.), Summer 1995.
"High School Pitching Aces Get St. Louis Cardinal Offer." *Panola (Tex.) Watchman*, March 12, 1942.
"Hondo, Adamson, Carthage, Mesquite in Semifinals of Baseball Tourney." *Dallas Morning News*, May 22, 1942.
McClanahan, Bill. "Adamson Battles Carthage for Title Today." *Dallas Morning News*, May 23, 1942.
McClanahan, Bill. "Adamson Beats Carthage in State Final, 12–0." *Dallas Morning News*, May 24, 1942.
McClanahan, Bill. "Carthage Is Rated Favorite to Win Diamond Title Here." *Dallas Morning News*, May 17, 1942.
McClanahan, Bill. "Hondo, Mesquite, McKinney and Sunset Nines Win Games." *Dallas Morning News*, May 16, 1941.
McClanahan, Bill. "Hondo Tackles Polytechnic in State Diamond Opener Today." *Dallas Morning News*, May 21, 1942.
McClanahan, Bill. "Sunset Defeats Carthage, 6 to 1, in High School Finals." *Dallas Morning News*, May 18, 1941.
McClanahan, Bill. "Sunset Plays Carthage High Tonight in Baseball Finals." *Dallas Morning News*, May 17, 1941.
Morrison, E.B. Interview with Cody Pierce. *Loblolly* (Gary, Tex.), Summer 1995.
Olien, Roger M. and Diana Davids Olien. *Life in the Oil Fields.* Austin, Tex.: Texas Monthly Press, 1986.
Presley, James. *A Saga of Wealth: The Rise of the Texas Oilmen.* New York: Putnam, 1978.
Shadowens, Jack. "Bulldogs Blanked Wolves for District Championship." *Panola (Tex.) Watchman*, May 15, 1941.

Shadowens, Jack. "Carthage Wins from Garrison 3 to 2." *Panola (Tex.) Watchman,*
   April 3, 1941.
Westmoreland, Lamar. "Bulldogs Win 5 to 1; Lose 4 to 5." *Panola (Tex.)*
   Watchman, April 18, 1940.
Author Interviews: June Graves, Mary Graves, Margaret (Rhiddlehoover) Hamlin,
   Louie (Reeves) McNeese, Margaret (Barnett) Reeves, Jenny Lee (Wimberly)
   O'Reilly, Carey Rhiddlehoover, Chester Studdard, Virgie (Reeves) Thomas.

Chapter Three
"Army to Take Two Cardinals Hurlers Soon." *The News* (Lynchburg, Va.), April 5,
   1945.
"Colts Defeat Cards, 13–5, In Easy Win." *The News* (Lynchburg, Va.), June 7, 1945.
Creamer, Robert W. *Baseball in '41.* New York: Penguin, 1991.
"Dodgers Hand Cards Fourth Loss In Row." *The News* (Lynchburg, Va.), May 12, 1945.
"Double Rally Wins Night Cap by 10 to 9 Score." *Natchez (Miss.) Democrat,* June 2,
   1946.
"Errors Prove Costly for Alexandria." *Alexandria (La.) Daily Town Talk,* August 2,
   1946.
Gilbert, Bill. *They Also Served: Baseball and the Homefront, 1941–1945.* New
   York: Crown, 1992.
"Intrasquad Games Scheduled at Stadium This Afternoon." *The News* (Lynchburg,
   Va.), April 8, 1945.
Lee, Ray. "Aces Will Open Evangeline Loop Season in Natchez." *Alexandria (La.)*
   Daily Town Talk, April 15, 1947.
Lee, Ray. "Baton Rouge Gets 14 Hits in Easy Victory." *Alexandria (La.) Daily Town*
   Talk, August 7, 1946.
Lee, Ray. "Once Over Lightly." *Alexandria (La.) Daily Town Talk,* August 3, 1946.
Lee, Ray. "Once Over Lightly." *Alexandria (La.) Daily Town Talk,* August 7, 1946.
Lee, Ray. "Once Over Lightly." *Alexandria (La.) Daily Town Talk,* August 24, 1946.
"Locals Defeat Thibodaux, 6–4, in 12 Innings." *Alexandria (La.) Daily Town Talk,*
   May 24, 1947.
"Marshall Hangs Up Fourth in Row; Reeves Checks Henderson, 3 to 2. *Marshall*
   (Tex.) News Messenger, June 8, 1947.
"Marshall Takes Lone Star Lead with 11–4 Victory Over Texas." *Marshall (Tex.)*
   News Messenger, July 18, 1947.
"Near Riot." *Henderson (Tex.) Daily News,* July 27, 1947.
"Oilers vs. Lufkin Tonight and Fri." *Henderson (Tex.) Daily News,* August 14, 1947.
"Reeves Outduels Henson, Comets Defeat Jacksonville in Opener." *Marshall (Tex.)*
   News Messenger, July 14, 1947.
Reeves, Jim. Letter to Chester Studdard, April 25, 1944.
"Richmond Blasts 2 Lynchburg Hurlers for 7–1 Victory." *The News* (Lynchburg,
   Va.), May 20, 1945.
"Seventeen Oilers Left On Base Tuesday Nite." *Henderson (Tex.) Daily News,* July
   31, 1947.
"Tyler Edges Marshall, 3 to 2 for Comets Fourth Loss in Row." *Marshall (Tex.)*
   News Messenger, June 4, 1947.

Author Interviews: Shep Baron, Cloyd Boyer, Alan Cross, Mary Graves, Margaret (Rhiddlehoover) Hamlin, Louis (Reeves) McNeese, Frank O'Hare, Floyd Reeves, Hugh Sooter, Chester Studdard, Elvin Tappe, Charlie Thompson, Art Trieschman, Art Visconti, Leroy Youngblood.

Chapter Four
Anderson, Pat. "Jim Reeves Is Still A Satisfied Man." *Nashville Tennessean*, January 17, 1960.
Caro, Robert A. *The Years of Lyndon Johnson: Means of Ascent.* New York: Knopf, 1990.
Deen, Dixie. "Mary Reeves: The Woman Behind the Man." *Music City News*, October 1967.
"Jim Reeves: Panola's Good Will Ambassador of Music." *Panola (Tex.) Watchman*, July 5, 1962.
Perryman, Tom. Interview with John Rumble. Country Music Foundation Oral History Project, June 19–22, 1990.
Reeves, Mary. Interview with Alanna Nash, c. 1980.
Sippel, Johnny. "Folk Talent and Tunes." *Billboard*, February 2, 1952.
Sippel, Johnny. "Folk Talent and Tunes." *Billboard*, June 7, 1952.
White, John A. "In Spite of It All." Self-published, 1997.
"White-Reeves Marriage Told." *Marshall (Tex.) News Messenger*, September 7, 1947.
Author Interviews: John Bolin, Paul Brown, Alan Cross, John Grimes (a.k.a. Billy Barton), Leo Ferguson, Bobby Garrett, Margaret (Rhiddlehoover) Hamlin, Burton Harris, Kenneth "Little Red" Hayes, Horace Logan, Caesar Massey, Bill Morris, Douglas Reeh, Barney Vardeman.

Chapter Five
"Folk Talent and Tunes." *Billboard*, December 27, 1952.
"Folk Talent and Tunes." *Billboard*, June 13, 1953.
Hall, Lillian Jones. "A Historical Study of Programming Techniques and Practices of Radio Station KWKH, 1922–1950." Diss. Louisiana State University and Agricultural and Mechanical College, 1959.
Author Interviews: Norman Bale, John Bolin, Charles Greenberg, Kenneth "Little Red" Hayes, Sleepy LaBeef, Horace Logan, Hi Roberts, Bob Sullivan, Mitchell Torok, Billy Walker.

Chapter Six
"Reeves Ankles Abbott Waxery." *Billboard*, February 26, 1955.
Author Interviews: Luckey Brazeal, Jack Gale, Bobby Garrett, Charles Greenberg, Kenneth "Little Red" Hayes, Ginny (Wright) Henderson, Leo Jackson, Horace Logan, Bob McCluskey, Hi Roberts, Del Roy, Russell Sims, Bob Sullivan.

Chapter Seven
Deen, Dixie. "Mary Reeves: The Woman Behind the Man." *Music City News*, October 1967.

Killen, Buddy with Tom Carter. *By the Seat of My Pants: My Life in Country Music*,
New York: Simon and Schuster, 1993.
Sachs, Bill. "Folk Talent and Tunes." *Billboard*, August 13, 1955.
Sachs, Bill. "Folk Talent and Tunes." *Billboard*, November 26, 1955.
Sachs, Bill. "Folk Talent and Tunes." *Billboard*, March 3, 1956.
Author Interviews: Chet Atkins, Cy Coben, Bobby Garrett, Charles Grean, Don
Helms, Anita Kerr, Leo Jackson, Horace Logan, Bill Morris, Katherine Shucher.

Chapter Eight
"Bon Voyage Fete for RCA Country Unit." *Billboard*, April 6, 1957.
Horstman, Dorothy. *Sing Your Heart Out, Country Boy*. New York: Dutton, 1975.
Killen, Buddy with Tom Carter. *By the Seat of My Pants: My Life in Country Music*.
New York: Simon and Schuster, 1993.
Reeves, Jim. Letter to Doris and Elmer Gath, c. December 1958.
Sachs, Bill. "Folk Talent and Tunes." *Billboard*, April 29, 1957.
Sachs, Bill. "Folk Talent and Tunes." *Billboard*, October 14, 1957.
"Sholes Bucks Tradition Again." *Billboard*, May 26, 1956.
Simon, Bill. "Victor Singles to Go International." *Billboard*, November 3, 1956.
Wilson, John S. "You Can't Take the Country Out of Chet." *New York Times*,
April 7, 1974.
Author Interviews: Dick Broderick, Bobby Garrett, Don Helms, Leo Jackson, Anita
Kerr, Jeff Miller, Katherine Shucher, Velma Williams Smith.

Chapter Nine
Horstman, Dorothy. *Sing Your Heart Out, Country Boy*. New York: Dutton,
1975.
Killen, Buddy with Tom Carter. *By the Seat of My Pants: My Life in Country Music*.
New York: Simon and Schuster, 1993.
Rumble, John W. "Behind the Board: Talking with Studio Engineer Bill Porter, Part
One." *Journal of Country Music*, Vol. 18, No. 1.
Sachs, Bill. "Folk Talent and Tunes." *Billboard*, November 9, 1959.
Author Interviews: Auggie Blume, Gordon Bossin, Jack Burgess, Bobby Garrett,
Leo Jackson, Anita Kerr, James Kirkland, Louis Nunley, Johnny Rosica, Katherine
Shucher.

Chapter Ten
de Meillon, Bill. Interview with Arie den Dulk, November 1978.
"Guitarist is Jim Reeves' Star." Unidentified South African newspaper, August 29,
1962.
"Nashville Sound Travels Toward African Veldt." *Billboard*, August 25, 1962.
Rumble, John W. "Behind the Board: Talking with Studio Engineer Bill Porter, Part
One." *Journal of Country Music*, Vol. 18, No. 1.
Simon, Bill. "All's Veldt With U.S. Pop Disks in S.A." *Billboard*, September 8,
1956.
"Tweetalige Texan Delights City Fans." *Eastern Province Herald* (Port Elizabeth,
South Africa), August 29, 1962.

Author Interviews: Dick Broderick, Leo Ferguson, Leo Jackson, James Kirkland, Clive Parnell, Alex Zanetis.

Chapter Eleven
Clark, Peter. "Mr 'Velvet Voice' Reeves talks to Peter Clark about his Irish Tour." *Spotlight* (Dublin, Ireland), June 6, 1963.
Deen, Dixie. "Mary Reeves: The Woman Behind the Man." *Music City News,* October 1967.
"Jim Plays An Ace." *Pretoria News* (South Africa), April 4, 1963.
Sachs, Bill. "Country Music Corner." *Billboard,* March 9, 1963.
Variety's Film Reviews, 1964–1967. New York: R. R. Bowker, 1983.
Author Interviews: Leo Jackson, Anita Kerr, Billy Livingstone, Clive Parnell, Jerry Rice, Peter Smith, Bill Walker.

Chapter Twelve
Campbell, Pat. "We Want To Play Britain!" *New Musical Express* (Great Britain), July 17, 1964.
"CMA Shows Its Wares To Nashville's C. of C." *Billboard,* January 18, 1964.
Deen, Dixie. "Mary Reeves: The Woman Behind the Man." *Music City News,* October 1967.
Dietz, Eugene. "Storm Stuns Heart of City." *Nashville Tennessean,* July 30, 1964.
"Jim Reeves, Companion Found Dead." *Dallas Morning News,* August 3, 1964.
"Jim Reeves, Dean Manuel Found Dead After Plane Crashes Near Nashville." *Batesville (Ark.) Guard,* August 3, 1964.
"RCA Victor's Overseas P.A. Drive." *Billboard,* April 11, 1964.
"Reeves and Bare Get Norwegian Silver." *Billboard,* May 1, 1964.
Reeves, Jim. Interview with Kitty Prinsk, April 20, 1964.
Reeves, Mary. Interview with Alanna Nash, c. 1980.
"Stickbuddies Do It Again." Unidentified U.S. military newspaper, April 26, 1964.
Thompson, Jerry. "Jim Reeves Feared Aboard Missing Plane." *Nashville Tennessean,* August 1, 1964.
Thompson, Jerry. "Reeves Hunt Ends for Night." *Nashville Tennessean,* August 2, 1964.
Thompson, Jerry and Frank Sutherland. "Reeves Found Crash Victim." *Nashville Tennessean,* August 3, 1964.
"Two Thousand GIs Wait on Stickbuddies." Unidentified U.S. military newspaper, April 19, 1964.
Author Interviews: Shep Baron, Dick Broderick, Bob Ferguson, Leo Jackson, John D. Loudermilk, Louis Nunley, Bill Pursell, Chuck Seitz, Henry Strzelecki, Bill Walker, John White.

Epilogue
Deen, Dixie. "Mary Reeves: The Woman Behind the Man." *Music City News,* October 1967.
Killen, Buddy with Tom Carter. *By the Seat of My Pants: My Life in Country Music.* New York: Simon and Schuster, 1993.
Thompson, Jerry. "Reeves Ring Found, But No Clue." *Nashville Tennessean,* August 4, 1964.
Author Interviews: Leo Jackson, James Kirkland, James O'Gwynn, Cindy Walker, Alex Zanetis.

Discography

Record companies in America and around the world have considered Jim Reeves in far greater volume and detail than many of his country music contemporaries. In 1998, while music of artists such as Eddy Arnold, Bill Anderson, and Sonny James languishes in hidden vaults, every recording Reeves made for the Macy's, Abbott, and RCA labels is as close as the nearest CD store or on-line music catalog. For the continued availability of Jim's recordings, we can thank the vast international following he amassed before his death and the life-giving breath that Mary Reeves gave her husband's music after his death. One can own a set that includes Jim Reeves's entire catalog or a $3.99 cassette tape that skims a few songs from his list of hits.

For anyone who truly wishes to become intimate with the development of the Jim Reeves sound, I recommend the aforementioned collection that corrals every official recording. The German company Bear Family released *Welcome to My World* (BCD 15656 PI) in 1994, revealing more about Reeves and his career than had any other source to that point. The album's sixteen compact discs include everything from his late 1940s Macy's sides to his last RCA session, on July 2, 1964. Also packed onto the discs are interesting demos that Jim recorded when he wasn't spinning records at KRGI Radio in Henderson, Texas, as well as his many basement tapes that would evolve into posthumous hits. For many years after 1964, Chet Atkins produced the recordings by lifting Jim's voice from the raw "basement" material and dubbing it over new instrumentation. The hits that resulted, including macabre 1980s duets with Patsy Cline, show up on Bear Family's *Welcome to My World*. Colin Escott's liner notes and Richard Weize's virtually complete sessionography are useful companions to the music in the mammoth collection. In 1999 Bear Family plans to release another installment in its consideration of Jim Reeves: a multi-disc set of transcriptions that the country-pop star recorded for the U.S. armed services. It promises to add another layer to the understanding of Reeves's performing legacy.

Those who are unwilling to invest the money (and time!) in Bear Family's *Welcome to My World* have countless other options available to them. BMG, the company that now owns the entire RCA catalog, has two surveys of Reeves's career that hit many of his highlights. The 1993 *Welcome to My World: The Essential Jim Reeves Collection* (RCA 07863-66125-2) starts with Macy's "My Heart's Like a Welcome Mat" from the late 1940s, hits the Abbott years with the inclusion of "Mexican Joe," and then sifts through many of the RCA Victor recordings. *The Essential Jim Reeves* (RCA 07863-66589-2) of 1995 sticks strictly to the RCA Victor recordings, highlighting the big ones: "Four Walls," "He'll Have to Go," and others. Unfortunately, neither presents much of the early, unvarnished sound that Fabor Robison created with Jim during the Abbott period. BMG tacked seven Abbott numbers onto 1991's *Four Walls: The Legend Begins* (BMG 2493-2-R), but for a comprehensive mining of the legendary Reeves's association with Fabor Robison, two record albums released in 1982 by RCA International are the best bet. *The Abbott Recordings*, volumes one and two (INTS 5222 and INTS 5223), features every song Jim Reeves waxed for Abbott, accomplishing what the three aforementioned BMG releases do not.

Unfortunately, vinyl albums such as *The Abbott Recordings* may be hard to locate. But to dig deeper into the Jim Reeves catalog—without investing in the Bear Family releases—one must resort to flipping through record albums in the world's secondhand record shops. BMG, which has done an admirable job reissuing the greatest hits of RCA Victor's country artists, has not made available again anything that delves below the surface of Jim Reeves's catalog. Thus, the necessity to hunt for old records and to hope that BMG begins to unveil, in compact disc form, a more complete consideration of Jim Reeves's recorded legacy, as well as the recorded legacies of labelmates such as Eddy Arnold, Skeeter Davis, Don Gibson, and others.

Below, I have listed several RCA albums released in America over the past forty years that promise good listening and mark important developments in Reeves's recording career. Collectively, the albums reveal more about Jim's recording career than do the skimpy greatest-hits packages currently on the market. Several companies around the world have leased Jim's songs from BMG and marketed albums on their own labels, but they are not widely available. The RCA albums below—which are mostly American releases—perhaps can be more easily located.

Singing Down the Lane **(LPM-1256), 1956:** A compendium of Reeves's earliest RCA Victor recordings that hints at the "Four Walls" style to come but also highlights Jim and RCA's reluctance to stray very far from the Fabor Robison sound. The album's "Ichabod Crane," "Roly Poly," and "Tweedle O'Twill" are well in the Abbott mold.

Jim Reeves **(LPM-1576), 1957:** The new Jim Reeves! In the glow of "Four Walls," Chet Atkins produced this decidedly pop-leaning set that ditched the fiddle and steel guitar in favor of the crooning Jordanaires. Jim's breezy interpretations of "Yours," "Everywhere I Go," and "I Get the Blues When It Rains" lift the album.

Girls I Have Known **(LPM-1685), 1958:** By the time it released this concept album featuring songs about girls with names such as "Charmaine," "Juanita," and "Linda," RCA Victor had clearly stepped up its efforts to establish Jim in the pop album market. This album could have passed for a Perry Como or an Eddie Fisher collection, and the instrumentation suggests New York, rather than Nashville. Cindy Walker's composition "Anna Marie," which is included, was a country-pop hit for Reeves in 1957.

Songs to Warm the Heart **(LSP-2001), 1959:** After the drastic swing away from country on *Girls I Have Known*, and in the absence of a follow-up single to rival "Four Walls," RCA Victor pulled Reeves back toward his country base in this collection. The guitars of Chet Atkins and Hank Garland, and country standards like "Just Call Me Lonesome" and "How's the World Treating You?" (penned by Chet Atkins and

Discography   231

Boudleaux Bryant) offer a concession to the country sound. Standing out are the tender "Scarlett Ribbons," the perky "Dear Hearts and Gentle People," and a reworking of Jim's 1957 hit "Am I Losing You?"

He'll Have to Go (LPM-2223), 1960: When Jim's version of "He'll Have to Go" exploded in late 1959 and early 1960, he and RCA Victor had nailed the elusive follow-up to "Four Walls." The song's surging performance almost certainly caught RCA by surprise, forcing the company to hastily assemble an LP around Reeves's big hit. *He'll Have to Go* gave the title track another forum, but the package lacks the common thread of earlier RCA Victor albums. In its rush to release the album, the label reached back to 1957 for filler songs. "I Love You More," "Wishful Thinking," and "Theme of Love (I Love to Say 'I Love You')," all waxed in 1957, feature the fiddle and steel guitar, instruments that, in the studio, Jim had all but abandoned by 1960. However, the album is an appealing potpourri of Reeves's late 1950s work. In addition to "He'll Have to Go," his 1959 hits "Home" (written by Roger Miller), "Partners," and "I'm Beginning to Forget You" are included. This was the first Jim Reeves album to hit the pop album charts, peaking at number eighteen in 1960.

According to My Heart (CAL-583), 1960: Like *He'll Have to Go*, this release on RCA Victor's Camden budget label incorporates a smattering of Reeves's styles, reaching back to 1955 for the enjoyable title track (which reached number four on the country charts in '56) and including four more recent songs cut during a January 1960 session. The free-flowing "Stand at Your Window" stands out among the January 1960 recordings and features the steel guitar work of Bobby Garrett and the reliable picking of Leo Jackson.

Tall Tales and Short Tempers (LPM-2284), 1961: This release represents Jim's effort to adapt to the stream of saga songs that were invading country music in the late 1950s and early 1960s. The instrumentation and background vocals sparkle, illustrating the cohesion of the Nashville session scene, but Jim is unconvincing in his interpretations of ballads that deal with trains, blizzards, and the frontier. His voice lacks the weathered quality that best translates the feeling of such ballads. Jim Reeves was better suited to romantic numbers. Folk writer and documentalist Jimmie Driftwood penned the liner notes for this album. The cuts "Danny Boy," "Streets of Laredo," and "Rodger Young" feature the instrumental backing of the Blue Boys: Leo Jackson, James Kirkland, Mel Rogers, and Dean Manual.

Talkin' to Your Heart (LPM-2359), 1961: Arranger and background vocalist Anita Kerr lists *Talkin' to Your Heart*, another LP in the saga style, as one of her favorite Jim Reeves albums. She loves the sound of Jim's recitations, which comprise the entirety of this collection. Thankfully, Jim mostly steered away from train songs here and instead tackled numbers about the human condition that had more general plot lines.

The International Jim Reeves (LPM-2704), 1963: The handsome glossy photo of Jim standing with his monogrammed suitcases in front a jet airliner is itself worth the search for this album. A concept album that returns to the pop sound, *The International Jim Reeves* takes Jim around the world with numbers like "The Old Kalahari" and "Tahiti." The interpretations of the chestnut "(There'll Be Bluebirds Over) The

White Cliff of Dover" and Cindy Walker's "Blue Canadian Rockies" are musts for any Jim Reeves collection. "Guilty," the country-pop hit penned by Alex Zanetis, is tacked onto this LP. Chet Atkins and Anita Kerr shared producer's credit on this outing.

Good 'n' Country (CAL-784), 1963: Jim recorded this album specifically for release on the Camden budget label. It is a sprightly visit with the country sound and features the talented steel guitarist Pete Drake. Jim Carroll's "Little Old Dime" and "Before I Died," and Johnny Elgin's "Lonely Music" are more than good vehicles for Jim's voice, they are examples of good songwriting.

Kimberley Jim (LPM-2780), 1964: The importance of this release is twofold: It is the soundtrack of Jim's only film and it also highlights the emphasis on vowels that Jim employs in his singing. He acquired an enunciation associated with a Broadway vocalist, eschewing the emphasis on consonants so common to country and rock singers. He would continue to linger on the vowel sounds until his death. Listen for Alex Zanetis's "Could I Be Falling in Love?" the rueful "Diamonds in the Sand," and the expansive title track, "Kimberley Jim."

Moonlight and Roses (LPM-2854), 1964: Perched on the pop and country album charts at the moment of Jim Reeves's death, *Moonlight and Roses* is laden with standards such as "Mexicali Rose," "Carolina Moon," and "Oh What It Seemed to Be." However, Jim's version of Cindy Walker's Latin-flavored "Rosa Rio"—not exactly a standard—sits above all other songs on the LP. *Moonlight and Roses* reached number one on the country album charts, illustrating Jim's acceptance in that market despite his decidedly un-country sound. Pop markets also welcomed the album, giving Jim a place alongside such luminaries as Andy Williams and Johnny Mathis.

The Jim Reeves Way (LPM-2968), 1965: The first Jim Reeves album released after his death, this LP features cuts from his last session (July 2, 1964) and a couple of Jim's songs performed in the Afrikaans language.

Distant Drums (LPM-3542), 1966: On February 9, 1966, Chet Atkins dubbed Jim's vocals over new instrumentation for the first time. Jim had recorded the title track of *Distant Drums* as a demo for Cindy Walker, but on that date in 1966, it would be varnished and then released to a market with a considerable taste for Jim Reeves product. Subsequently, Chet would redo several songs that Jim had recorded in his basement or at other studios. The new recordings would become part of the core of Jim Reeves's posthumous career.

Yours Sincerely, Jim Reeves (LPM-3709), 1966: A nice collection of Jim Reeves songs, but this LP is most remarkable for its inclusion of a newscast that Jim read in 1948 at KGRI Radio in Henderson.

Jim Reeves on Stage (LSP-4062), 1968: This album is one of the few examples available of Jim before a concert audience. Recorded somewhere in Pennsylvania during the early 1960s, the LP offers a glimpse of Jim pacing through his hits and clowning around in a free and easy style. For other glimpses of Jim in live performance, I recommend *Live at the Opry* (Country Music Foundation Records, 1993) which documents twenty of Jim's *Grand Ole Opry* performances between 1956 and 1960, and *Jim*

Reeves: Louisiana Hayride Anthologies of Legends which offers fifteen songs recorded on the *Hayride* in the years after Jim left Horace Logan's cast. The *Hayride* CD is available through the Collector's Choice Music of Itasca, Illinois.

The Best of Jim Reeves, Volume Three (LSP-4187), 1969: One of those skimpy greatest-hits albums, this is still worth a search in order to find Jim's 1962 hits "I'm Gonna Change Everything" and "Pride Goes Before a Fall," as well as Chet Atkins's reworkings of "Distant Drums" and "The Storm."

Greatest Hits: Jim Reeves and Patsy Cline (AHL1 4127), 1981: RCA Victor perhaps crossed the line when it collaborated with MCA to splice together the voices of Jim Reeves and Patsy Cline. In 1979 RCA had teamed Jim's voice with the very much alive and up-and-coming Deborah Allen, a union that produced three Top Ten country hits. Allen, though, could adapt her voice to Jim's. On the two Cline-Reeves songs, "Have You Ever Been Lonely" and "I Fall to Pieces," tapes of the two singers had to be electronically welded together. The union seemed unnatural but illustrates the lengths to which both RCA and MCA were willing to go to exploit their deceased singers. ("I Fall to Pieces" was released on an MCA album.)

Index